Kenne[illegible]

New College, Edinburgh

December 1957

THE EIGHTEENTH CENTURY BACKGROUND

By the same Author

THE SEVENTEENTH CENTURY BACKGROUND

NINETEENTH CENTURY STUDIES

★

Chatto & Windus

The Eighteenth Century Background

Studies on the Idea of Nature in the Thought of the Period

By

BASIL WILLEY

FELLOW OF PEMBROKE COLLEGE
KING EDWARD VII PROFESSOR OF ENGLISH LITERATURE
IN THE UNIVERSITY OF CAMBRIDGE

1950
CHATTO & WINDUS
LONDON

PUBLISHED BY
Chatto & Windus
LONDON

*

Clarke, Irwin & Company Ltd
TORONTO

FIRST PUBLISHED 1940
FOURTH IMPRESSION 1950

PRINTED BY THE REPLIKA PROCESS
IN GREAT BRITAIN BY
LUND HUMPHRIES
LONDON · BRADFORD

Preface

LIKE its predecessor *The Seventeenth Century Background* (1934), this book is the outcome of lectures delivered in the Faculty of English at Cambridge. It is intended as a companion volume to the other work, and continues the story down to the end of the eighteenth century. Whereas for the seventeenth century 'Truth' seemed to be the key-word, this time it is 'Nature'. I have not presumed to write even an outline 'history' of eighteenth century thought in general, but have tried to illustrate the importance, in that century, of the idea of 'Nature' in religion, ethics, philosophy and politics, and in particular to indicate some stages in that divinization of 'Nature' which culminates in Wordsworth. This is the central theme of the book, and from this it derives whatever unity it may have—though I have at times elaborated the study of certain representative writers to cover a wider field. Much of what follows can be regarded as prolegomena to the study of Wordsworth and Coleridge. The whole book is addressed, partly to the general reader who takes an unprofessional interest in the history of ideas, and partly to the literary student who may care to seek for explanations or analogies outside the sphere of 'pure' literature.

The closing chapters of the book were written under the shadow of approaching war, and when the catastrophe finally came I wondered at first whether it was fitting to come forward, at such a time, with studies so remote from actuality. But possibly if it is ever worth while to study past modes of thinking and feeling, it is none the less so now, and it happens that the eighteenth century can perhaps offer us, not merely escape or refreshment, but even actual guidance in our present troubles.

My acknowledgments are due, and are gratefully given, to the Clarendon Press for permission to include, as the first chapter, my contribution to *Seventeenth Century Studies Presented to Sir Herbert Grierson* (1938).

B. W.

PEMBROKE COLLEGE, CAMBRIDGE,
November 1939.

Contents

CHAPTER I

The Turn of the Century

Nature and Nature's laws lay hid in night:
God said, Let Newton be! *and all was light!*

THE eighteenth century—'the silver age of the European Renaissance'—virtually begins in the final decades of the seventeenth. When we enter those decades we recognize on all sides the familiar eighteenth century landmarks, lit by the familiar illumination of the time. Glory and loveliness may have passed away, but so also have the fogs and glooms of history; the common daylight which now descends upon a distracted world may be prosaic, but at least it is steady and serene, and has not yet become dark with excessive light. One meets everywhere a sense of relief and escape, relief from the strain of living in a mysterious universe, and escape from the ignorance and barbarism of the Gothic centuries. Nature's laws had been explained by the New Philosophy; sanity, culture, and civilization had revived; and at last, across the vast gulf of the monkish and deluded past, one could salute the ancients from an eminence perhaps as lofty as their own. In England there was added to the general feeling of emancipation from historic spectres a sense of security from the upheavals of the Civil War period. 'We have been so long together bad Englishmen', wrote Dryden in 1668, 'that we had not leisure to be good poets'; but now, 'with the restoration of our happiness, we see revived Poesy lifting up its head, and already shaking off the rubbish which lay so heavy on it'.

In this 'noble Eluctation of Truth, wherein, against the tenacity of Prejudice and Prescription, this Century now prevaileth', no conception played a more significant part than that of 'Nature', and in the present chapter it is proposed to examine some of the uses to which that idea was put at the end of the seventeenth and the beginning of the eighteenth centuries. 'Nature' has been a controlling idea in Western thought ever since antiquity, but it has probably never been so universally active as it was from the Renaissance to the end of the eighteenth century. Nature was the grand alternative to all that man had made of man; upon her solid ground therefore—upon the *tabula rasa* prepared by the true philosophy—must all the religion, the ethics, the politics, the law, and the art of the future be constructed. Leslie Stephen has said that 'Nature is a word contrived in order to introduce as many equivocations as possible into all the theories, political, legal, artistic or literary, into which it enters'. An American scholar has recently distinguished sixty different senses of the term. Even in the seventeenth century Robert Boyle,[1] the natural philosopher, could enumerate eight senses of the word as used in philosophy and natural science, and Pierre Bayle,[2] complaining of the ambiguity of the same word, mentions that eleven different meanings for it can be discovered in 1 Corinthians. Nevertheless in our period it was not the ambiguity of 'Nature' which people felt most strongly; it was rather the clarity, the authority, and the universal acceptability of Nature and Nature's laws. The laws of Nature are the laws of reason; they are always and everywhere the same, and like the axioms of mathematics they have only to be presented in order to be acknowledged as just and right by all men. The historic rôle of 'Nature' at this time was to introduce, not further confusion, but its precise opposites,—peace, concord, toleration, and progress in the affairs of men, and, in poetry and art, perspicuity, order, unity, and proportion.

[1] *A Free Inquiry into the Vulgarly Received Notion of Nature*: Works (1744), vol. iv.

[2] *Réponse aux questions d'un Provincial* (1706 ed.), vol. ii, ch. cv, p. 391.

1. *Natural Science and Natural Religion*

This was the Golden Age of natural theology and deistical freethinking: the age of Spinoza and of Bayle, of the Cambridge Platonists, of Locke, Toland, Blount, Collins, Clarke, Wollaston, Shaftesbury, Tindal, and the rest. During the Christian centuries religion had rested upon revelation; now it rested largely upon 'Nature', and even the orthodox, who retained the supernatural basis, felt that faith must be grounded firmly upon Nature before one had recourse to super-nature. 'All the duties of Christian religion', says Archbishop Tillotson himself, 'which respect God, are no other but what natural light prompts men to, excepting the two sacraments, and praying to God in the name and by the mediation of Christ.' 'And even these', continues Anthony Collins[1] (after quoting this passage), 'even these, he justly observes, are of less moment than any of those parts of religion which in their own nature tend to the Happiness of human Society'. Whereas 'Nature', in one sense, had been opposed to 'Grace', and in another sense—as 'natural Light'—could at best conduct the Christian pilgrim to the point where Beatrice must supersede Virgil, now 'Nature' (in perhaps yet another sense) was to furnish the principal evidences of religion, while a somewhat embarrassing Revelation must be harmonized with it as best might be. How had this situation arisen? To account fully for the change would be an intricate task; let us merely remind ourselves of two relevant forces—the scientific movement of the sixteenth and the seventeenth centuries, and the religious conflicts following the Reformation. By the 'scientific movement' is meant the work of (for example) Copernicus, Kepler, Galileo, Bacon, Harvey, Gilbert, Descartes, Boyle, the Royal Society, and Newton. For our purposes the results of this great movement were twofold. First, it produced a 'climate of opinion' in which supernatural

[1] *Discourse of Freethinking* (1713), p. 136.

and occult explanations of natural phenomena ceased to satisfy, and the universe came more and more to be regarded as the Great Machine, working by rigidly determined laws of material causation. The supernatural, in both its divine and its diabolical forms, was banished from Nature. But, if one may put it so, Satan was banished on harsher terms than his divine Antagonist: and this brings us to the second point, namely, that though the new philosophy was anti-supernaturalist, it was not at first anti-religious. Most of the great scientists just mentioned conceived that they had rendered the highest services to religion as well as to science, and Descartes, Boyle, and Newton, as is well known, were notable theists. As Bacon had said (and Sir Thomas More before him), science was the study of the *works* of God, and this should be almost, if not quite, as pious a pursuit as the study of his *word*. A little learning might be a dangerous thing, but deeper draughts of philosophy would bring us back to sober faith. This view involved a changed attitude towards Nature and natural science; it meant that Nature was rescued from Satan and restored to God. For the physical world, in spite of its divine origin, was traditionally held to have shared in the fatal consequences of the fall of man, and to have become the chosen abode of the apostate spirits. Science in the Middle Ages was largely black magic; Nature was full of pagan divinities turned devils, and to meddle with it was to risk damnation. Friar Bacon was imprisoned as a sorcerer, and the Faust story illustrates the fascinated horror with which, as late as the sixteenth century, the popular mind regarded scientific knowledge. But now the more fortunate Francis Bacon could announce with conviction and authority that science was not the forbidden knowledge; that God had provided two channels of revelation, not one merely: the Scriptures, of course, but Nature also. Did not the Psalmist write *Coeli enarrant gloriam Dei*? And Bacon's follower, Sir Thomas Browne, assured his readers that 'there is no danger to profound these mysteries', and that God prefers a 'devout and learned admiration' of his works to that 'gross rusticity'[1] which stares and gapes at Nature, or trembles at portents where none were intended.

Science, then, it may be said, played an all-important part in producing the divinized 'Nature' of the eighteenth century (and ultimately of the 'romantic' generation). That science was thus able, for a time, to furnish natural religion with one of its two indispensable foundations —belief in a divine universe—was perhaps due to the fact that the findings of science, up to date, could fuse harmoniously with the presuppositions inherited from Christianity, which, though shaken by controversy, still remained as almost unquestioned certainties in men's hearts. For what had science revealed? Everywhere design, order, and law, where hitherto there had been chaos. Whether one contemplated the infinitely great through the optic glass of the Tuscan artist, or the infinitely little through the microscope of Malpighi, one received at every turn new assurance that all was 'according to the Ordainer of order and mystical mathematicks of the city of heaven'. Biology had as yet revealed no disturbing ancestries, and man was still unassailed by anthropology and psycho-analysis. Materialism itself could scarcely dispense with a divine hypothesis (though this soon followed): the Great Machine presupposed the Divine Mechanic. And when Newton bound together in one dazzling synthesis the great and the little, the stars in their courses and the fall of an apple, a thankful generation, at once scientific and pious, could exclaim with its spokesman, Alexander Pope:

> Nature and Nature's laws lay hid in night:
> God said, *Let Newton be!* and all was light!

and with its other spokesman, Addison:

> The spacious firmament on high
> With all the blue aethereal sky
> And spangled heavens, a shining frame,
> Their great Original proclaim.

[1] *Religio Medici*, i, sect. xiii.

Secondly, how did the religious conflicts of the sixteenth and seventeenth centuries lead up to the growth of natural religion in our period? Briefly, by calling in doubt all the points of the faith, and reducing them to the level of controversy. Christianity, instead of producing Christian individuals and societies, seemed for so long to have been producing disputes, persecutions, and wars, and had, in the Protestant countries, not only renounced the Holy See but split up further into so many sects, that a desire arose during the seventeenth century to formulate a creed which should be acceptable to all good and reasonable men. Christianity was based upon Revelation: well and good, but what had in fact been revealed? No one seemed to know, or rather—which was worse—everybody seemed to know that his own version was the only correct one. As Anthony Collins complained in his *Discourse of Free-thinking*, the Bible might be divinely inspired, but this had not prevented its official interpreters from disagreeing on all fundamentals; there was hardly in those days one clergyman 'that has consider'd and examin'd things with care, that believes all the Thirty-Nine Articles, in their proper and original meaning'. 'All Faiths have been shaken', writes Charles Blount, 'but those only which stand upon the Basis of Common Reason.'[1] What then? Must we abandon religion itself along with the metaphysical jargon bequeathed by our uncouth forefathers? By no means; there were ways of escape. The Cambridge Platonists, for example, adopted the technique of setting religion in a new framework, and changing the vocabulary of exhortation. The Platonic and neo-Platonic tradition was ready at hand to supply them with both. To platonize was to avoid the controversial danger-zone; it was to suggest that salvation did not depend upon the correct solution of the credal puzzles. Platonism had after all been, if not the Church's one foundation, at any rate (as John Smith observed) the 'Church's loving Nurse'. The values which Christians and all men respected had been taught by Plato,

[1] *Religio Laici: Written in a letter to John Dryden, Esq.*, 1683, p. 85.

and the advantage of approaching them by the Hellenic route was that it led you direct to the summits, and avoided all the theological morasses which beset you on the Christian side. But above all, there was the Grand Alternative, Nature; that at least proclaimed its divine Original unmistakably. 'The works of Nature everywhere sufficiently evidence a Deity', said Locke; sufficiently, that is, for us to be able to dispense with a troublesome and controverted revelation. Nature simply obtruded upon us its evidence for divine activity and wisdom: why then seek the living amongst the dead? why seek for evidence of what we already know? and especially why seek it in the 'historical' annals of an illiterate Semitic tribe? But that was not all. Natural religion reaches God not only through the starry heavens above, but also through the moral law within: through Reason as well as Nature. *Intra te quaere Deum;* look for God within thyself. And what exactly would you find when you looked within? Not the questionable shapes revealed by psycho-analysis, but something much more reassuring: the laws of God and Nature inscribed upon the heart, the 'ideas of first impression', 'truths of first inscription', 'common notions (*communes notitiae*)'—to mention a few of the names by which they were then known. From these clear imprints Lord Herbert of Cherbury had already formulated his fundamentals of natural religion: acknowledgment of God's existence, duty towards Him and our neighbour, necessity for repentance, future state of rewards and punishments. The knowledge of these points, as even the Schoolmen had held, could be attained without revelation, by that Reason which, in Locke's phrase, is

> 'natural Revelation, whereby the Father of Light, and fountain of all knowledge, communicates to mankind that portion of truth which he has laid within the reach of their natural faculties.' [1]

These are the saving truths vouchsafed not merely to a 'chosen people', but to all mankind, 'Enacted by the All-

[1] *Essay Concerning Human Understanding*, bk. iv, 19, sect. 4.

wise and Supreme Being from the beginning of the World, and therefore not to be destroyed or altered by every whiffling Proclamation of an Enthusiast'.[1] To the question, What must I do to be saved?, therefore, natural religion made answer: 'We want not so much knowledge to tell us what to do, as Wills to do that which we may know!' You know perfectly well what to do: your own nature informs you. Follow Reason, the God within; look after your conduct and your creed will take care of itself. In short, whether you looked without or within, Nature (without any supernatural revelation) offered you all that was needful for salvation. One should endeavour to realize how persuasive, and how sound, these injunctions must have seemed at that time. You had then upon the surface a great deal of obvious and clamorous dissension about doctrinal principles, but below the surface a far greater mass of real unanimity about the nature of the good life—the end and purpose of living. To this body of beliefs and attitudes, the product of the blended traditions of Greece and of Palestine, appeal could confidently be made, as to Nature itself. However furiously the sects might brawl, these common notions would remain. Whether this attitude can seem so obviously wise and so available to-day as it did to the Platonists and Deists of our period, and to such later followers as Matthew Arnold, Tulloch, or Dean Inge, is open to question. We cannot now be so sure that it is God we shall find if we look without, and perhaps still less if we look within. Even in the seventeenth century some warning notes were heard. Pascal found nothing but terror in the thought of inter-stellar space; Nature only proved God to one who already believed. And even Dryden could write with well-affected conviction:

> These truths are not the product of thy Mind,
> But dropt from Heaven, and of a Nobler Kind.
> *Reveal'd Religion* first inform'd thy Sight,
> And Reason saw not till *Faith* sprung the Light.

[1] Charles Blount, *op. cit.*, p. 94.

> Hence all thy *Natural Worship* takes the Source:
> 'Tis *Revelation* what thou thinkst *Discourse*.[1]

But few believed this report: on the contrary, the light sprung by faith had become so dimmed by controversy that Nature now seemed to supply the true divine sunshine. 'Twas discourse what we thought revealed. Let us not evade the issues, says Toland, by prating about our sinful and corrupted state since the Fall. We have got reason enough if only we will take the trouble to be reasonable. And the Gospel 'affords the most illustrious Example of close and perspicuous Ratiocination conceivable'.[2] 'What is revealed in Religion, as it is most useful and necessary, so it must and may be as easily comprehended, and found as consistent with our common Notions, as what we know of Wood or Stone, of Air, of Water, or the like. . . . As for God, we comprehend nothing better than His Attributes.'[3] The essence of the New Testament revelation was, for Toland, that it did really reveal, that is, make plain and comprehensible, things formerly mysterious. Had it been otherwise, where would have been the superiority of Christianity over 'the idle dreams of the philosophers', the 'impieties and fables of the Alcoran', or the other esoteric quackeries with which the world was already overstocked? Faith itself is 'entirely built upon ratiocination', since it consists in trusting those to whom we believe God has spoken, and the latter belief must be established by evidence. As for 'the vulgar', who are said to be incapable of rational conviction—'the vulgar are more oblig'd to Christ, who had a better Opinion of them'. It is the gibberish of the divinity schools which is above their heads, not the plain, easy truths of Christianity. Jesus taught pure morals, a reasonable worship, and just conceptions of heaven; He 'stripp'd the Truth' bare of all ceremonial and symbolical trappings, and made it 'easy and obvious to the meanest Capacities'.[4] Strip-

[1] *Religio Laici* (1682), 66-71.
[2] Toland, *Christianity Not Mysterious* (1702), p. 46.
[3] *ibid.*, pp. 79-86.
[4] *ibid.*, p. 151.

ping the truth bare was what that age and generation felt itself to be mainly engaged upon: stripping it bare of mythology and all the accretions of paganism and popery. Protestantism, which evolved in England (and elsewhere) through Puritanism into 'rationalism', had always been in almost equal measure anti-pagan and anti-Catholic; the sin of popery was that in proselytizing the pagans it had absorbed so many of the pagan beliefs and practices. Now more than ever it was felt that the late era of controversy had obscured the divine simplicity and rationality of early Christianity, which had really been so exactly like the natural religion of the reign of William and Mary. That the freethinkers should have thought their deism more 'natural' than paganism or popery illustrates a familiar ambiguity in the meaning of that term. If 'natural' means what is original or primitive, natural religion would be that which was most deeply grounded in prehistory and the collective unconscious, while deism of the Stoical or eighteenth century varieties would appear as a late product of civilized sophistication. But, for our deists, 'natural' meant what is congenial to the mind of an abstract Man whose traits corresponded to those of the *honnête homme*, the man of parts and sense, who had become the moral norm of the age.

Speaking broadly, we are confronted, on approaching the eighteenth century, with a steady decline in what has been called the tragic sense of life. We have gone on too long, it was felt, repeating that we are miserable offenders, and that there is no health in us. We must change these notes to something more cheerful, something more befitting a polite and civilized age. As that excellent representative of the time, Halifax, puts it in *The Character of a Trimmer* (1684): 'there should not always be Storms or Thunder; a clear Sky would sometimes make the Church look more like Heaven',—our Church, especially, which (thank Heaven) is itself 'a Trimmer between the phrenzy of Platonick visions and the Lethargick Ignorance of Popish Dreams'. 'Religion', says the same author in his

Advice to a Daughter (the daughter who became the mother of Lord Chesterfield), 'is a chearful thing, so far from being always at Cuffs with Good Humour, that it is inseparably united to it.' 'A wise Epicure would be religious for the sake of Pleasure.' 'No other thing is the better for being Sowre, and it would be hard that Religion should be so, which is the best of things.' Exorcize from religion, therefore, its sombre and tragic elements—its jealous and offended God, its conviction of sin; put in place of Jehovah the Supreme Being, in whom there is no darkness at all, and see in Adam's posterity a race who would always have loved the highest if only designing priests had not prevented them from seeing it. Against the *Deus absconditus*, the *Dieu irrité* of Pascal, Shaftesbury puts forward a deity who is 'the best-natured Being in the world'. 'What a charming Idea does he give us of the Deity', says Collins of Tillotson[1]: 'it is alone sufficient, without any further Argument, to make the Atheist wish there were a Deity.' M. Paul Hazard has recently described the deists of this time 'as rationalists with a nostalgia for religion': men, that is, who had allowed the spirit of the age to separate them from orthodoxy, but who liked to believe that the slope they had started upon was not slippery enough to lead them to atheism. Meanwhile, one might delete from the Beatitudes 'Blessed are they that mourn':

> 'On veut détourner les yeux du Christ douloureux, crucifié pour le salut des hommes; on ne veut plus entendre l'appel muet de ses bras. Le bonheur est l'expansion d'une force qui se trouve spontanément en nous-mêmes, et qu'il suffit de diriger. L'acceptation des peines, l'appétit du sacrifice, la lutte contre l'instinct, la folie de la croix, ne sont plus que des erreurs de jugement, des habitudes mauvaises. Le Dieu-Raison nous défend de concevoir notre existence mortelle comme une préparation à l'immortalité.'[2]

---

[1] *op. cit.*, p. 136.

[2] *La Crise de la Conscience Européenne* (Paris, 1935), vol. ii, p. 93.

Meanwhile significant confirmatory evidence for natural religion and natural morality had for some time been pouring in from the accounts of voyagers, both real and imaginary, to non-Christian lands in distant parts of the earth. The noble savage had made an important entry upon the European stage in the sixteenth century, when Pigafetta, who voyaged round the world with Magellan, wrote that the Brazilians followed Nature, wore no clothes, lived to be 140 years of age, and were free from the civilized vices. Montaigne, whose essay *Of Cannibals* is best known as the source of Gonzalo's Utopian speech in *The Tempest*, describes therein the conduct of three savages at the court of Charles IX, and declares that what he had seen of their manners surpassed 'all the pictures with which poets had adorned the golden age'. In the seventeenth century a host of travellers repeated the same tale. Most remarkable of all, perhaps, not only merchants and philosophic dreamers, but even Jesuit missionaries to Paraguay, Brazil, Canada, China, and elsewhere agreed to praise the virtues of the unspoilt natural man, whose physique and whose morals everywhere, it seemed, put those of Christendom to shame. The Utopian method of satirizing or criticizing one's own civilization was of course a well-established convention, and many Utopias appeared during this time: for example, Foigny's *Terre Australe Connue* (1676)—describing an ideal island in the Southern Seas inhabited by hermaphroditic deists enjoying perfect liberty and equality—or 'La Bétique' in Fénelon's *Télémaque* (1699). But the interesting point is that so many actual travellers and missionaries wrote in like fashion. Evidently they wrote rather as moralists and satirists than as anthropologists. Noting what seemed to be the absence from savage society of the characteristic institutions of Europe, especially property, inequality, coercive government and the Church, they concluded that the primitives lived in the Paradise lost long since for us by Adam. In any case such accounts provided a safe means of indirectly attacking the institutions of one's own country. As Geoffroy Atkinson says:[1]

> 'En parlant des indigènes de l'Amérique, les auteurs de voyages ne risquaient pas d'alarmer les autorités qui auraient très mal reçu, probablement, un traité sur le communisme.'

But even so, the ecclesiastical authorities in France became seriously perturbed by the end of the century, for there were awkward theological implications in all this primitivism. These good savages, these sage Chinese, these noble Indians, these honest negroes, these wise and tolerant heathens of every colour—had they somehow escaped the curse of Adam? It was not to be thought of; though Foigny had indeed suggested that his Australians were descended, not from Adam, but from a previous being —an androgyne unmentioned by Moses—who had never fallen. What seems finally to have awakened the orthodox to the menace from beyond Christendom was a book about China by the Jesuit Father Le Comte (1696), in which he asserted that the Chinese had preserved the true knowledge of God for more than two thousand years, and had practised all the while a purer morality than most Christians. This book was condemned by the Paris Faculty of Theology in the following terms:

> 'Si tous ceux qui ont vécu selon la raison, soit Juifs, soit Gentiles, ont été véritablement et proprement Chrétiens et en état de salut, comme ceux qui ont eu la foi et à qui Jésus-Christ a été révélé, on peut donc se sauver par les forces de la nature, et la foi en Jésus-Christ Médiateur n'est nullement nécessaire.' [2]

On the whole, this was in fact very much what the age wanted to believe. For centuries Christian kings and Christian priests had been spreading the dark blight of tyranny and superstition over a portion of the world's sur-

[1] *Les Relations de Voyages du 17e Siècle et l'Évolution des Idées* (Paris, 1926), p. 40. I am indebted, for the above references, to this work and to the same author's English work, *The Extraordinary Voyage in French Literature before 1700* (Columbia Univ. Press, 1920).

[2] Atkinson, *Relations de Voyages*, p. 97.

face: only pass beyond that shadow, and you would find unspoilt Nature, still apparelled in celestial light. These generations, especially in France, were anxious to escape from the tragic glooms of history, and they willingly adopted the touching belief that *là-bas on était bien*. *Là-bas*, for Montaigne and the sixteenth century, had mostly meant America, but closer acquaintance with that country drove the mirage further and further off, until it finally settled, for the eighteenth century, in Tahiti. It happened that Bougainville, the explorer, published his glowing account of Tahiti just at the time when Rousseau had made the noble savage fashionable. Once again, in Bougainville's narrative, the dreams of philosophers and poets seemed to be confirmed by fact. Diderot, in his *Supplément au Voyage de Bougainville*, made use of Tahiti, as his editor says, 'to verify, localize, and render more real the hypothetical reconstruction of the earliest ages in Rousseau's second *Discourse*'.

> 'Voulez-vous savoir [he wrote] l'histoire abrégée de presque tout nôtre misère? la voici. Il existoit un homme naturel: on a introduit au dedans de cet homme un homme artificiel, et il s'est élevé dans la caverne une guerre civile qui dure toute la vie.'[1]

2. *Natural Law*

Samuel Pufendorf was the first to occupy a Chair as Professor of the Law of Nature and of Nations (at Heidelberg, *c.* 1662), but the idea which he expounded had behind it a long and venerable history. In antiquity the cry 'Follow Nature' was raised by Cynics, Stoics, and Epicureans; and the Stoics, like their later counterparts, linked together the starry heavens and the moral law within: the law that preserved the stars from wrong was also the rule of duty. The Stoic law of Nature, as the source and test of morality, fused with the *jus gentium* of the Roman Jurists, which,

[1] Diderot, *Supplément au Voyage de Bougainville*, ed. G. Chinard (Johns Hopkins Press, 1935), quoted in editor's Introd., p. 57.

originally a body of customary usages employed between Romans and aliens, came later to be identified with the laws of that Nature before which all men are equal. The writings of Cicero (who, by the way, was held in exaggerated esteem at the end of the seventeenth century) seem to have helped towards this fusion:

> 'Nations and princes may make laws, but they are without the true character of law if they are not derived from the original source of law, which existed before the State was established.'[1]

Gaius defines the *jus gentium* as *jus quod naturalis ratio constituit*, and in Justinian the identification is complete. The pagan conceptions of the Natural Law and of a life according to Nature were assimilated and modified by Christianity. The Law of Nature now becomes the Law of God, or rather, as St Thomas Aquinas puts it, that part of the Law Eternal which is made known to man through his reason.[2] Though in Pauline and Augustinian teaching our legal righteousness is mere dross, and our loftiest virtues only splendid vices, yet Christianity had in Adam and his prelapsarian bliss a type of the natural man, and of a State of Nature which, unlike the fabulous *Saturnia regna* of the pagan poets, had really once existed. Christianity was thus able to use the conception of a natural state, i.e. of a state in which the laws of God and of reason, and we may add, the Gospel laws especially, should prevail, as a perpetual check upon existing ways of life. From the first, however, Christian Natural Law had two aspects corresponding to the 'original' and the fallen natures of man; there was, on the one hand, what was natural in Eden, and on the other, what was natural in Europe. Private property, in the opinion of St Ambrose, for example, is not an institution of Nature; Nature gave all things to all men in common: it was usurpation and greed which created dominion. Things being as they are since the Fall, however, property is not necessarily an evil. Similarly, men made in the image of God are 'by nature'

[1] *De Legibus*, i, 7.

[2] *Summa*, Ia IIae, Q. xciv, 2.

free, yet sin has made serfdom and all the paraphernalia of coercion a necessity. The Gospel rule that we should do as we would be done by was a law of Nature, yet man in his depravity must be compelled by positive law to obey this natural law. On the whole, then, the existing system was sanctioned by God and Nature for the preservation of order, and departures from it would be unnatural. Yet still the idea of the first and purer Natural Law hovered in the background, and man, though severely damaged by the Fall, could feel that he had not yet lost all his original brightness. Liberty, equality, and fraternity were still the perquisites of his ideal if not of his actual nature, and even in the Middle Ages the established order could be criticized from this standpoint. For instance, as goods were originally or by nature held in common, Natural Law still demands that the rich shall relieve the poor out of their superfluity. Similarly, slavery was supposed to be contrary to Nature (in spite of Aristotle, who had thought it quite natural), and the various radical revolts of the Middle Ages were partly inspired by Natural-Law doctrine. On the whole, however, one may perhaps risk the generalization that it was the idea of a controlling *Law* of Nature which officially dominated the Middle Ages, rather than that of the liberating *Rights* of Nature; and that in passing into the seventeenth and eighteenth centuries, 'Nature' ceases to be mainly a regulating principle, and becomes mainly a liberating principle. The Middle Ages condemned usury as unnatural ('a breed of barren metal'), contrary to Scripture and to Aristotle; and it also condemned, in the names of Scripture and Nature, precisely 'that effort to achieve a continuous and unlimited increase in material wealth which modern societies applaud as meritorious'.[1] The centuries following the Renaissance liberated the acquisitive impulses, also in the name of Nature, and severed economic ethics from control by any comprehensive conception of the ultimate purpose of human (not to say Christian) living. The inhabitants of

[1] Tawney, *Religion and the Rise of Capitalism*, p. 35.

the brave new world could feel that the world was all before them, and Providence their guide. For, as the eighteenth century discovered,

> Thus God and Nature fixed the general frame,
> And bade self-love and social be the same.

So beneficently had God planned the world, that by giving full rein to his acquisitive appetites the individual was, in fact, adding his maximum quota to the sum of human happiness. Thus, instead of Dante ascending to Paradise under the guidance of Reason and Grace, instead of Spenser's Arthur, fashioned in noble and gentle discipline, instead of Bunyan's Pilgrim, setting forth with his load of sin to escape from the wrath to come, the new world offers us as its symbolical figure Robinson Crusoe, the isolated economic man, pitting his lonely strength successfully against Nature in a remote part of the earth, and carrying on a little missionary activity as a side-line. The Law of Nature, which in the Middle Ages had been a check on unregenerate impulse, had now been transformed into a sanction for *laissez-faire*, and free competition for the spoils of the world.

Somewhat similarly the idea of a State of Nature, especially after Locke, came to be used as a means whereby the new ruling classes could vindicate, against the surviving restraints of the old feudal and ecclesiastical order, their cherished rights of individual freedom and of property. But further, the eighteenth century was haunted by the philosophical mirage of the State of Nature, and used it as an ideal standard by which an obsolete actuality could be condemned. It has often been pointed out that Locke's vindication of the Whig Revolution inspired both the American and the French Revolutions, both of which were accompanied by declarations of the natural and inalienable Rights of Man. It was especially his successors, the French *philosophes*, who (in Bryce's somewhat rhetorical phrase) converted 'that which had been for nearly two thousand years a harmless maxim, almost a commonplace of morality', into 'a mass of dynamite which shattered an ancient monarchy and shook the European continent'.[1] Natural Law, sanctioning liberty and progress, was to be the basis of the modern liberal-bourgeois State.

3. *Nature in Literary Theory*

First follow Nature, and your judgment frame
By her just standard, which is still the same.

Critics and poets, no less than theologians, jurists, and political philosophers, were at this time referring habitually to Nature as their standard. The protean ambiguity of the term is well illustrated in the circumstance that it was Pope, commonly regarded by the nineteenth century as the chief exemplar of an 'artificial' poetry, who wrote the lines just quoted, and who described Nature as 'at once the source, and end, and test of Art'. The Nature of one age becomes the Art of the next, and each new school has to fight against the Nature of the last age. Wordsworth himself, when rejecting the 'gaudy and inane phraseology' of the eighteenth century, hardly felt more conscious of making a salutary return to Nature than Dryden when abandoning 'metaphysics' and Jacobean over-luxuriance in favour of the style of Sir John Denham, whose *Cooper's Hill*, he wrote, 'is, and ever will be, the exact standard of good writing'. The 'Nature' of the critics doubtless borrowed some of its authority from physics and theology, but the special problem in criticism was to reconcile adherence to Nature with adherence to the rules of Art, and both with the requirements of reason and good sense. The favourite solution, that of Rapin and Pope, was to identify Nature, the ancients, the rules, and sound reason, so that to follow any was to follow all. 'Art', says Rapin, is 'good Sense reduc'd to Method'; and again, the Rules were 'made only to reduce Nature into Method'.[2] The Rules, in fact,

[1] *Studies in Jurisprudence*, vol. ii, p. 163.
[2] *Reflections on Aristotle's Treatise of Poesie* (1674): Rymer's translation, 1706 ed., vol. ii, pp. 146 and 240.

are those laws in whose service is perfect naturalness; only by following them does the poet's work become 'just, proportionate, and natural': they are founded on 'good sense and sound reason, rather than on Authority and Example'—though, of course, the ancients exhibit these qualities in the highest degree, and 'it is in these great Originals that our modern poets ought to consult Nature'. Further, 'the only certain way to please, is by Rules'; hence, what pleases must be in accordance with the Rules, and must therefore also be an imitation of Nature. What, for instance, is 'natural' in poetic diction? Dryden answers:

> 'Virgil and Horace, the severest writers of the severest age, have made frequent use of the hardest metaphors, and of the strongest hyperboles; and in this case the best authority is the best argument; for generally to have pleased, and through all ages, must bear the force of universal tradition. And if you would appeal from thence to right reason, you will gain no more by it in effect, than, first, to set up your reason against those authors; and, secondly, against all those who have admired them. . . . I grant you, that the knowledge of Nature was the original rule; and that all poets ought to study her, as well as Aristotle and Horace, her interpreters. But then this also undeniably follows, that *those things, which delight all ages, must have been an imitation of Nature.*'[1]

Here 'imitation of Nature' seems to approach the sense of 'satisfying to the mind or heart or imagination of man'—an interpretation made explicitly in the next century by Reynolds:

> 'My notion of Nature comprehends not only the forms which Nature produces, but also the nature and internal fabric and organization, as I may call it, of the human mind and imagination. . . . He who thinks Nature, in the narrow sense of the word, is alone to be followed, will produce but a scanty entertainment for the imagination: *everything is to be done with which it is natural for the mind to be pleased. . . . In short, whatever pleases has in it*

---

[1] *Apology for Heroic Poetry and Poetic Licence* (1677), in Ker's edition of Dryden's *Essays*, vol. i, p. 183. (My italics.)

what is analogous to the mind, and is, therefore, in the highest and best sense of the word, natural.' [1]

Whatever pleases *whom*? The principle would seem to sanction the most unlimited individualism in taste. In fact, however, most educated people between Rapin and Reynolds were pleased with much the same things, and 'whatever pleases' meant whatever pleased them; their preferences and aversions could well seem those of average educated humanity. 'Natural' in this context (as in most others at this time) has lost all reference to what is original or primitive, and has come to mean what is congenial to those in whom human nature is most fully developed, that is, to the educated in the most polite nations of the civilized world. To establish the 'natural' in art we must follow the method of Grotius in establishing the authority of Natural Law: we must refer to what is received amongst the 'most civil', since 'what is natural we must judge by those in whom nature is least corrupt, and not by the depraved'. [2] What pleased the Goths is not natural, for in their time poets 'suffered their Wits to ramble in the Romantick way'. [3] And what qualities in poetry best pleased the most civil of our period? All must be 'just, uniform and proportionable'; design or 'ordonnance' is the first consideration. The Epic or Heroic poem is 'the greatest Work that Human Wit is capable of', and the weightiest critical remarks of the age refer to this, or to Tragedy. The Fable should combine the astonishing with the probable 'in such a just Temperament as may please the Fancy without shocking the Reason'. Poetic probability is preferable to 'Truth' (realism): 'Nothing is brought into the World that is not remote from the Perfection of its Idea from its very Birth. Originals and Models are to be search'd for in Probability, and in the Universal Principles of Things, where nothing that is Material and

[1] *Discourse VII,* pp. 193 and 197 in Roger Fry's edition. (My italics.)

[2] *Of the Law of Warre and Peace*, Eng. trans., London, 1655, First Part, sect. v.

[3] Rapin, *op. cit.*, p. 158. The ensuing quotations are from the same treatise.

Singular enters to corrupt them'. In this theory the two meanings of 'Natural'—(*a*) what is 'true' and (*b*) what is 'pleasing'—are harmonized. *We are in fact pleased by what is 'true'*, but 'true' here means the universal, not the particular. 'Nature' for the poet is the idea, the form, the potentiality which in history, and in 'fact', strive to realize themselves in refractory matter. Art completes what Nature leaves imperfect; Nature offers a brazen world—the poets only deliver a golden. The problem was that which has exercised poets and critics in all ages, namely, how to intensify Nature without distorting it; how to attain the universal without abandoning the particular; how to 'subject the shows of things to the desires of the mind' without producing chimaeras; how to be poetical without ceasing to be natural; how to be natural without becoming mean or insipid. The critics of the neo-classic age could solve the problem in their own way because they knew what pleased them, and they surmised that this corresponded with Nature's own intentions. A play, says Dryden, 'to be like Nature, is to be set above it'; a serious play 'is indeed the representation of Nature, but 'tis Nature wrought up to an higher pitch'.[1] We must not follow Nature on foot, but mounted upon Pegasus. So, the characters in our heroic poems or plays must be types, not individuals; their thoughts, sentiments, and expressions must be suited to their Age, Sex, Quality, Employment, and Fortune. In our Eclogues, our shepherds and nymphs must not be real rustics, nor should their talk run too much upon the technicalities of their calling. We must avoid alike the gross bucolicism of Theocritus and Ronsard, and the over-sophistication of Guarini or Marino. 'L'illusion et en même temps l'agrément des bergeries', wrote Fontenelle,[2] 'consiste donc à n'offrir aux yeux que la tranquillité de la vie pastorale, dont on dissimule la bassesse: on en laisse voir la simplicité, mais on en cache la misère.' Similarly our diction

[1] *Essay of Dramatic Poesy*, Ker, vol. i, pp. 100 and 102.
[2] *Discours sur l'Églogue* (1688): Works (1790-2 ed.), vol. v, p. 16.

must be 'Apt, Clear, Natural, Splendid, and Numerous';[1] one must be simple, but nobly simple—not base, dull, or without sinew; one should aim at the grand manner, but without conceit or extravagance. *Decorum* is the most universal of all the Rules.

All this decorum—this propriety of thoughts and words, this unity and proportionableness, this mending of Nature by Nature herself—to what purpose is it? For delight, certainly, Dryden and others will say; but Rapin's statement is sufficiently representative:

> ''Tis true, Delight is the end Poetry aims at, but not the principal End, as others pretend. In effect, Poetry being an Art, ought to be profitable by the quality of its own Nature, and by the essential Subordination that all Arts should have to Polity, whose end in general is the publick Good. . . . Heroick Poesie proposes the Example of great Virtues and great Vices, to excite Men to abhor these, and to be in love with the other. . . . Tragedy rectifies the use of Passions, by moderating our Fear, and our Pity, which are obstacles of Virtue.'[2]

But as the immediate aim is delight, the poet tries 'to give the most common and natural things a fabulous Gloss, to render them more Admirable, and heighten Truth by Fiction'. 'The common and ordinary Terms are not proper for a Poet.'

As the seventeenth century wore to its close, Nature and Reason began on the whole to gain upon Aristotle and the Rules. The great influence of Descartes, who had taught men to look within for their first certainties, and had spread abroad the clear light of geometric reasoning, told strongly on behalf of 'Moderns' versus 'Ancients'. It was not that one adopted any new standards: supporters of both parties in that controversy seem to have shared the same general scale of values. It was a sense that the world's great age was beginning anew, and that pupilage to antiquity was now unnecessary. Now that right Reason had down returned to men, we

[1] Rapin, *op. cit.*, p. 163. [2] *ibid.*, p. 140.

could address ourselves direct to her, and neglect the mediation of Aristotle and Horace, her interpreters. But with the triumph of the Cartesian spirit a new and disquieting question did suggest itself: now that we were delivered from ancient error, now that our minds were filled with clear and distinct ideas, should we really need poetry any more?—poetry, which heightens Truth by fiction, and imparts to all things a fabulous gloss? Perhaps poetry was the 'mental rattle' which awakened the attention of man in the infancy of society, and perhaps we should now put away childish things? Let us hear, on 'the geometric spirit', a writer whose range of interests and whose longevity render him singularly representative of the period under discussion, Fontenelle—poet, critic, mathematician, historian, philosopher, and popularizer of Descartes.

> 'L'esprit géométrique n'est pas si attaché à la géométrie, qu'il n'en puisse être tiré, et transporté à d'autres connoissances. Un ouvrage de morale, de politique, de critique, peut-être même d'éloquence, en sera plus beau, toutes choses d'ailleurs égales, s'il est fait de main de géomètre. L'ordre, la netteté, la précision, l'exactitude, qui règnent dans les bons livres depuis un certain temps, pourraient bien avoir leur première source dans cet esprit géométrique, qui se répand plus que jamais, et qui en quelque façon se communique de proche en proche à ceux même qui ne connoissent pas la géométrie. Quelquefois un grand homme donne le ton à tout son siècle; celui [i.e. Descartes] à qui on pourroit le plus légitimement accorder la gloire d'avoir établi un nouvel art de raisonner, étoit un excellent géomètre.'[1]

An age which has produced such a man, and in which truth has so mightily prevailed against prejudice, should look forwards to a glorious future, not backwards to the infancy of society. History, the past, is a nightmare from which we are trying to awake. The sciences are only recently born, yet what exhilarating advances they have already made! We might, indeed, be grateful to the

[1] Preface, *Sur l'Utilité des Mathématiques et de la Physique*, etc.: Works, vol. vi, pp. 67-8.

ancients for having exhausted all the wrong theories for us in advance. It might have been easy, we may think, to perceive that

> 'tout le jeu de la nature consiste dans les figures et dans les mouvemens des corps: cependant, avant que d'en venir lâ, il a fallu essayer des idées de Platon, des nombres de Pythagore, des qualités d'Aristote; et *tout cela ayant été reconnu pour faux, on a été réduit à prendre le vrai système*.' [1]

But although we so easily surpass the ancients in physics, mathematics, and medicine, which depend upon experiment or exact reasoning, it may be otherwise with poetry. Eloquence and poetry only require a limited outlook, a little vivacity of imagination, and a few rules, in order to arrive at all the perfection of which they are capable, and thus in these accomplishments—'*quoiqu'elles ne soient pas en elles-mêmes fort importantes*' [2]—the ancients may have excelled. Fontenelle thinks that they attained this limited perfection in the century of Augustus. Virgil's versification was the finest in the world, though in ordonnance, variety, and nobility of characters our romances have revealed new possibilities. Poetry, moreover, is essentially something primitive; it began before prose, and it was bound up with all that pertains to the childhood of man—with fable and myth, which even now are so congenial to us that 'nous retombons aisément en enfance'. But now that we have reached maturity, now that Descartes and Newton have sprung the light, what of poetry? '*Ce qui n'est fondé que sur d'agréables fantômes, n'aurait-il rien à craindre?*' [3] Fontenelle echoes such writers as Thomas Sprat, and anticipates Johnson and Wordsworth, in his opinion that the 'fabulous' images of poetry have now worn very thin—they are 'extrèmement usées', though he admits that they 'mettent de la vie dans tout cet univers': this universe which is becoming so mechanical. Nothing

[1] Fontenelle, *Digression sur les Anciens et les Modernes*: Works, vol. v, p. 287. (My italics.)

[2] *ibid.*, pp. 290-1. (My italics.)

[3] Fontenelle, *Sur la Poésie en général*: Works, vol. iii, p. 195.

else is exempt from the touch of cold philosophy, and it is unlikely that poetry will escape it. Poetry must save itself, if at all, by becoming philosophic, by concerning itself less with surface ornament and more with underlying realities. It must use 'real' or 'material' images, in defiance of those who think its function is merely 'se jouer sur la superficie des choses, la décorer, l'embellir'.

> 'Et que seroit-ce si l'on venoit à découvrir et à s'assurer que ces ornemens, pris dans un système absolument faux et ridicule, exposés depuis longtems à tous les passans sur les grands chemins du parnasse, ne sont pas dignes d'être employés, et ne valent pas la peine qu'ils coûtent encore à employer? Qu'enfin . . . il y a de la puerilité à gêner son langage uniquement pour flatter l'oreille, et à le gêner au point que souvent on en dit moins ce qu'on vouloit, et quelquefois autre chose?' [1]

When opening a book of poetry, wrote Jean Le Clerc in the last year of the seventeenth century, the reader should remember that he is about to peruse 'the Work of a Liar, who intends to entertain him with Fictions. . . . The poets are full of false thoughts, by which if we are not deceived, yet we insensibly lose a good Taste and right judgment, which are the finest ornaments of human nature.' [2]

Cut off by philosophy from their traditional 'machinery' because it was too fabulous, and cut off (in spite of all that Perrault and Dryden [3] could urge) from Christian material because it was too sacred, the poets of the new century may well seem to have stood shivering in a spiritual east wind. Boileau is reported to have said that Descartes had cut the throat of poetry; however, it was only pseudo-poetry that he helped to destroy. Great new subterranean forces—political, social, and economic—were indeed to be required in order to break the glittering surface of the silver age; but meanwhile, by shifting off the dead weight

[1] *ibid.*, pp. 195-6.

[2] *Parrhasiana* (1699), Eng. trans., 1700, p. 6.

[3] Cf. *Parallèle des Anciens et des Modernes* (1692), vol. iii, pp. 7 ff., and Ker's *Dryden*, vol. ii, pp. 30 ff.

of antique authority, and by clearing away the neo-classic lumber, the geometric spirit was preparing the way for the return to a new Nature, and for a poetry which should devote itself 'moins au talent qu'à l'esprit, moins aux ornemens qu'au fond des choses'.

CHAPTER II

The Wisdom of God in the Creation

'*The works of Nature everywhere sufficiently evidence a Deity.*'
[Locke.]

THE proposition quoted above was, as we have seen, very generally accepted as self-evident at the beginning of the eighteenth century. I propose to illustrate the manner of its acceptance by briefly examining three works which enjoyed considerable vogue in their own day: Thomas Burnet's *Sacred Theory of the Earth* or *Telluris Theoria Sacra* (1681-9), John Ray's *Wisdom of God manifested in the Works of the Creation* (1691), and William Derham's *Physico-Theology* (1713). It is the last two of these which I am taking as representative of the period of the Newtonian illumination, when heaven and earth were felt to be so obtrusively proclaiming their divine original. But the quality of this 'physico-theology' will perhaps be better appreciated if we first consider, by way of contrast, the work of Thomas Burnet, in which an older, darker theology is seen blending with the temper of the new philosophy.

1. THOMAS BURNET'S *Sacred Theory of the Earth*

Thomas Burnet (1635?-1715), successively pupil of Tillotson at Clare, friend of Cudworth, Fellow of Christ's, Master of the Charterhouse, and finally Chaplain-in-Ordinary to William III, deserves to be read, if only for his stately prose, which, no less than his theory of the world, places him unmistakably within the seventeenth century penumbra. The *Sacred Theory*, for all its eccentricity, has about it a certain epic grandeur both in conception and style, and Burnet might be described as a kind of prose Milton thirty years nearer to Addison.

Burnet grants, with the physico-theologians, that in the

general economy of Nature there is enough—and more than enough—evidence of design to prove a Deity. Where he differs from them is in not regarding the world in its present state as the best of possible worlds. The world, as we know it, is not the world as God designed it, and it is therefore both unscientific and blasphemous to ground our devotion upon its alleged perfections. On the contrary, the world is a mighty ruin, a damaged paradise—majestic, no doubt (the work of the divine architect could scarcely be otherwise, even in decay), but a ruin none the less. It may furnish evidence of God's anger, but not of his original intention; disproportioned sin has jarred against Nature's chime. Burnet rests his argument upon three main points: the chaotic state of the terraqueous globe as it presents itself to the unflinching eye, the certainty that this condition arose from sin, and the theory that the cataclysm which produced it was the Flood. It will be seen, then, that Burnet's high argument is blended of aesthetic, moral, theological, and pseudo-scientific ingredients. Indeed (as I hope to show in a moment), his belief in the parallel and synchronized working of the scientific laws along with God's dispensations is one of the most significant points in the book.

Casting his eye, then, over the physical world, Burnet (not unlike Pascal contemplating the stellar scene) is appalled by what he sees.

> 'Oratours and Philosophers treat Nature after a very different manner; Those represent her with all her graces and ornaments, and if there be anything which is not capable of that, they dissemble it, or pass it over slightly. But Philosophers view Nature with a more impartial eye, and without favour or prejudice give a just and free account, how they find all the parts of the Universe, some more, some less perfect.'[1]

If we are to describe the earth as it really is,

> 'though it be handsome and regular enough to the eye in certain parts of it, single tracts and single Regions; yet if we consider the

[1] *Theory of the Earth* (1684 ed.), p. 109.

whole surface of it, or the whole Exteriour Region, 'tis as a broken and confus'd heap of bodies, plac'd in no order to one another, nor with any correspondency or regularity of parts: And such a body as the Moon appears to us, when 'tis look'd upon with a good Glass, rude and ragged. . . . They are both in my judgment the image or picture of a great Ruine, and have the true aspect of a World lying in its rubbish.'

Still greater would be our horror if we could descend into the hideous catacombs below the surface of the earth, 'some filled with smoak and fire, some with water, and some with vapours and mouldy Air'; if we saw all this, 'we should not easily believe that God created it into this form immediately out of nothing; It would have cost no more to have made things in better order; nay, it had been more easie and more simple; and accordingly we are assured that all things were made at first in Beauty and proportion.'[1]

Or again, consider the sea: how aesthetically unsatisfying is its arrangement! how unlike what we should have supposed to be the taste of the divine artificer in world-planning!

'If the Sea had been drawn round the Earth in regular figures and borders, it might have been a great Beauty to our Globe, and we should have reasonably concluded it a work of the first Creation, or of Nature's first production; but finding on the contrary all the marks of disorder and disproportion in it, we may as reasonably conclude, that it did not belong to the first order of things, but was something succedaneous, when the degeneracy of mankind, and the judgments of God had destroy'd the first World, and subjected the Creation to some kind of Vanity.'[2]

And the very idea of the ocean-bed, with all its slimy circumstance, fills Burnet with disgust; such things must not be put down to divine omnipotence. 'Nature doth not fall into disorder till mankind be first degenerate and leads the way.' Occasionally, it is true, Burnet slips into a mood of admiration even of our lost planet, and he

[1] *ibid.*, p. 125. [2] *ibid.*, p. 129.

writes then more in the tone of a *Spectator*-reverie on the Sublime or on the ruins of antiquity. Mountains, for example, move him strongly (and perhaps rather unexpectedly), and he gives us a passage which Derham could quote in support of his own very different argument:

> 'The greatest objects of Nature are, methinks, the most pleasing to behold; and next to the great Concave of the Heavens, and those boundless Regions where the Stars inhabit, there is nothing that I look upon with more pleasure than the wide Sea and the Mountains of the Earth. There is something august and stately in the Air of these things that inspires the mind with great thoughts and passions; We do naturally upon such occasions think of God, and his greatness, and whatsoever hath but the shadow and appearance of Infinite, as all things have that are too big for our comprehension, they fill and over-bear the mind with their Excess, and cast it into a pleasing kind of stupor and admiration.'[1]

Almost all that Addison, Gray, Burke, or even Wordsworth could claim for mountains, one might reflect. Yet this mood, so akin, apparently, to that in which Gray wrote of Gordale Scar or 'that huge creature of God Ingleborough', soon deserts him, and he returns to his point. The mountains are majestic ruins, and he receives from them only a sense of awe, 'as from old Temples and broken Amphitheaters of the Romans we collect the greatness of that people'. Burnet has crossed the Alps and the Apennines, and the sight of 'those wild, vast and indigested heaps of Stones and Earth' seems to have been what first set him upon devising a theory to account for such prodigies. Apparently there were no 'physical' maps in those days—only 'political', for Burnet deplores the absence of the former. He also desiderates rough Globes (i.e. with mountains shown in relief) instead of the smooth ones used in the schools, for then we should see 'what a rude lump our World is which we are so apt to dote upon'.

How, then, was the world formed when fresh from the

[1] *ibid.*, p. 139.

hands of God? and how did it fall into its present state? Burnet's answers to these questions are not greatly to our purpose, but they may be briefly indicated for the sake of their 'period' interest. When the earth was formed from chaos the elements were arranged in their 'proper' order, with Earth as the centre, surrounded by the Water, and this in turn by the Air. 'Water', however, includes all fluids, and consequently the watery surface of the globe had a top coating of oil. Further, before the process of creation had quite settled down, the air was full of particles of dust—earthy matter which had not yet found its true location. All this sifted down, and formed a thick crust by mixing with the oily matter on the surface. This became the first crust of the world, and was absolutely smooth, as befitted the paradise which God had designed for man. Paradise was not confined to one spot of ground; it covered the whole earth. Burnet refutes with great composure and surprising resourcefulness all the possible scientific objections which might be raised against his theory. The earth was originally in a 'right posture' to the sun, and so it enjoyed perpetual equinox. How was the earth watered, if there were no seas and no mountains? Vapours arose, he replies, from the waters below the crust, passed through the surface into the air, and then condensed at the Poles. Thence the precipitated water ran in radiating streams towards the equator—(why? because, the earth being slightly oval, the Poles were 'higher' than the equator), and there evaporated. In this beautifully geometrical world, then, so much worthier of its divine original than the 'torn troubled form we know' to-day, man lived awhile in peace and innocence, enjoying the tranquil climate and attaining great longevity. This was the true Golden Age dreamed of by the poets, and Burnet, like all 'primitivists' who have sung or discoursed of such an age, tells us that it was a time of 'great easiness and simplicity', whereas now we have to endure 'a more pompous, forc'd and artificial method'. Let no one think this paradise fabulous or 'unnatural': ''Tis we that have left the tract of Nature, that are wrought and screw'd up into artifices, that have disguis'd our selves; and 'tis in our World that the Scenes are chang'd, and become more strange and fantastical'.[1]

What, then, of the cataclysm which shattered this spherical and world-wide Eden? It was the Flood, of course, which produced the heavy change; that must be unquestioned. But it is precisely here that Burnet produces his most triumphant pseudo-scientific hypothesis. The Flood? Yes, but Burnet, strongly tinged with the scientific curiosity of his age, is dissatisfied with what Browne had called the 'popular exposition of Moses'. Assuming that the earth was in its present state at that time, how could the available waters have covered the earth, even granting the most torrential downpour of rain throughout the specified forty days and nights? It was inconceivable; there was simply not enough water for the purpose. What really happened was this: in the fulness of time the earth's crust, which had been imperceptibly drying and shrinking throughout the patriarchal period, began to crack. And when sin had gathered sufficient head, parts of the crust collapsed and fell inwards upon the waters below, forcing them out over all the earth. Here, says Burnet, is the true explanation of that mysterious phrase 'the fountains of the great deep were opened'—a phrase insufficiently regarded by the holders of the rainfall theory. When the force of the convulsion had abated, and the water found its level again, the world was left as we now see it, the collapsed portions constituting the ocean-beds, and the rest the dry land with its fretted coastlines and broken surfaces. The blend, in Burnet, of the theologian and the follower of the 'new philosophy', is well seen in his ingenious way of linking together the laws of matter and the decrees of God. How was the world ruined? By the operation of natural causes which, one might suppose, would have produced their result even if man had retained his first innocence. But the things

[1] *ibid.*, p. 249.

which come to pass in the ordinary course of Nature are no less 'providential' than special interpositions; on the contrary, the regular mechanism of second causes is the best evidence of God's wisdom. And Burnet actually postulates a kind of pre-established harmony between the material and the moral worlds:

> 'This seems to me to be the great Art of Divine Providence, so to adjust the two Worlds, Humane and Natural, Material and Intellectual, as seeing through the possibilities and futuritions of each, according to the first state and circumstances he puts them under, they should all along correspond and fit one another, and especially in their great Crises and Periods.'[1]

For once at least, it would seem, disproportion'd sin chimed punctually with Nature's crash.

Burnet's eschatology (Books III and IV—'The Burning of the World' and 'The New Heavens and New Earth') may be mentioned, in conclusion, to complete the picture. The last conflagration, like the Flood, will have natural causes. All the volcanoes and more will vomit at once, aided by 'fiery meteors' from above. And if you desire further inflammable material, consider 'our Brittish Soyl', which contains so much coal that England will be a particularly hot corner when the catastrophe arrives. The fire will, however, *begin* at Rome, as being the seat of Antichrist. After the fire, the precipitation of the elements from the vast smoke-cloud begins, and the original paradisal earth is reproduced. The thousand years' reign of Christ and the Saints follows (Satan being in chains), and at the end of this period Gog and Magog, and the 'earthborn' (a second race produced from the new Earth), will arise in a final conflict, in which Satan and the giants will be destroyed, and the saints translated to heaven. The Earth will become a fixed star.

This theory, of which its author seems justly proud, carried many difficulties in its wake, but Burnet tackles them all with that intrepidity which later brought his

[1] *ibid.*, p. 107.

orthodoxy into suspicion, and lost him his Clerkship to William III. For instance, how does he account for the diffusion of Noah's progeny after the Flood? How was America peopled from Ararat? Perhaps each continent had its Noah's Ark, he replies; we may only have been apprised by Moses of the particular Ark which concerns our own part of the world. He is excused by his own theory from assuming more than one Adam, though he is ready to surmise that other planets have had their floods, and so, presumably, their original sins. But the point which, when later developed in his *Archaeologiae Philosophicae* (1692), cost him his preferment, is already touched upon in the *Review* of the *Theory* (dated 1690). What explanation was to be offered to anyone who should object that, after all, Moses described a terraqueous globe, and not Burnet's paradise? Moses, replies Burnet, did not 'Philosophize or Astronomize in that description'; ''tis a narration suited to the capacity of the people, and not to the strict and physical nature of things'. Moses must be interpreted so as not to be 'repugnant to clear and uncontested science'. ''Tis a dangerous thing to ingage the authority of Scripture in disputes about the Natural World, in opposition to Reason, lest Time, which brings all things to light, should discover that to be evidently false which we had made Scripture to assert.'[1] This argument (no new one even in Burnet's time) was worthy, one may feel, of a better kind of 'science' than Burnet's.

2. John Ray's *Wisdom of God in the Creation*

Of the two physico-theologians whom we are now to consider, John Ray (1627-1705) was by far the more distinguished. Ray has been called 'the Aristotle of England and the Linnaeus of his age', and he is usually accounted the founder of modern botany and zoology. He was the son of an Essex blacksmith, and became a Fellow of Trinity College, Cambridge, the same year as Barrow (1649). In that age of harmony between science and religion it is not

[1] *ibid.*, Preface.

surprising to find that he took orders (1660), though he resigned them two years later over the question of the 'Bartholomew' Act, remaining, however, in lay communion all his life. His *Wisdom of God in the Creation*, which became something of a classic in the eighteenth century (it was used by two such diverse teachers as Wesley and Paley), was written as a College exercise, but was not published until 1691.

In passing from Burnet to Ray and Derham we become aware of a change of outlook none the less profound for being unstated. What we are witnessing is simply the emergence from the tragic shadows of the past into the common daylight of the eighteenth century. The Fall is no longer a haunting obsession, and whatever may be true of Man, Nature is now to be contemplated as the finished and unimprovable product of divine wisdom, omnipotence, and benevolence. 'How manifold are thy works, O Lord!' represents the prevailing mood of Ray's book. With a confident assurance that his words will be readily acceptable to his readers, he disposes first of the classical arguments for atheism, sometimes working out his own refutation, and sometimes referring merely to some unimpeachable authority. The heresy of Aristotle, that the world is eternal, has been exploded by Archbishop Tillotson and Bishop Wilkins. That of the Epicureans, that the world can be accounted for by postulating matter, a void, and the declination of atoms, has been exposed by Cudworth and Stillingfleet, but had in fact been effectively refuted long since by Cicero, who of all the ancients seemed, at that time, perhaps the most entirely admirable. '*Caelestem ergo admirabilem ordinem, incredibilemque constantiam, ex qua conservatio et salus omnium omnis oritur, qui vacare mente putat, nae ipse mentis expers habendus est?*' Had Cicero known of the Copernican simplification, and all that we have since learned, could he have said more? But what of that more subtle modern atheism, that Cartesian teaching which, by reducing the Deity to an abstract first cause, leaves us with a dead universe of matter and motion, virtually untenanting Creation of its God? As a biologist, Ray was able to attack mechanical materialism, if not with new arguments, at least with new evidence and a new degree of confidence. The laws of motion fail to account for the very class of phenomena in which he was most interested—the organization of the bodies of plants and animals, their adaptation to their environment, and all the details of their development and structure:

> 'These mechanick Philosophers being no way able to give an account thereof from the necessary Motion of Matter, *unguided by Mind for Ends*, prudently therefore break off their System there, when they should come to Animals.' [1]

To account for 'vital motions', and the existence and preservation of species, Ray demands a 'vegetative soul' or a 'plastick Nature', which will both relieve God from setting his hand to every work, and at the same time bear the responsibility for what may seem to us 'Errors and Bungles'. But for all the marvels of instinct in the animal kingdom—the parental solicitude of birds, the non-appearance of wasps until the 'plumbs' are ripe, the organization of the bee-hive, and so forth, as well as for the maintenance of the due proportion of the sexes in animals—for all these and the other manifold instances of design, he postulates a superintendence by a principle superior to the 'plastick or spermatick Nature'. No matter how closely we pry into Nature, the evidence all repeats the same tale. Had Pliny looked through one of our microscopes, and seen the animalculae in a drop of water, how would he have been 'rapt into an Extasie of Astonishment and Admiration'? The study of Nature is the true 'preparative to Divinity'; let us then 'converse with Nature as well as Books', not confining our studies (as is unfortunately too much the custom in 'this University') to tongues, philology, history, and antiquity. The large-scale phenomena of Nature, no less than the microscopic, point to their divine original, and of mountains Ray can write with a much more com-

[1] *Wisdom of God* (1701 ed.), p. 48.

placent sensibility than Burnet. So far from being 'Warts and superfluous Excrescencies',

> 'They are very Ornamental to the Earth, affording pleasant and delightful Prospects, both 1. To them that look downwards from them, upon the subjacent Countries; as they must needs acknowledge, who have been but on the Downs of Sussex, and enjoyed that ravishing Prospect of the Sea on one hand, and the Country far and wide on the other. And 2. To those that look upward and behold them from the Plains and low Grounds, which what a refreshing and pleasure it is to the Eye, they are best able to judge who have lived in the Isle of Ely, or other level Countries.'[1]

God has placed man in a 'spacious and well-furnished world', and it is man's duty as well as privilege to exploit and improve it as much as he can. Ray is with the Baconians and the moderns against the older theologians and moralists; the world we are to exploit is no ruin, blasted by God's vengeance for mortal sin. It is the brave new world of science which lies before us. Ray decisively rejects the golden-age 'primitivism' of such as Burnet—that half-belief in a lost paradise which is the natural corollary of belief in the Fall. Like Voltaire later, he prefers civilization to Arcadia:

> 'If a Country thus planted and adorned, thus polished and civilized, thus improved to the height . . . be not preferred before a barbarous and inhospitable Scythia . . . or a rude and unpolished America peopled with slothful and naked Indians, instead of well-built Houses, living in pitiful Huts and Cabans, made of poles set end-ways; then surely the brute Beasts Condition, and manner of Living . . . is to be esteem'd better than Man's, and Wit and Reason was in vain bestowed on him.'[2]

The world and the creatures in it were not, indeed, 'so made for Man that they have no other use', but they were made for our study, and the Creation can only praise God through us. And, of course, the grand and pre-eminent instance of design is the human body itself—its erect posture

[1] *ibid.*, p. 221. [2] *ibid.*, p. 185.

(proved by anatomical evidence to be intentional), the admirable and convenient disposition of all its parts, and so forth (for further testimony we are referred to Mr Boyle on the teeth, and Mr Clopton Havers on the bones):

> 'it seems to me impossible that Matter divided into as minute and subtle Parts as you will or can imagine, and those moved according to what Catholick laws soever can be devised, should without the Presidency and Direction of some intelligent Agent, by the mere agitation of a gentle Heat, run itself into such a curious Machine, as the Body of Man is.'[1]

Ray anticipates the theory of the survival of the fittest, or natural selection in the struggle for existence, and condemns it as a 'grand subterfuge of Atheists'. Such a theory, for him, implies spontaneous generation, which, besides being theologically unacceptable, can be disproved scientifically. The contracting muscle of the armadillo and the hedgehog is no accident of adaptation, as it might have seemed if it had been bestowed upon a soft-haired creature. Nature has not produced all sorts of creatures at random, and then allowed the unfit to be eliminated; were this so, we should surely now have many 'monsters' which, though undesigned and unwanted, had nevertheless managed to survive. One might ask, why has God made creatures other than Man, and so less perfect? Ray answers, with all who have held that whatever is, is right, that the lower ranks in the scale of being were made 'for the manifestation and displaying of his Infinite Power and Wisdom.'

Finally Ray appends an eloquent discourse, much in the vein of the Cambridge Platonists, on the use of the body in the service of God:

> 'the Body is but the dark Lanthorn, the Soul or Spirit is the Candle of the Lord that burns in it.'[2]

And he concludes with a quotation from Bishop Wilkins embodying the celebrated wager-argument so much in

[1] *ibid.*, p. 304. [2] *ibid.*, p. 407.

vogue at the end of the seventeenth century: even if there were no God, it behoves us to live as though there were, for then we at least enjoy the benefits of virtuous living on earth, while if God does exist we stand to gain an everlasting reward.

3. Derham's *Physico-Theology*

William Derham (1657-1735), though in no way remarkable either as scientist or as theologian, is a worthy representative of that class of eighteenth century country parsons who pursued both avocations with confident assurance of their essential harmony. As vicar of Upminster he made notable collections of birds and insects, and studied meteorology, astronomy, bird-migration, the habits of wasps and the death-watch beetle, and 'mechanics'. Nor did these preoccupations cause him to neglect his cure, for we learn that this 'strong, amiable and healthy' ecclesiast served his parishioners faithfully both as physician and as pastor. His researches brought him to the notice of his scientific contemporaries, and he became a Fellow of the Royal Society (1702). In 1711 and 1712 he was summoned from his rural parish to deliver the Boyle Lectures—a mark of high distinction, considering that such men as Bentley and Clarke had been amongst his predecessors. These lectures were embodied in his *Physico-Theology, or a Demonstration of the Being and Attributes of God from his Works of Creation* (1713), a work whose wide acceptance can be gauged by its having reached a twelfth edition within half a century, and by its having been translated into French, Swedish, and German.

Derham opens with proper acknowledgments to Boyle himself, of whom he says that

> 'it was his settled Opinion, that nothing tended more to cultivate true Religion and Piety in a man's Mind, than a thorough Skill in Philosophy.' [1]

The effects of this skill were everywhere manifest in

[1] *Physico-Theology*: To the Reader.

Boyle's own writings and in his life; they are evident, says Derham,

> 'from his constant Deportment in never mentioning the Name of God without a Pause, and visible Stop in his Discourse; and from the noble Foundation of his Lectures for the Honour of God, and the generous Stipend he allowed for the same.'

There is little intellectual excitement in Derham's book: indeed, it well illustrates what happens when there descends upon a whole generation the 'deep slumber of a decided opinion'. He follows Ray very closely, and constantly refers to him, though he assures us that he has deliberately refrained from reading him, immediately before and during composition, so as to make his own contribution more original. *Physico-Theology* consists mainly of a long catalogue of relevant characteristics of the terraqueous globe and its living inhabitants, punctuated frequently by pious exclamations. The globe is 'a Work too grand for any thing less than a God to make'. Earlier orthodoxy, from Aristotle to Sidney, had represented Nature as 'inferior' to Art: Art completes what Nature has left imperfect; Nature's world is brazen—'the poets only deliver a golden'. But the eighteenth century begins to reverse this teaching:

> 'Let us cast our Eyes here and there, let us ransack all the Globe, let us with the greatest accuracy inspect every Part thereof, search out the inmost Secrets of any of the Creatures; let us examine them with all our Gauges, measure them with our nicest Rules, pry into them with our Microscopes, and most exquisite Instruments, still we find them to bear Testimony to their infinite Workman; and that they exceed all humane Skill so far, as that the most exquisite Copies and Imitations of the best Artists, are no other than rude bungling Pieces to them.'[1]

And Derham supports his argument by a quotation from Bishop Wilkins, who had written, in his *Natural Religion*,

[1] *ibid.*, p. 38.

that 'whatever is Natural, doth by that appear adorned with all imaginable Elegance and Beauty . . . whereas the most curious Works of Art, the sharpest, finest Needle, doth appear as a blunt rough Bar of Iron, coming from the Furnace or the Forge. . . . So vast a Difference is there betwixt the Skill of Nature, and the Rudeness and Imperfection of Art.'

Derham defends the Globe against the strictures of Thomas Burnet by reasonings which, in their bland inconsistency, well illustrate the speculative inadequacies of his book, and perhaps indicate the strength of the will-to-believe in his age. Even if the Globe were such a 'rude, confused, inconvenient Mass as he [Burnet] pretends, yet is it *well enough for a sinful World*'.[1] Poisonous or noxious creatures are to be regarded as 'Rods and Scourges to chastise us', or as 'Means to excite our Wisdom, Care and Industry'. But it is on the material rather than the moral utility of the monstrosities of creation that Derham prefers to dwell. 'Vulcano's', for example (or 'Ignivomous Mountains'), though of undoubted value as 'Emblems or presages of Hell itself', are also physically essential as safety-valves for the fires and vapours that would otherwise 'make dismal Havock' ('and oftentimes'—he adds, with engaging thoughtlessness—'actually do so'!). As for ordinary mountains, Derham appeals beyond Burnet to the ancient and modern poets, and to the common sense of mankind, to confirm his opinion that they are beautiful. Who would care to travel, if the earth were everywhere 'of an even, level, globous Surface'? But above all, mountains are useful: they are health-giving, they furnish pasturage for sheep, they contain minerals, they provide gradients for streams, and so forth. In the end Derham stands the argument on its head in a fashion not unknown to other theologians, declaring that we must not pretend to 'censure what God doth', or to 'know the Ends and Purposes of his Infinite Will'. This, when alleged 'blunders' are in question; in the rest of the book

[1] *ibid.*, p. 48 n. (My italics.)

Derham knows enough about these very ends and purposes.

> 'All the Works of the Lord, from the most regarded, admired, and praised, to the meanest and most slighted, are great and glorious Works, incomparably contrived, and as admirably made, fitted up, and placed in the World.' [1]

God did not spend so much skill on his creatures to have them ignored; it is our pious duty, therefore, as well as our interest, to study Nature. What was true for Galen or Cicero is still truer for us Christians: did not St Bernard declare that '*Natura Codex est Dei*'?

[1] *ibid.*, p. 465.

CHAPTER III

Cosmic Toryism

'Tous les évènements sont enchainés dans le meilleur des mondes possibles.' [Pangloss.]

All partial evil, universal good,
All discord, harmony not understood.

[Pope.]

IT is not surprising to find that a certain type of metaphysical optimism was prevalent in this age of physico-theology, and that at least two of the most celebrated works of the time are theodicies. If Nature is God's own codex, then certainly the mighty maze of things cannot lack a plan—indeed, it must have the best of all possible plans, and the world must be the best of all possible worlds. The task confronting all makers of theodicies is to demonstrate the divine wisdom in creating this particular universe, in which 'evils' appear to exist.

The affirmation that 'whatever is, is right' may be and has been made at many different levels, and consequently may mean many different things. It may represent the last insight of the mystic when, in a rapture of contemplation, he has transcended good and evil, and reached an acceptance of all existence as part of a divine pattern. Such insight can only be purchased at a tremendous price —at the price, indeed, of the temporary extinction of one's separate individuality. To reach it, one must be 'laid asleep in body, and become a living soul', and we are told that even Plotinus reached this condition only four or five times in his life. What is seen from these visionary heights the mystics cannot tell; their experience is essentially incommunicable, and can only be hinted at in metaphor or negation. In such high hours, Wordsworth says, 'thought was not: in enjoyment it expired'. Traherne, who had the gift of seeing the world as heaven, wrote of his moments of vision:

> 'I was (as Plato saith, *In summa rationis arce quies habitat*) seated in a throne of repose and perfect rest. Whereupon you will not believe how I was withdrawn from all endeavours of altering and amending outward things. They lay so well, methought, they could not be mended: but I must be mended to enjoy them.'

Optimism at this level—the level at which Spinoza could declare that *omnis existentia est perfectio*—so far from being a facile or complacent creed, is admittedly almost impossibly hard to attain, and can never be long sustained by flesh and blood. For what it demands is no less than the performance, by one's own unaided strength, of the miracle which, if achieved, would wind up the universe for good and all: the resolution of the many into the one—the annihilation by sheer will-power of the gulf between the absolute and the fallen world. No wonder that in Stoicism, which tried to translate such vision into terms of daily living, the special note should have been a sad earnestness, a fatigued endurance of an almost intolerable burden.

But these high moods are rare, and much more often the affirmation that 'whatever is, is right' may be a cry of satisfaction from a complacent and conservative individual or generation. With a Spinoza or a Leibniz, unquestionably, it represents the conclusion of long and arduous metaphysical reflection. But with Pangloss, and with many of our Hanoverian poets and moralists, as with such nineteenth century exponents as Thoreau ('God himself culminates in the present moment') or Browning ('All's right with the world'), it generally seems to denote contentment with the existing state of things. In the early and middle years of the eighteenth century the wealthy and the educated of Europe must have enjoyed almost the nearest approach to earthly felicity ever known to man.

Centuries of superstition, error, and strife lay behind; most of the mediaeval ghosts had been laid; a revolutionary era had been successfully weathered; liberty and philosophy and the arts were raising their heads once more. 'The vulgar', not yet indoctrinated with the Rights of Man, were contented with the lot to which an inscrutable Providence had fortunately assigned them, or else consoled themselves, as they were advised to do by the clergy and moralists, with thoughts of the future life. Most of the English writers of the time felt that they were living in an age of enlightenment. The universe had been explained, and—what gave added zest to their satisfaction—explained by an Englishman, and a pious Englishman at that. This feeling of enlightenment was confined, of course (then, as perhaps always), to a small group who were conscious of being in touch with the best that was being thought and said. Thomson, for example, referring (in *The Seasons*) to popular superstitions about comets, says:

> But, above
> Those superstitious horrors that enslave
> The fond sequacious herd, to mystic faith
> And blind amazement prone, the enlighten'd few,
> Whose godlike minds Philosophy exalts,
> The glorious stranger hail.[1]

And, elsewhere:

> While thus laborious crowds
> Ply the tough oar, Philosophy directs
> The ruling helm . . . [2]

—a very gratifying state of affairs (for the philosophers), and one can understand, and even envy, the satisfaction felt in it by such men as Shaftesbury, Pope, Addison, Thomson, or Chesterfield. It is significant that 'Chearfulness' is one of the qualities that Addison most highly recommends: the 'chearfulness' which 'keeps up a kind

[1] *Summer*, l. 1710. [2] *ibid.*, l. 1776.

of Day-light in the Mind, and fills it with a steady and perpetual Serenity', [1] and disposes us to regard the whole Universe as 'a kind of Theatre filled with Objects that either raise in us Pleasure, Amusement, or Admiration'. Addison can even use Locke's epistemology to demonstrate the kindly intentions of Providence:

> 'if Matter had appeared to us endow'd only with those real Qualities which it actually possesses, it would have made but a very joyless and uncomfortable Figure; and why has Providence given it a Power of producing in as such imaginary Qualities as Tastes and Colours, Sounds and Smells, Heat and Cold, but that Man, while he is conversant in the lower Stations of Nature, might have his Mind cheared and delighted with agreeable Sensations?' [2]

The perfections of the universe (and, we may add, of the existing social order) could be taken as established, and the main business of the philosopher was to vindicate them against all subversive criticisms.

There had long been a conflict, in Western thought, between the idea that God made all things 'good', and the experience that much exists, both in the material and the moral worlds, which is 'evil'. On the whole this had been resolved, for Christendom, by the doctrine of the Fall and the divine malediction which ensued. Through this doctrine it had been possible to recognize evil as such, and to see meaning in human life as a struggle to escape or to conquer it. But in the new mental climate of the enlightenment this was no longer generally acceptable. What was now desired, as we have seen, was a more favourable interpretation of the scheme of things. The Newtonian universe certainly seemed to work as perfectly as if no Fall had taken place: perhaps, then, *all* things are even now still in their proper order? perhaps the status quo *is* what God intended and intends? Even man is not vile, but exactly what he should be—since everything that exists contributes perforce to the 'good' of the whole system?

[1] *Spectator*, 381. [2] *ibid.*, 387.

In that case, it might seem, we need no longer foster any gloomy conviction of sin, nor any enthusiastic yearning for salvation, but should aim simply at a sober understanding—or at least acknowledgment—of the wisdom of God in the creation.

[1] Apart altogether from the Christian doctrine of the Fall, the Western mind had been confronted, since at least the time of Plato, with the fundamental opposition between the One and the Many, the Absolute and the world of 'things'. How or why had the unchanging One, or Total Being, generated the Many—this variegated, 'imperfect' world of corruptibles? Apparently the accepted explanation was that of Plato in the *Timaeus*: that the One was 'Good', that is to say, it desired to communicate existence to the not-itself, and having desired this self-overflowing, it could not deny existence to any possible kind of being. As Thomas Aquinas expresses it, God's love did not permit him to remain self-absorbed, without production of the creatures; the seeds of all things were latent in his mind, and he could not deny them germination. Thus we get the paradox that it was the 'goodness', the 'love' of God which impelled him to generate things which not only in the sight of God, but even of man, must seem imperfect or evil. It was argued, however, that any thing less than God himself must be imperfect, and, in its degree of imperfection, evil, but that the disadvantage of creating such things is outweighed by the one grand advantage of giving existence to all possibles. From this standpoint it was 'better' to create one angel and one man than two angels; one man and one monkey than two men, and so on. The realization of a 'full' universe is the greatest of all 'goods'.

By the first half of the eighteenth century it had come to be generally accepted that the universe presented the spectacle of a continuous scale or ladder of creatures,

[1] On the topic of the next few pages see Prof. A. O. Lovejoy's admirable work *The Great Chain of Being* (Harvard, 1936), to which I am here much indebted.

extending without a break from the worm to the seraph. In this scale there must be such a creature as Man:

> Of Systems possible, if 'tis confest
> That Wisdom infinite must form the best,
> Where all must full or not coherent be,
> There must be, somewhere, such a rank as Man.[1]

If we don't like the rank or position assigned to us, we must console ourselves by reflecting that there would be a gap in the chain without us, and that, after all, we are fairly high up in the scale of creation, having all the animals below us, and probably only the conjectural angels or 'superior beings' between us and God. Man may be unhappily unique, 'plac'd on this isthmus of a middle state' between animal and angel, but this uniqueness is due, not to the Fall or to Satan, but to the requirements of plenitude.

Eighteenth century optimism was thus not essentially a joyous or hopeful creed, though it may well have suited the complacent and the shallow. It was in essence an apologia for the status quo, presenting you with a God who loved abundance and variety better than happiness or progress, and a universe whose 'goodness' consisted in its containing the greatest possible range of phenomena, many of which seem evil to all but the philosophers. Cease then, nor order imperfection name! Submit! This glorification of Things as They Are, and of the God who wills them so, naturally had social implications (or shall we say, a social basis?) of the kind that would be expected. These, and other aspects of the doctrine, are well illustrated in Soame Jenyns's *Free Enquiry into the Nature and Origin of Evil* (1757), a book which is not only noteworthy as containing a full statement of the position I have outlined, but has acquired an adventitious fame from the very unfavourable review written upon it by Dr Johnson. It is not surprising that Johnson should have rejected Jenyns's version of the official optimism of the eighteenth century.

[1] *Essay on Man*, i, 42.

As Leslie Stephen has remarked, in an age of shallow optimism the deeper natures are apt to be pessimists, and Johnson, who though not a profound thinker had deep convictions, had been taught by hard experience that human life is a state in which there is little to be enjoyed, and much to be endured. Even Voltaire, who in dealing with Pascal seems an optimist, reacted into pessimism when confronted with the philosophy of Dr Pangloss, and *Candide* teaches much the same moral as *Rasselas*. I give here, by way of illustration, an outline of some of Jenyns's arguments, together with a few extracts from Johnson's review.

Speaking of 'evil' in general, Jenyns maintains at the outset that all evils owe their existence to 'the necessity of their own natures':

> 'all that infinite power and wisdom could do, was to make choice of that method, which was attended with the least and fewest; and this not proceeding from any defect of power in the Creator, but from that imperfection which is inherent in the nature of all created things.' [1]

It will be noticed that the 'nature of things' here becomes the culprit. But what things? Those which God has chosen. Jenyns and his school seem to represent God as choosing the best out of many samples, but it is not emphasized that the samples are of his own manufacture. Evils of imperfection, Jenyns goes on, are only 'privations', and are essential to the whole system, which is based on the principle of 'just subordination':

> 'the beauty and happiness of the whole depend altogether on the just inferiority of the parts.'

Do we want a picture devoid of shade or variety? a universe of archangels? No, plenitude demands the ant and the bee (he does not specify the tsetse-fly or the mosquito), with their own inferior 'happiness', as well as angel or man with theirs. At this point we encounter what I referred

[1] *Free Enquiry* (1790 ed.), p. 37.

to as the social implications of this teaching: the social order, we are now told, is as much divinely ordained as the natural order. Just as the lower animals enjoy their ignorant bliss, so the human poor are happy in their inferior way. Ignorance, says Jenyns, is the 'opiate' (it is Jenyns's own word) of the poor, 'a cordial, administered by the gracious hand of providence'.[1] And is it for us to frustrate the kindly purposes of providence? No, let us not presume to deprive the poor of their opiate by 'an ill-judged and improper education'. This sentiment evokes a protest from Johnson:

> 'The privileges of education may sometimes be improperly bestowed, but I shall always fear to with-hold them, lest I should be yielding to the suggestions of pride, while I persuade myself that I am following the maxims of policy; and under the appearance of salutary restraints, should be indulging the lust of dominion, and that malevolence which delights in seeing others depressed.'[2]

Pain, poverty, toil, and the rest, Jenyns argues, are merely instances in our own sphere of the imperfection inhering in all created things, of which he has already demonstrated the necessity; they are

> 'the necessary consequences of human nature; from which it can no more be divested than matter from extension, or heat from motion, which proceed from the very modes of their existence.'

In short, we cannot imagine human beings any otherwise than as we have known them, and though doubtless God might have made us other than we are, some other creatures would then have had to 'occupy our stations in the universal system'. On this, Johnson (who knew that slow rises worth by poverty depressed) comments:

> 'This author and Pope perhaps never saw the miseries which they imagine thus easily to be borne.'

Are we, because we are philosophers, and therefore cosmic

[1] *ibid.*, pp. 49-50. [2] Works (Pickering ed., 1825), vol. vi, p. 57.

Tories, to 'entail irreversible poverty upon generation after generation'? But Jenyns has no misgivings; the 'world' (meaning eighteenth century society?) could not subsist without poverty, though of course by *charity* we may—and indeed must—try to mitigate the evils 'now and then pinching a few'. 'We are therefore little enlightened', Johnson concludes, 'by a writer who tells us, that any being in the state of man must suffer what man suffers, when the only question that requires to be resolved is, Why any being is in this state?'

We now come to the most notorious passage in the book, the passage on which Johnson poured his choicest scorn. Jenyns professes to be persuaded

> 'that there is something in the abstract nature of pain conducive to pleasure; that the sufferings of individuals are absolutely necessary to universal happiness.'[1]

Whose happiness? This universal good, this universal happiness for the realization of which the creation was framed, and for which the sufferings of individuals are essential—who enjoys it? Could it be the enlighten'd few whose godlike minds Philosophy exalts, while laborious crowds ply the tough oar? One may suspect it, though naturally this is not Jenyns's reply. His technique (that of his age, and probably of all ages, is to project his own social order upon the universal screen, and interpret it as part of the unchanging structure of creation. For this purpose the theory of the Great Chain of Being was ready to hand. Addison, elaborating upon Locke in his blandest tones, had argued that

> 'Infinite Goodness is of so communicative a Nature, that it seems to delight in the conferring of Existence upon every degree of perceptive Being,'

and that,

> 'If the scale of Being rises by such a regular Progress, so high as Man, we may by parity of Reason suppose that it still proceeds

[1] *op. cit.*, pp. 67-8.

gradually through those Beings which are of a Superior Nature to him, since there is an infinitely greater Space and Room for different Degrees of Perfection, between the Supreme Being and Man, than between Man and the most despicable Insect.' [1]

—though there must, he adds, always remain an infinite gap between the highest created being and God himself. Here then we have our answer: it is these Superior Beings who enjoy the universal happiness—it is for their pleasure that man agonizes. Do not our own pleasures depend upon the sufferings of other creatures? Are not empires and flourishing cities founded upon slavery and degradation? Must not the pheasant or the deer yield up their lives to furnish us with sport, and the pleasures of the banquet?

> 'Man is one link of that vast chain, descending by insensible degrees, from infinite perfection to absolute nothing. As there are many thousands below him, so must there be many more above him. If we look downwards, we see innumerable species of inferior beings, whose happiness and lives are dependent on his will; we see him cloathed by their spoils, and fed by their miseries and destruction, inslaving some, tormenting others, and murdering millions for his luxury or diversion; is it not therefore analogous and highly probable, that the happiness and life of man should be equally dependent on the wills of his superiors? . . . The fundamental error in all our reasonings on this subject, is that of placing ourselves wrong in that presumptuous climax of beast, man and God; from whence, as we suppose falsely that there is nothing above us except the Supreme Being, we foolishly conclude that all the evils we labour under must be derived immediately from his omnipotent hand: whereas there may be numberless intermediate beings who have power to deceive, torment, or destroy us, for the ends only of their pleasure or utility, who may be vested with the same privilege over their inferiors, and as much benefited by the use of them, as ourselves.' [2]

This hypothesis, which evidently seems to Jenyns quite consonant with the perfections of the Creator and his creation, illustrates this curious feature of most attempts to

[1] *Spectator*, 519. [2] *Free Enquiry*, pp. 71-2.

vindicate the ways of God to man: that the more you demonstrate the rightness of whatever is, the more desperate, because the more inescapable, the plight of man appears. Johnson, who looked to literature not for explanations of the riddle of existence, but for moral and religious support, was roused to satire by Jenyns's theory:

> 'Many a merry bout have these frolick beings at the vicissitudes of an ague, and good sport it is to see a man tumble with an epilepsy, and revive and tumble again, and all this he knows not why. As they are wiser and more powerful than we, they have more exquisite diversions, for we have no way of procuring any sport so brisk and so lasting, as the paroxysms of the gout and stone, which undoubtedly must make high mirth, especially if the play be a little diversified with the blunders and puzzles of the blind and deaf.'

Another diversion of the Superior Beings, Johnson continues (pressing home his point more closely), is to fill the heads of proud mortals with false opinions, 'till in time they make their plaything an author':

> 'Many of the books which now croud the world, may be justly suspected to be written for the sake of some invisible order of beings, for surely they are of no use to any of the corporeal inhabitants of the world. *The only end of writing, is to enable the readers better to enjoy life, or better to endure it:* and how will either of those be put more in our power by him who tells us, that we are puppets, of which some creature not much wiser than ourselves manages the wires?'[1]

Having proved to his own satisfaction that God is the author of all the natural evils in the universe, 'that is, of the fewest possible in the nature of things', Jenyns proceeds to ask why God may not be the author of all moral evil in the same manner and on the same principle. Here again we see him clinging to his 'optimism' only at the price of transforming the Deity into the moral equivalent of Shelley's Jupiter. Quite apart from the interests of the Superior Beings, which may again be served, there may

[1] Johnson, *op. cit.*, pp. 65-6. (My italics.)

be another justification for moral evil: natural evil once admitted, some men 'must' be created bad enough to deserve it!

> 'Men may be inclined to vice in order to render them proper objects of such a degree of misery as was unavoidably necessary.'[1]

This, says Johnson,

> 'is given as a satisfactory account of the Origin of moral Evil, which amounts only to this, that God created beings whose guilt he foreknew, in order that he might have proper objects of pain, because the pain of part is, no man knows how or why, necessary to the felicity of the whole.'

On the subject of political evils, where he can forget the perfections of the universe and write from experience, Jenyns talks better sense. His main point is that many political institutions are absurd and irrational, but that as man is an absurd and irrational creature they suit him all the better for that reason. In politics as in metaphysics, then, Jenyns supports the existing order, and his argument is blended of ingredients suggestive both of Hobbes and of Burke. He gives a Hobbist account of humanity: self-interest is, he says, 'the great principle that operates in the political world in the same manner that attraction does in the natural'. But his conservatism rests mainly on a Burkean sense of the relation between politics and human nature. Enthusiastic reformers are usually wrong-headed, he declares; they see the undoubted abuses, but not the necessities from which they spring: 'It is a strange, but a certain truth, that in politics most principles speculatively right are practically wrong.' The pageantries of patriotism, war, and religion are of course ludicrous, yet it is only by such deceits that men can be successfully manipulated. Every flourishing nation endeavours to improve the arts, and to cultivate reason and good sense, 'yet, if these are extended too far', he says (echoing Mandeville), 'no national government or national religion

[1] Jenyns, *op. cit.*, pp. 104-5.

can long stand their ground; for it is with old establishments as with old houses, their deformities are commonly their support, and these can never be removed without endangering the whole fabric'. These considerations apply also to Christianity, which (without derogation!) lacks authenticity and perspicuity, and is subject, like all other human institutions, secular or religious, to corruption. The deists, like the political reformers, are intellectually right in their criticisms, but practically wrong in their conclusions. They are wrong in thinking that the really divine religion would be perfectly plain and rationally convincing. No such religion is possible, and we must therefore not pretend that Christianity is such. The argument somewhat resembles Butler's in the *Analogy*, save that Jenyns, cynical and unimplicated, clearly enjoys showing up the necessary irrationalities of religion, while Butler is earnestly toiling to defend it. On the whole book, Johnson concludes:

> 'All our effort ends in belief, that for the Evils of life there is some good reason, and in confession, that the reason cannot be found. This is all that has been produced by the revival of Chrysippus's untractableness of matter, and the *Arabian* scale of existence.'

What emerged, then, as the chief outcome of this kind of 'optimism', was a gospel of hopelessness. The status quo represents the last word of divine wisdom and goodness; the scale of being is fixed and unimprovable: what then is left to us but to content ourselves with the station, both in the cosmical and the social scale, to which it has pleased God to call us? No improvements are to be expected; to demand them is in fact impious. In this state of affairs it is not to be wondered at that many of the really dynamic men of the century—men like Voltaire, Rousseau, Diderot, or Holbach in France, and I think we must add John Wesley in England—should have been men who disliked the status quo much too intensely to want to explain it favourably. And the main tenor of later eighteenth century thought was towards the abolition of avoidable evils, and an indefinite progress towards perfection. Man need *not* 'stay put'; perfectibility, as Godwin later said, is one of his main distinguishing marks. An optimism of progress supersedes the optimism of acceptance.

CHAPTER IV

Natural Morality

I. SHAFTESBURY (1671-1713)

The generous Ashley thine, the friend of man;
Who scann'd his nature with a brother's eye,
His weakness prompt to shade, to raise his aim,
To touch the finer movements of the mind,
And with the moral beauty charm the heart.

[Thomson's *Seasons.*]

WE have seen how some of the most powerful forces of the early eighteenth century, scientific, philosophical, and social, were tending to divinize the idea of Nature, either in the sense of the physical universe, or in that of the whole order of creation, including the moral order. The ways of God had been many times vindicated by physico-theologians, metaphysicians, and popular writers; let us now consider the work of one who, though he also largely treats that theme, may be regarded as especially important for his vindication of the ways of man. Shaftesbury is the 'friend of man' in the sense that he makes it his business to defend *human* nature against the traditional detractions, particularly those of religion on the one hand, and of Hobbes on the other. This 'virtuoso of humanity' (as Herder called him) or the 'elegant' and 'sublime' Lord Shaftesbury (as he appears in Fielding and Hume) was the grandson of Dryden's Achitophel. He was educated partly under Locke's direction, and afterwards at Winchester; then, after a period of aesthetic foreign travelling, and a three years' spell in Parliament, the remainder of his short life was spent in retirement ('intellectual luxury', says Macaulay), and in the composition of works of which the tone is uniformly serene and sanguine, in spite of their author's precarious health.

Shaftesbury is the typical English moralist of the 'enlightenment', and is usually accounted the founder of the 'moral sense' school. Hume says that he was the first who gave occasion to remark the distinction between two theories of ethics, that which derives them from Reason, and that which derives them from 'an immediate feeling and finer internal sense', and in recent times Babbitt has signalized him as the precursor of the 'Rousseauist' moralists who transform the conscience from an inner check into an expansive emotion. His writings, collected in *Characteristicks of Men, Manners, Opinions and Times* (1711), had an immense vogue in the first half of the eighteenth century, both at home and abroad. Montesquieu described him as one of the four great 'poets' (of whom the other three are Plato, Montaigne, and Malebranche!), and Herder declared (1794) that he had 'signally influenced the best heads of the eighteenth century.'[1] Certainly most of the English philosophers, moralists, and essayists of the period, and some of the poets and novelists as well, refer to him, not always with approval, but generally with respect.

Of the seventeenth century moralists, it was the Cambridge Platonists whose doctrine had pointed most clearly towards an exaltation of the natural moral sense of man; to act aright, they taught, we need but look within, and read the natural law written upon the heart. It is therefore interesting to find that Shaftesbury's first published work was an edition, with Introduction, of Whichcote's *Select Sermons* (1698). We have, here, in Shaftesbury's Introduction, a useful link between seventeenth century latitudinarian thought and its eighteenth century offspring. He begins by whimsically apologizing for publishing yet more sermons, when so great a number have already been preached and printed, with so little apparent effect. Why is it that men who profess such a religion as Christianity

[1] See J. M. Robertson's Introduction to his edition of the *Characteristicks*.

live such lives as they do? Not, he suggests, on account of any radical depravity in mankind, but rather because exhortation has been misdirected. Religion has been perverted to serve political ends—and here Shaftesbury proceeds to the first of his attacks on Hobbes, who, in reckoning up the passions and affections which produce society, 'forgot to mention Kindness, Friendship, Sociableness, Love of Company and Converse, Natural affection, or anything of this kind', and substituted only the master-passion Fear, and the passion for power which never ends but in death. But Hobbes is not the only culprit; divines, also, in their efforts to prove the necessity of revealed religion, have denigrated human nature, 'as if Good-nature and religion were enemies'. The view that there is no natural sociability and goodness in man is thus acceptable both to atheists and to defenders of religion. Shaftesbury finds it strange that those who profess to believe in a Supreme Being who is wholly good, and is actuated exclusively by love and good-will toward men, should think it unsuitable to a rational creature derived from Him to follow His example, and find pleasure in 'goodness without Prospect'. 'That Virtue is her own reward', Sir Thomas Browne had written (in the *Religio Medici*), 'is but a cold principle, and not able to maintain our variable resolutions in a constant and settled way of goodness.' But this 'cold principle' had now, for 'enlightened' moralists, become of greater importance than the older sanctions. With the growth of the secular and scientific spirit, it had come to seem more and more desirable to base morality not upon rewards and punishments in the hereafter, but upon human nature, and what was known as 'the nature of things'. Writers like Locke and Samuel Clarke do not, indeed, abandon Revelation, but with them the centre of gravity has shifted, and Revelation has become an adjunct, not a first consideration. Clarke went as far, perhaps, as it is possible to go in deriving good and evil from the Eternal Fitnesses and Relations of Things. God, he declares, has chosen to establish these

Fitnesses, not thereby constituting them 'good' *ex arbitrio*, but choosing them because they were antecedently 'best', and the ground of morality lies in these: we, also, ought to act in accordance with the Fitness and Reason of Things. When men do wrong, they are 'Setting-up their own unreasonable Self-Will in opposition to the Nature and Reason of Things', and attempting to 'make Things be what they are not and cannot be', thus destroying 'that Order by which the Universe subsists'.[1] The injunction to do as you would be done by, has for Clarke the same force as the proposition 'if A=B, B=A', and disobeying it is acting a contradiction.[2] 'That which is truly the Law of Nature, or the Reason of Things, is in like manner the Will of God',[3] he subjoins; but it is observable that 'the Will of God' takes second place here, as if its function were merely to ratify the enactments of the natural legislature. It was Clarke who wrote that 'Moral Virtue is the Foundation and the Summ, the Essence and the Life of all true Religion'[4]; whose thesis for the Cambridge D.D. was an argument 'that no article of Christian faith is opposed to right reason'; and whom Bishop Gibson is reported to have described to Queen Caroline as the most learned and honest man in her dominions, but with one defect—he was not a Christian.

From the standpoint of Clarke, then, and still more from that of Shaftesbury, Browne's conclusion that we cannot hope 'to be honest without thought of Heaven or Hell', or his pronouncement upon Charity: 'I draw not my purse for his sake that demands it, but His that enjoined it', seemed both unchristian and in a sense utilitarian. We must not, Browne himself had said, 'make the consequences of virtue the end thereof', but to perform virtuous actions for the sake of a heavenly reward—what is this but to reintroduce utilitarian considerations

[1] Samuel Clarke, *Demonstration of the Being and Attributes of God* (Boyle Lectures, 1704), pp. 256-7.

[2] *Discourse Concerning the Unchangeable Obligations of Natural Religion* (1705), p. 86.

[3] *ibid.*, pp. 147-8.

[4] *ibid.*, p. 141.

on another level? To be honest without thought of heaven and hell is, for Shaftesbury, precisely the mark of the disinterested lover of virtue, and an act of charity springing from an impulse of sympathy for a fellow-creature would be, in his view, morally superior to one discharged mechanically as a mere routine duty. He thought it strange that religious teachers should 'refer all to Reward', thereby excluding spontaneous goodness of heart—the very thing that 'true Christianity' demands. The truth is, he says, that they were afraid of conceding too much to 'good Nature' lest they might be diminishing the need for Revelation ('a thing so highly important to Mankind', says Shaftesbury, not without irony), and have been 'willing to wound Virtue' rather than 'admit a sort of rival to the faith of Divine Revelation'. Thus, with both atheists and believers uniting to decry human nature, there was all the more need for someone to come forward in its defence, and 'here it is that our author [Whichcote] has appeared so signally'. Whichcote, whom Shaftesbury recognizes as his spiritual predecessor, had inculcated that human nature is not so untoward, but that it retains 'a secret sympathy with virtue and honesty'; he had taught that virtue is the foundation of happiness, and that sin punishes itself. Shaftesbury can therefore describe him as 'a truly Christian Philosopher, whom for his appearing thus in defence of Natural goodness, we may call the preacher of Good Nature'. This is his excuse for reprinting the sermons in an age when many are prejudiced against pulpit exhortations, and indeed against religion itself. To such readers the sermons should, he hopes, have a special appeal on account of the divine temper shown in them, while they will make professing Christians like Christianity better.

We may now consider a few of the leading notions in the *Characteristicks*. 1. As might be expected, Shaftesbury insists upon the divine perfection of 'Nature' (in the sense of the whole order of creation). Here he presents again the optimistic theory which we have already glanced at, and which, reaching Pope chiefly through Bolingbroke, is versified in the *Essay on Man*. Nature, for him, is a vast system of interconnected and interdependent parts, of which we see little, but enough to be convinced that it is an admirable Cosmos, moving majestically according to unalterable laws. What we call 'evils' only appear such to our ignorance, because we are unable to see their justifying relationship to the Whole. The divinity of Nature (like the 'good-nature' of man) is affirmed by Shaftesbury both against the atheists, who think the universe a distracted chaos of atoms, and against the orthodox, who hold that we live in a world which has been permanently ruined by the fall of Adam. The quality of Shaftesbury's nature-worship can best be illustrated from the concluding sections of his dialogue entitled *The Moralists: A Philosophical Rhapsody*,[1] in which Theocles and Philocles discourse upon natural and moral subjects. In these sections Shaftesbury casts aside his customary serenity, and through the lips of Theocles indulges in an astonishing outburst, in 'number'd prose', on the wonders and perfections of Nature, revealing here a degree of 'enthusiasm' which he will not permit in any other context. This sermon-panegyric of Theocles is delivered, 'with the Advantage of the Rural Scene around us', partly during an 'Evening-Walk in the Fields', and partly at dawn in similar 'solemn Places of Retreat'. It illustrates how the philosophical passion for the best-of-possible-worlds could already, in the opening eighteenth century, pass into fondness for 'the country' and for what is 'natural', in contrast to town life and the 'artificial'. The quality of the writing is singular: Shaftesbury seems, in this semi-iambic prose, to be trying to generate a Platonic *furor poeticus*, in which elements from Milton, the pastoral tradition, and perhaps Lucretius, are also interfused. His normal prose-style is not to be judged from the samples I am about to give, but it is instructive, I think, to find so much emotion displayed, in however spurious a rhetoric, on such a subject at such a period (1709).

[1] See especially pt. ii, sect. 4, and pt. iii.

'[*Theocles*] Ye Fields and Woods, my Refuge from the toilsome World of Business, receive me in your quiet Sanctuarys, and favour my Retreat and thoughtful Solitude. Ye verdant Plains, how gladly I salute ye. . . . Bless'd be ye chaste Abodes of happiest Mortals, who here in peaceful Innocence enjoy a Life unenvy'd, tho Divine; whilst with its bless'd Tranquillity it affords a happy Leisure and Retreat for Man; who, made for Contemplation, and to search his own and other Natures, may here best meditate the Cause of Things; and plac'd amidst the various Scenes of Nature, may nearer view her Works.

'O Glorious *Nature*! supremely Fair, and sovereignly Good! All-loving and All-lovely, All-divine! . . . Whose every single Work affords an ampler Scene, and is a nobler Spectacle than all which ever Art presented! O mighty *Nature*! Wise Substitute of *Providence*! impower'd *Creatress*! Or Thou impowering Deity, supreme Creator! Thee I invoke, and Thee alone adore. To thee this Solitude, this place, these Rural Meditations are sacred; whilst thus inspir'd with Harmony of Thought, tho unconfin'd by Words, and in loose Numbers, I sing of Nature's Order in created Beings, and celebrate the Beautys which resolve in Thee, the Source and Principle of all Beauty and Perfection.[1]

'All Nature's Wonders serve to excite and perfect this Idea of their *Author*. 'Tis here he suffers us to see, and even converse with him, in a manner suitable to our Frailty; How glorious is it to contemplate him, in this noblest of his Works apparent to us, The *System* of *the bigger World*.'[2]

Philocles listens enraptured to all this and much more, for Theocles, before he utters these impassioned strains, has enunciated a complete nature-philosophy, surveying in turn the various orders of animals and plants, the stars, the earth and all that it contains, man, and the problem of evil, and shown how all work together to form that admirable Order and Proportion which we admire as Beauty, and try to reproduce in our lives as Goodness. Convinced, amazed, Philocles at length assents in the following terms:

'I shall no longer resist the Passion growing in me for Things

[1] Works, vol. ii (1727 ed.), pp. 344-5. [2] *ibid.*, vol. ii, p. 370.

of a *natural* kind; where neither *Art*, nor the *Conceit* or *Caprice* of Man has spoil'd their *genuine Order*, by breaking in upon that *primitive State*. Even the rude *Rocks*, the mossy *Caverns*, the irregular unwrought *Grotto's*, and broken *Falls* of Waters, with all the horrid Graces of the *Wilderness* itself, as representing NATURE more, will be the more engaging, and appear with a Magnificence beyond the formal Mockery of princely Gardens.'[1]

At this point, however, Philocles remembers with disquiet that those who are 'deep in this *romantick* way' (lunatics, lovers and poets, for the most part) 'are look'd upon, you know, as a People either plainly out of their wits, or over-run with *Melancholy* and ENTHUSIASM'. Shaftesbury had written against Enthusiasm[2] in the manner and spirit of his time, but the rapture inspired by the contemplation of natural beauty is permissible (he replies through Theocles), provided that we remember, with Plato, that 'whatever in Nature is beautiful or charming, is only the faint Shadow' of the 'first Beauty'.

Thus far, then, had the divinization of Nature proceeded a hundred years before Wordsworth. Already the injunction 'First follow Nature' had passed beyond the region of ethics and poetics, and the Wordsworthian nature-religion can be regarded, less as something wholly new, than as the culmination of a process which had been implicit in the 'humanist' tradition ever since the Renaissance. Mr Aldous Huxley has said (in his essay *Wordsworth in the Tropics*) that 'for the last hundred years or so it has been an axiom that Nature is divine and morally uplifting', and that 'for good Wordsworthians a walk in the country is the equivalent of going to church, a tour through Westmorland is as good as a pilgrimage to Jerusalem'. But, if we leave Westmorland out of account, these were axioms for good Augustans a hundred years earlier, and we need not proceed much further than the middle of the century to find Westmorland appearing as a Holy Land also (in Gray's Letters). Shaftesbury was

[1] *ibid.*, vol. ii, pp. 393-4.

[2] *Letter Concerning Enthusiasm* (1708).

not the only apostle of the new religion; Addison, that most accurate reflector of contemporary moods, can also write, in one of his papers on 'Chearfulness':

> 'The Creation is a perpetual Feast to the Mind of a good Man, every thing that he sees chears and delights him; Providence has imprinted so many Smiles on Nature, that it is impossible for a Mind which is not sunk in more gross and sensual Delights to take a survey of them without several secret Sensations of Pleasure. . . . Natural Philosophy quickens this Taste of the Creation, and renders it not only pleasing to the Imagination, but to the Understanding. It does not rest in the Murmur of Brooks, and the Melody of Birds, in the Shade of Groves and Woods, or in the Embroidery of Fields and Meadows, but considers the several Ends of Providence which are served by them, and the Wonders of Divine Wisdom which appear in them. It heightens the Pleasures of the Eye, and raises such a rational Admiration in the Soul as is little inferior to Devotion. . . . Such an habitual Disposition of Mind consecrates every Field and Wood, turns an ordinary Walk into a morning or evening Sacrifice, and will improve those transient Gleams of Joy, which naturally brighten up and refresh the Soul on such Occasions, into an inviolable and perpetual State of Bliss and Happiness.' [1]

2. It follows from all this that in Shaftesbury's view 'true religion' should be based on 'Nature' rather than on Revelation. We have seen that he considered religion to be the enemy of virtue in so far as it depreciated 'good nature' and recommended reliance on future rewards and punishments. 'Little were you aware', exclaims Theocles,

> 'that the cruel Enemy oppos'd to Virtue shou'd be Religion itself! But . . . Virtue is often treated so, by those who wou'd magnify to the utmost the Corruption of Man's Heart; and in exposing, as they pretend, the Falshood of *human Virtue*, think to extol Religion. How many sacred Orators turn all their edge this way, and strike at *moral Virtue* as a kind of Stepdame, or Rival to Religion!' [2]

---

[1] *Spectator*, 393 (1712).

[2] *The Moralists*, pt. ii, sect. 2: Works, vol. ii, p. 256.

He concludes:

> 'That by building a future State on the Ruins of *Virtue*, Religion in general, and the Cause of *a Deity* is betray'd; and by making Rewards and punishments the principal Motives to Duty, the Christian Religion in particular is overthrown, and its greatest Principle, that of *Love*, rejected and expos'd.' [1]

But there is a further implication: orthodoxy is also the enemy of 'true' (i.e. 'natural') religion, because it invites us to base our faith, not on the beautiful and harmonious Order of Things—the best and only genuine external evidence—but on miracles, that is, on infractions of that Order. The contemplation of the Universe, its Laws and Government, is

> 'the only means which cou'd establish the *sound Belief* of a Deity. For what tho innumerable *Miracles* from every part assail'd the Sense, and gave the trembling Soul no respite? What tho the Sky shou'd suddenly open, and all Kinds of Prodigys appear, Voices be heard, or Characters read?' [2]

This would only prove that there were certain Powers capable of producing these effects, not that they were wise or foolish, good or bad Powers. 'Power can never serve as a Proof for *Goodness*; and Goodness is the only Pledg of *Truth*.' Perpetual breaches of that admirable Order, 'from whence the One infinite and perfect principle is known', would merely unhinge Nature, and bring back the '*Chaos* and *Atoms* of the Atheists', or 'the *Magic* and Daemons of the Polytheists':

> 'Yet is this tumultuous System of the Universe asserted with the highest Zeal by some who wou'd maintain a Deity. . . . As if *Atheism* were the most natural Inference which cou'd be drawn from a regular and orderly State of Things!' [3]

If by harmony and concord we are to be made atheists, how shall we be convinced of Deity by irregularity and

[1] *ibid.*, vol. ii, p. 279.
[2] *ibid.*, vol. ii, p. 333.
[3] *ibid.*, vol. ii, p. 336.

discord? It was fantastic, he thought, to suppose that 'the World is a mere Accident, if it proceeds in Course; but an Effect of Wisdom, if it runs mad!' It is perhaps not surprising that the Bible was not a book which Shaftesbury could highly recommend, and we find him, in the *Advice to an Author*, using a disparaging irony, of the Voltairean type, about certain Old Testament characters. The stories and characters of the Bible, he warns his Author, are no fit subjects for a 'mere poet', since they are divinely inspired and thus beyond his comprehension:

> 'The Wit of the best Poet is not sufficient to reconcile us to the Campaign of a Joshua, or the Retreat of a Moses, by the assistance of an Egyptian *Loan*. Nor will it be possible, by the *Muses* Art, to make that Royal *Hero* appear amiable in human Eyes, who found such favour in the Eye of Heaven.' [1]

—a passage which may be compared with the conclusion of Hume's Essay on Miracles.

3. We next come to that part of Shaftesbury's teaching which more especially justifies Thomson in calling him the 'friend of Man'. Like 'Nature', Man is essentially 'good', and—in opposition to the view of Hobbes—'naturally' social. Shaftesbury faces up to Hobbes with the gestures of one who is so confident of victory that he need do little more than sport with his opponent. How shall we most effectively deal with so 'Gothick' a philosopher? Not, assuredly, by holding up hands in horror:

> 'If we fall presently into Horrors, and Consternation, upon the hearing Maxims which are thought *poisonous*, we are in no disposition to use that familiar and easy Part of Reason, which is the best *Antidote*.' [2]

No, let us approach Hobbes in the spirit of raillery; let us tell him that it is most friendly of him to communicate his

[1] Works, vol. i, p. 358.
[2] *Essay on the Freedom of Wit and Humour*: Works, vol. i, p. 91.

views to us, and that by so doing he has given us the surest token that he is not the savage wolf he seemed to be. When he, or any of his school, tries to persuade us that there is no such thing as natural faith or justice, that Force alone constitutes right, or that we have no natural impulses tending towards public good, let us thus address him:

> 'Sir! The Philosophy you have condescended to reveal to us, is most extraordinary. We are beholden to you for your Instruction. But, pray, whence is this Zeal on our behalf? What are *We* to *You*? . . . Is there then such a thing as *natural Affection*? If not, why all this Pains, why all this Danger on our account? Of what advantage is it to You, to deliver us from the Cheat? The more are taken in it, the better. 'Tis directly against your Interest to undeceive Us, and let us know that only private Interest governs You; and that nothing nobler, and of a larger kind, shou'd govern us whom you converse with. Leave us to ourselves, and to that notable *Art* by which we are happily tam'd, and render'd thus mild and *sheepish*. 'Tis not fit we shou'd know that *by Nature* we are all *wolves*. Is it possible that one who has really discover'd himself such, shou'd take pains to communicate such a Discovery?'[1]

The Hobbists show up human nature in the worst light, so that we may be on our guard, whereas real impostors usually speak well of it, 'that they may the easier abuse it'. Shaftesbury adds, in the more sober tone of a disciple of Locke, that we shall best provide against human ambition, not by surrendering to a Leviathan, but by a 'right Division and Ballance of Power, and by the Restraint of good Laws and Limitations, which may secure the publick Liberty'.

Shaftesbury's criticism of Hobbes's 'state of nature' has some importance as one of the earliest attempts to replace that philosophical abstraction by a historical and evolutionary view of the origin of society. In order to refute the idea that the state of nature is a state of war of all against all, he asks what sort of existence we consider

[1] *ibid.*, vol. i, pp. 92-3.

to be the most 'natural' to man as man: to live solitary and unassociated? No, he replies, man was a social being from the start, or at any rate a family man—and from the family grew the tribe, and thence the state, by natural evolution.

> 'If *Eating* and *Drinking* be natural, *Herding* is so too. If any *Appetite* or *Sense* be natural, the *Sense of Fellowship* is the same. If there be anything of Nature in that Affection which is between the Sexes, the affection is certainly as natural towards the consequent Offspring; and so again between the Offspring themselves, as Kindred and Companions bred under the same Discipline and Oeconomy. And thus *a Clan* or *Tribe* is gradually form'd; *a Publick* is recognized. . . .'[1]

In short, 'to *cantonize* is natural', not artificial, and 'how the Wit of Man shou'd so puzzle this Cause, as to make Civil Government and Society appear a kind of Invention, or Creature of Art, I know not'. It is absurd, too, to argue that there were no moral obligations in the state of nature before the compact; the compact itself was made in the state of nature, and 'the *Natural Knave* has the same reason to be a *Civil one*'. But Shaftesbury is no 'primitivist',[2] no dreamer of dreams about ages of gold. For him the 'natural' condition of a thing, and so of man, is not its 'original' state, but rather that state in which it realizes most fully its inner intention, or individuating principle. Just as, for him, the grace of a trained dancer is more 'natural' than the uncouth movements of the rustic who has been taught by 'Nature' (in the other sense) only,[3] so society is for man the true State of Nature. Shaftesbury's naturalism is on the whole of the progressivist rather than the primitivist type.[4] We shall often have

[1] *ibid.*, vol. i, p. 110. (See also *The Moralists*, pt. ii, sect. 4.)

[2] On the whole subject of 'primitivism' see Lovejoy and Boas, *Documentary History of Primitivism & Related Ideas* (Baltimore, Johns Hopkins Press, vol. i, 1935).

[3] *Advice to an Author*, pt. i, sect. 3: Works, vol. i, p. 190.

[4] On this distinction see L. Whitney, *Primitivism and the Idea of Progress in English Popular Literature of the Eighteenth Century* (Baltimore, 1934).

occasion, in the course of these studies, to remark upon the ambiguities arising from these two leading senses of 'Nature'.

4. Human virtue consists in 'following Nature', in the sense that it is a reproduction, within the individual microcosm, of the harmony and proportion so manifest in the greater world. The cry 'Follow Nature' had of course been raised of old by the Cynics, Stoics, and Epicureans, for all of whom virtue meant the 'life according to Nature' in varying senses; it had been revived by More, Montaigne, and other humanists of the Renaissance, and then forgotten for a while during the struggles of the seventeenth century. With Shaftesbury the emphasis often seems to fall upon the converse of the proposition 'that to be moral means to be natural', for, as we have already partly indicated, he thought it 'natural' to be moral.

In the *Inquiry Concerning Virtue or Merit* (1699) he proposes to determine which are the 'good and natural', and which the 'ill and unnatural' Affections. We possess by nature a faculty whereby we are able to distinguish and prefer what is right—the celebrated 'moral sense'. This faculty is closely akin to the aesthetic sense, by which we recognize and approve of that which is harmonious and proportionate. The moral sense might be called 'good taste in the art of living', and, like other forms of taste, it may be improved by training. The man of virtue, then, like the man of *virtù*, is the man who recognizes what is good by its beauty. The virtue of a rational creature consists in a 'rational affection' towards right: a 'just sentiment' or 'proper disposition'. Thus a man begins to be virtuous when he makes 'the Conception of *Worth and Honesty* to be an Object of his Affection' [1]; he is a 'good' man when the natural bent of his affections is towards the good of society. Shaftesbury does not dissolve morality entirely into sentiment: Reason also has its function,

[1] Works, vol. ii, p. 31.

which is to 'secure a right application of the Affections'. But we are not truly virtuous unless feeling coincides with reason; reluctant or merely dutiful well-doing is not genuine virtue. He defines the Moral Sense as 'a real Affection or Love towards *Equity* and *Right*, for its own sake, and on the account of its own natural Beauty and Worth'.

There may, however, be wrong conceptions of right behaviour, and it is typical of Shaftesbury that he mentions Religion, as well as superstition and false ideas of honour, as one of the sources of such errors. Religion may, for instance, pervert our natural moral sense by inculcating false conceptions of the Deity: 'the ill *Character* of a God does injury to the Affections of Man'.[1] The fact is, he believes our natural sense of right and wrong to be antecedent to, and independent of, any religious beliefs. It is characteristic of him, and of his comparatively 'unhistorical' age, that he should regard a correct theism as a piece of refined speculation—the last outcome of refinement and civilization, whereas the simple notions of morality, however refinable by cultivation, are imprinted on the heart by 'nature'. If there be 'a' God, He can do no more than ratify the immutable and self-existent distinctions of right and wrong, beauty and deformity. On the other hand, Shaftesbury concedes that an enlightened theism—belief in a Deity who represents the loftiest conceptions of justice and benevolence, and who, as the universal Mind, must necessarily be the '*best-natur'd one in the World*' [2]—cannot fail to reinforce the dictates of the moral sense. In effect, we may cultivate a judicious belief in the Supreme Being of the eighteenth century, but we must keep clear of Jupiter or Jehovah. An atheist may have a firm grasp of the fundamental principle of ethics: That virtue causes happiness and vice misery, yet the atheistic belief that the Whole is 'a vast and infinite deformity', 'a distracted universe', must weaken that love for everything

[1] *ibid.*, vol. ii, p. 51.
[2] *Letter Concerning Enthusiasm*: Works, vol. i, p. 40.

harmonious and proportionable in which virtue consists. Whereas

> 'Admiration and Love of Order, Harmony and Proportion, in whatever kind, is naturally improving to the Temper, advantageous to social Affection, and highly assistant to *Virtue*; which is it-self no other than the Love of Order and Beauty in Society. In the meanest Subjects of the World, the Appearance of Order gains upon the Mind, and draws the Affection towards it. But if *the Order of the World it-self* appears just and beautiful; the Admiration and Esteem of *Order* must run higher, and the elegant Passion or Love of Beauty, which is so advantageous to Virtue, must be the more improv'd by its Exercise in so ample and magnificent a Subject. For 'tis impossible that such a *Divine Order* shou'd be contemplated without Extasy and Rapture.' [1]

As for the belief in future rewards and punishments, this (at any rate in its cruder forms) robs our actions of moral value, yet it can be useful as a safeguard against sudden temptations, and still more as a general curb upon those whose moral sense is undeveloped.

Shaftesbury next deals with the motives or obligations to virtue, and the thesis he tries to prove is that celebrated one, that self-love and social are the same. He divides the 'affections' into three kinds: the 'natural affections', which tend towards the public good, the 'self-affections', which tend towards one's private good, and the 'unnatural' affections, which tend towards neither. Virtue depends upon the maintenance of a proper balance between the two first. The animals exhibit 'an exact Proportionableness, Constancy and Regularity' in the balancing of their impulses; they are, in fact, 'natural' without strain and effort. It is only man who is sometimes vile, that is to say, who does not always live according to *his* nature. Since man's most usual moral deformity is the predominance of self-love over social, we must show that it is precisely through the social affections that we do, in fact, obtain the maximum of self-enjoyment. To begin with, it is generally admitted that the completely anti-social man of Hobbes's state of

[1] *Inquiry Concerning Virtue*: Works, vol. ii, p. 75.

nature is not only 'morose, rancorous and malignant', but also thoroughly miserable. Further, Shaftesbury takes it to be 'allow'd by most people' that the pleasures of the mind are superior to those of the body. But these mental pleasures, what are they but the 'natural affections' themselves, or their effects? There should be little need of proving this, he thinks, to any human being 'who has ever known the Condition of the Mind under a lively Affection of Love, Gratitude, Bounty, Generosity, Pity, Succour,' etc. 'The very outward Features, the Marks and Signs which attend this sort of Joy, are expressive of a more intense, clear, and undisturb'd Pleasure' than those attending the bodily delights. It can even be said that a man who knows 'the Principles of *Mathematicks*' will not fail to enjoy, in the discoveries of speculative truth which he makes in that fascinating field, pleasures superior to those of the senses. Or again, the emotion of sympathy is so pleasing to us that we actually prefer a Tragedy to any other entertainment of equal duration. The very pleasures of the senses derive any satisfying quality they may have from their social appendages: the banquet would be nought without the guests, the plate, and the equipage. To possess the social affections full and entire, then, is 'to live according to Nature, and the Dictates and Rules of supreme Wisdom. This is Morality, Justice, Piety, and natural Religion.' The 'self-affections', on the other hand, tend towards misery. Love of Life, Resentment of Injury, Love of Luxury, Interest, Ambition, Love of Praise, or of Rest—a certain degree of all these is indeed allowable and even necessary. But carried beyond this point they become anti-social and vicious, and so productive of wretchedness. Finally Shaftesbury easily shows that the third class of passions (the 'unnatural'), those which, like Inhumanity, Misanthropy, Tyranny, and the rest, lead to no advantage public or private, reduce the lives of their victims to perpetual misery 'agitated by a thorow active Spleen, a close, and settled Malignity, and Rancour', converting their minds into a wilderness 'where all is laid waste, everything fair and goodly remov'd, and nothing extant but what is savage and deform'd'.

> 'Thus the Wisdom of what rules, and is First and Chief in Nature, has made it to be according to the *private Interest* and *Good* of every-one, to work towards the *general Good*.' [1]

Shaftesbury feels that he has reduced his subject to a 'Scheme of Moral Arithmetick' having as much evidence as Mathematicks. What he has in effect done has been to maintain both that virtue should be disinterestedly pursued, and also that it should be cultivated for hedonist reasons. He favours disinterestedness when he is criticizing religion for securing virtue by promises and threats. But when he is refuting Hobbes and the doctrine of self-love he becomes a hedonist: the motive to virtue is the realization of the intensest kind of pleasure, and selfishness is bad and wrong because it is not *really* pleasant. As long as the reward of virtue comes here and now, he accepts it as part of the beautiful order of things; remove it beyond this life, and he rejects it with disdain.

5. As a practical moralist Shaftesbury lays stress on the value of Common-Sense, Good-Humour, Raillery, and the Free Play of Mind. All these were at a high premium in an age which welcomed antidotes for the maladies engendered by superstition, enthusiasm, or the spirit of faction. Addison also, as we have seen, recommended Chearfulness, and it seemed obvious to both writers that all the spectres of history could be laid much more effectually by banter than by zeal. ''Tis the persecuting spirit has raised the bantering one',[2] says Shaftesbury, and he adds that if the Jews had treated early Christianity with raillery and contempt, instead of persecuting it—'had they but taken the Fancy to act such Puppet-Shows in his [Christ's] Contempt as at this hour the Papists are acting

[1] *ibid.*, vol. ii, p. 175.

[2] *Essay on the Freedom of Wit and Humour*: Works, vol. i, p. 72.

in his Honour'[1]—they might possibly have done our religion more harm than they actually did. And had not the Gospel been in any case indisputable, its influence might have disappeared if the heathens had made a Bart'lemy Fair of 'our primitive founders', instead of throwing them to the lions or burning them at the stake. We must at all costs dissociate religion from melancholy and tragic moods; otherwise, instead of coming to know that God in whom there is no darkness at all, we shall be in danger of ascribing our own morosity or vindictiveness to him. Above all, let us not insult him by supposing that he resents free enquiry even about his own existence. If we really believed that God exceeds us as much in good-nature as in all else, we should be more alarmed at the idea of there being no God than at that of his existence—whereas, alas, it is often the other way round.

This free play of mind, however, means for Shaftesbury freedom 'amongst *Gentlemen* and *Friends*, who know one another perfectly well'.[2] The 'mere Vulgar of Mankind' may perhaps 'often stand in need of such a rectifying Object as *the Gallows* before their Eyes'[3] (just as they may need supernatural terrors to prevent them from defying the parson), but it is really only the enlightened few that Shaftesbury takes account of. The evening walk of Theocles and his interlocutor, which resulted in such lofty flights of speculation, was taken in fields 'from which the laborious hinds were now retiring'. Shaftesbury's confidence in the results of philosophical enquiries 'politely managed' presupposes a settled order of society, with no shadow of approaching change to perplex the gentlemen and friends who know each other perfectly well. It is no wonder that Shaftesbury became outmoded when, later in the century, the 'free play of mind' had ceased to be an aristocratic perquisite.

[1] *Letter Concerning Enthusiasm*: Works, vol. i, p. 29.
[2] *Essay on the Freedom of Wit*, etc.: Works, vol. i, p. 75.
[3] *ibid.*, vol. i, p. 127.

CHAPTER V

Natural Morality
(continued)

II. JOSEPH BUTLER (1692-1752)

> '*Others had established the historical and prophetical grounds of the Christian Religion, and that sure testimony of its truth which is found in its perfect adaptation to the heart of Man. It was reserved for him to develope its Analogy to the Constitution and Course of Nature; and laying his strong foundations in the depth of that great argument there to construct another and irrefragable proof: thus rendering Philosophy subservient to Faith, and finding in outward and visible things the type and evidence of those within the veil.*' [Epitaph in Bristol Cathedral.]

DEISM had found all-sufficient evidence of God's existence and of his moral government in 'Nature' and in the conscience of man. The Church had also moved with the times, and, although its basis was still held to be supernatural, it was itself penetrated with the spirit of the age. It admitted that Reason could look up through Nature to Nature's God, and eminent divines since the middle of the seventeenth century (Cudworth, Tillotson, Clarke) had been stressing the reasonableness of Christianity. Yet the Church could not concede that 'natural' religion was enough: its very *raison d'être* lay in the alleged need for Revelation as well. The main effort of orthodox apologetics was therefore directed towards demonstrating that Revelation was a necessary adjunct to natural religion, or, at the lowest, not inconsistent with it. The difficulty of this task arose in part from the growing suspicion that the Jehovah of the Old Testament could hardly be identified with the God of the philosophers: the God whom both deists and orthodox alike agreed to find in Nature. It would no longer do, in this polite age, to 'teach one's haggard and unreclaimed reason to stoop unto the lure of faith', or to lose oneself in an *o altitudo*. The old explanation of biblical difficulties, that these matters were 'mysteries' above our comprehension, could no longer be used except in the way of irony—as was done by Shaftesbury or Voltaire.

Of all the champions of orthodoxy in the first half of the eighteenth century, Bishop Butler is usually felt to be the most effective, and his *Analogy of Religion* (1736) has important bearings upon our main theme. I shall consider, first, the argument of this celebrated work; and secondly, Butler's attempt (in the *Three Sermons*) to ground morality upon human nature, noting especially his divergencies from the school of Shaftesbury.

I

THE ANALOGY OF RELIGION (1736)

The main thesis of the *Analogy* is summed up in the sentence Butler quotes from Origen, that 'he who believes the Scripture to have proceeded from him who is the Author of Nature, may well expect to find the same sort of difficulties in it as are found in the constitution of Nature'. What distinguishes Butler from most other defenders of the faith is the unusual way in which he effects the identification between the God of Revelation and the God of Nature. Instead of proving, in the manner of the physico-theologians, that all things are bright and beautiful, and that the good God made them all, he shows that Nature and Revelation are both baffling and in a sense unsatisfying, and that it is as such that they both appear to be the products of the same mind. He finds a place in his scheme for Revelation, but only by showing it to be as full of 'defects' as Nature itself. In passing from Shaftesbury to Butler we pass from an optimistic to a relatively pessimistic theory of the world. It is not strange that the champion of orthodoxy should be more pessimistic than the heretic, for the Christian tradition had always been associated rather with a sense of the imperfection of Nature and of man, in their present state, than with any optimism of the eighteenth century type. It is the predominance of this sense in Butler which constitutes the real strength of his arguments, as opposed to their ostensible purport, and makes the *Analogy*, after two hundred years, still one of the more impressive works of the period. Butler is not, indeed, exempt from the eighteenth century propensity to seek a favourable explanation for all things; not satisfied with recognizing 'evil', he also tries to explain why God was wise to include it in his plan. But his distinction is that he looks it more directly in the face, and with a more disillusioned eye, than the optimists of the time.

Butler's method of argument depended upon the fact (for us highly significant) that he could assume, as a matter of almost universal consent, the existence of a divine Author of Nature. It was here that one stood on firm ground in the early eighteenth century: the natural evidences for the Divine Original were, as we have seen, felt to be overwhelming; it was 'Revelation' which had to be substantiated by analogy. The deists found God in Nature and in the heart of man, but denied Revelation. If God had really revealed himself in the Hebrew Scriptures, they argued, he would not have left us in any doubt or perplexity; we should find none of the historical, textual, and spiritual difficulties which in fact we do find there, and the God so revealed would correspond with our highest spiritual and moral conceptions, which, however, is not always actually the case. To all this Butler replies that there are just as many difficulties in proving God from the constitution and course of Nature as there are in accepting Revelation, and they are difficulties of the same kind. If, then, in spite of these difficulties, we admit the sufficiency of the natural evidence, may we not learn to expect analogous difficulties in the sphere of revealed religion, and to accept them with as good a grace? For how does God in fact operate in Nature, and in the moral government of the world? It is not Butler's concern to demonstrate the wisdom of God in the Creation, after the manner of Ray or Derham; it is enough for him to reaffirm that Nature is an organized whole, working according to general laws without regard to particular persons or things (so that, e.g., gravitation will not cease if you should happen to step over a cliff). Natural 'evils' of course result from such a system, yet the system is admitted to be of divine workmanship. And how of the moral government of the world? Experience teaches that God's method of moral government does not always correspond with human expectations or desires. We might, for instance, have supposed that a Creator as omnipotent as he is benevolent would only have created beings entirely happy, virtuous, and safe from all physical and moral harm, whereas we know that men are not so created. (We are not certain, however, that either happiness or virtue would exist in such circumstances.) 'Evil' is often used by God for his own inscrutable purposes; God works, not directly, but indirectly, always using subordinate means and agents, and these are often disagreeable to us. This, whether we like it or not, is the actual state of affairs, and Butler does not defend it with any glib assurance. He merely intimates that, on the analogy of what we observe in the 'scheme of the natural world', 'the things objected to may be, upon the whole, friendly and assistant to virtue, and productive of an overbalance of happiness'.[1] But Butler is quite certain, however, that we can see enough evidences of a moral government to be assured that God is governing the world righteously. The weightiest evidence is to be found in our own conscience: we know, that is, that 'upon the whole', virtue produces happiness and vice misery. There is enough evidence for this to justify us in regarding happiness as the reward bestowed upon us for right conduct, and misery as the punishment for vice. In spite of many appearances to the contrary, therefore, it is possible to hold that all may very well be for the best, or at least that

[1] *Analogy*, ch. vii, sect. ii.

there is nothing ridiculous in so thinking. In thus stressing the significance of the moral sense (though not in the tone of his writing) Butler comes near to Shaftesbury, as he also does in declaring that the world is a complex structure of interconnected parts, of which no portion could be altered without injury to the whole. Our limited purview never takes in more than a fragment of this whole, so that in objecting to any part of it we must remember that this part 'may be relative to other parts unknown to us'. To all such objections, then, 'our ignorance is a satisfactory answer, because some unknown relation, or some unknown impossibility, may render what is objected to just and good'. Butler concludes, then, that these considerations are fully sufficient to engage us 'to live in the general practice of all virtue and piety, under the serious apprehension, *though it should be mixed with some doubt*, of a righteous administration established in nature, and a future judgment in consequence of it'.[1]

Throughout the First Part of the *Analogy* Butler is careful to refrain from using arguments derived from dogma. He makes, however, certain assumptions which he takes to be admitted even by those who deny Revelation. These are (*a*) That God exists (this has been proved in innumerable ways, he says, and is almost universally allowed), and (*b*) that the soul exists and is immortal (this he tries to prove by arguments not unlike those of Plato in the *Phaedo*). These being granted, his object in this Part has been merely to study, in the rather melancholy yet devout spirit which is characteristic of him, what, as a matter of experience, God's method of natural and moral governance really is. In Part II he deals with Revelation in the same manner, with the intention of proving that the analogies between Revelation and Nature afford strong presumption of their proceeding from the same Author. One must remember that Butler feels himself to be living in an age when unbelief could make out a case strong

[1] *ibid.*, pt. i, Conclusion. (My italics.)

enough to test the whole defensive armoury of orthodoxy:

> 'It is come, I know not how, to be taken for granted, by many persons, that Christianity is not so much a subject for enquiry; but that it is, now at length, discovered to be fictitious. And accordingly they treat it, as if, in the present age, this were an agreed point among all people of discernment; and nothing remained, but to set it up as a principal subject of mirth and ridicule, as it were by way of reprisals, for its having so long interrupted the pleasures of the world.'[1]

But the system of revealed religion, he replies (using his habitual technique of testing Revelation against Nature), 'is not a subject of ridicule, unless that of Nature be so too'[2]—and to suppose this was, for the eighteenth century, the worst of blasphemies. If the deists can accept Nature as divine, he says in effect, why can they not similarly accept Revelation?—for Nature, to which they habitually appeal, is full of 'defects' analogous to those alleged against Revelation. We have, so to speak, learnt to recognize God's style in his first book, the book of Nature, and we have found it to be—shall we say?—a somewhat uncongenial style; let us not wonder, then, if we find the same mannerisms (not to say 'defects') in his other work, Revelation. Tertullian of old could say *credo quia impossibile*; now an eighteenth century saint asks us to believe Revelation to be authentic *because* it is as bewildering as an admittedly divine Nature. In this paradoxical defence Butler may seem to have virtually wiped out the distinction between Revelation and Nature; indeed, he urges in one place that our notion of what is 'natural' is relative to our degree of knowledge, and that there may be superior beings in the universe so well informed that 'the whole Christian dispensation may to them appear natural, i.e. analogous or conformable to God's dealings with other parts of his creation; as natural as the visible known course of things appears to us'.[3] In dealing, then, with the deistical objection that Revelation lacks clarity,

[1] *Advertisement* to the first edition. [2] Introduction.
[3] *Analogy*, ch. i (*ad fin.*).

fails to proclaim its divine original, Butler answers: God does not inform us exactly how, and on what evidence, we are to act in ordinary life; why therefore should we expect his procedure to be different in Revelation? It is probable that God intends to test and prove our capacities as much in understanding Revelation as in the practical conduct of life, or in exploring the secrets of Nature. But, one feels, if this is so, what has become of the notion of Revelation? Has it not in fact been obliterated in the effort to defend it? If there is no more certainty or clarity in Revelation than in Nature, then Revelation is *part* of Nature? To this pass has orthodoxy come in the reign of George II, that it can only defend Revelation by denying that it reveals. Butler seems to have established precisely that complete oneness of Scripture with Nature which the 'freethinkers' then and since were striving to prove, though his conscious purpose was, of course, to demonstrate the analogy, not the identity, of Revelation and Nature. He deals in a similar way with the objection that Revelation was not universal, but communicated only to a small and barbarous tribe of whose doings a mere minority of mankind have heard even to this day. This, he says, is but an instance of what we already know by experience, that God effects his ends not by immediate acts, but indirectly, through limited human and other agents.

It appears that what chiefly distinguishes Revelation from Nature in Butler's own mind is the biblical prophecies and miracles, and on these he leans with his whole weight. As might be expected, he defends a belief in the miraculous by the usual appeal to human ignorance. What do we know of Nature, who only Nature know? How can we presume to disbelieve what transcends our narrow purview? A native of the tropics might with equal reason disbelieve in ice and snow (and so forth). Butler has another (a typically eighteenth century) argument: we may well imagine, he says, that certain manifestations—signs and wonders—which would be out of place in modern times, might have been quite proper in the early ages of the world. Just so the wise parson in *The Spiritual Quixote* warns Wildgoose that it is fantastic to attempt to evangelize Hanoverian England by methods appropriate enough in the apostolic age! We have no reason to suppose, Butler adds, that when man first appeared upon this planet he was able to reason out his religion as we do now. Therefore he must have acquired it by Revelation: no other alternative is contemplated. Similarly, if Revelation is not genuine, it must be an imposture, and it is easier to suppose it true than false; again—no alternative. Butler belongs, as such remarks indicate, to an age which had not yet learnt to apply historical methods of interpretation in the study of religion.

Butler's arguments carry little conviction to us now, and his main thesis has become obsolete and irrelevant. What remains significant in him is his attitude to the universe, his unusual power of looking dispassionately at the facts, and reporting upon them without distortion. This lends a sombre gravity to his tone, which makes him, like Johnson, more impressive than the optimists. He saw, what perhaps we feel now more habitually than was usual in the eighteenth century, that the universe is not a vast loud-speaker through which God proclaims himself to man,[1] and that life would not necessarily be a more desirable business if truth were really obtruded upon us by a system of divine broadcasting, whether 'natural' or 'supernatural'. A faith so easy of attainment, he felt, would be worth no more than a knowledge of the multiplication table—or, as Coleridge expressed it later, 'it could not be intellectually more evident without being morally less effective; without counteracting its own end by sacrificing the life of faith to the cold mechanism of a worthless because compulsory assent'.[2] Though Butler does not express his dissatisfaction as we should, he seems to discern the radical defect

[1] Cf. A. Huxley: 'The assertions of Christianity, when freed from their mythological incrustations . . . happen unfortunately to be true. Our universe is the universe of Behemoth and Leviathan, not of Helvetius and Godwin' (*Music at Night*, p. 87).

[2] *Biographia Literaria*, ch. x (Shawcross ed., vol. i, pp. 135-6).

of eighteenth century deism, namely that it makes man the measure of all things, and takes no account of the most significant elements of religious experience—those, namely, which involve an acknowledgment of paradox, even of irrationality at the heart of things, certainly of transcendence or 'otherness'; of God not merely as deified Reason but as *mysterium tremendum*. And his insistence that life is a state of probation comes far nearer than the optimists' creed to expressing the modern realization that action is necessary, that the world contains material and moral jungles, and that the onus of clearing them rests upon us. Voltaire, reacting against the same optimism, condensed, in the familiar words of Candide to Pangloss, his view of the proper attitude towards these jungles. After they had experienced almost every possible form of physical and moral evil, Pangloss (who, being a philosopher, can never contradict himself) repeats his old formula that all events are inter-related in the best of possible worlds. '*Cela est bien dit*', replies Candide, '*mais il faut cultiver le jardin.*' Butler's general attitude, his realism and his freedom from illusion, can be indicated (in conclusion) in his reply to the imaginary objector who urges (with much force) that 'it is a poor thing to solve difficulties in revelation by saying that there are the same in natural religion'. 'Indeed the epithet *poor*', he replies (and Johnson might have said the same), 'may be applied, I fear as properly, to great part or the whole of human life'.[1]

2

BUTLER AS MORALIST

Butler's ethical writings have been spoken of with uniform respect by all the historians of ethics I have met with. He is regarded, by most, as the greatest English moralist of the eighteenth century. In the middle of the nineteenth century, as we learn from Whewell, Butler's *Fifteen*

[1] *Analogy*, pt. ii, ch. viii.

Sermons, and particularly the *Three Sermons on Human Nature* with the *Dissertation on Virtue*, were accepted as the official moral philosophy of the University of Cambridge. Matthew Arnold, in his long essay on *Bishop Butler and the Zeitgeist* (*Last Essays on Church and Religion*), speaks of the corresponding reverence paid to him at Oxford (where, it seems, Butler's Sermons and Aristotle's Ethics shared equal honours), and quotes several lofty encomiums upon his work as moralist and philosopher of religion. And Professor Broad concludes the chapter on Butler in his *Five Types of Ethical Theory* (1930) by saying that 'though his system is incomplete, it does seem to contain the prolegomena to any system of ethics that can claim to do justice to the facts of moral experience'.[1] I propose now briefly to examine the *Three Sermons* and the *Dissertation* in order to illustrate, through Butler's attempt to find a 'natural' basis for morality, the controlling influence of the idea of 'Nature' in the eighteenth century over minds as diverse as we have found Shaftesbury's and Butler's to have been.

Whewell indicates Butler's cast of mind as a moralist by contrasting him with Paley (he might equally well be contrasted with any utilitarian moralist, that is to say, with most English moralists of the century):

> 'Paley makes virtue depend upon the consequences of our actions; Butler makes it depend upon the due operation of our moral Constitution. Paley is the moralist of utility; Butler, of conscience.'[2]

Of the two ways in which the subject of morals may be treated (1) by enquiring into the abstract relations of things, and (2) by enquiring into the nature of man, and distinguishing what course of actions is in conformity with that nature, Butler proposes to follow the second. He takes the old Stoic injunction, Follow Nature!—the old definition of virtue as life according to Nature—and subjects it to a careful examination. In Butler's deistical and

[1] *op. cit.*, p. 83. [2] Preface to *Three Sermons*, 3rd ed., 1855, p. v.

free-thinking age, when 'Nature' in some sense was ascendant over 'Grace', and morality seemed likely to be resolved into an easy following of impulse (even if the impulses should in fact be benevolent and social), a scrutiny of this key-word, 'Nature', in its ethical uses, seemed peculiarly desirable. Even Wollaston, in his *Religion of Nature Delineated*, had pointed out that 'to follow Nature' as an ethical maxim might turn out to mean 'acting as any of the several parts, without distinction, of a man's nature happened most to incline him'.[1] Butler, anxious to save the principle, asks us to consider what we mean by the 'nature' of man. Like a watch, man's moral nature is made up of parts: appetites, passions, affections, *and* the '*principle of reflection*'; but we have not fully described his nature in giving this catalogue. We must also give some account of the relationship of the parts, how they fit together, and what sort of a system they form as a whole. Human nature is not the sum of its parts but the constitution of the whole into an organism, with due 'subordination of its faculties to each other according to their relative worth and dignity' (if the Coleridgean phrase may be here applied). We can only form a true notion of human nature by considering that certain parts of it have a 'natural' prerogative to rule the whole system. Brutes, indeed, act according to their natures in following the determination of instinct and environment. But man, in addition to passions and affections, possesses the 'principle of reflection', or conscience, the faculty which approves and disapproves, and recognizes the higher and the lower. Human nature then is such that 'virtue', action according to the approval of conscience, is its end, just as timekeeping is the watch's end. The 'principle of reflection', Butler says:

> 'plainly bears upon it marks of authority over all the rest, and claims the absolute direction of them all, to allow or forbid their gratification.'[2]

---

[1] *ibid.*, Author's *Preface*, pp. 8-9. [2] *ibid.*, p. 15.

We are therefore *not* acting according to *our* nature if we allow no more weight to this principle than to the various impulses—if we allow first one and then another to determine our actions. The strength or prevalence of any impulse is thus no indication of its moral value. Moral action springs only from according to conscience the 'absolute authority which is due to it'. Butler criticizes Shaftesbury for not allowing any weight to this authority in his *Inquiry*. Shaftesbury has shown convincingly that virtue in fact produces happiness, and vice misery; he has furnished, that is, good utilitarian grounds for morality. But suppose that there may be exceptional cases where virtue and happiness are not coincident, or suppose a resolute sinner or sceptic refuses to believe in their coincidence? We must then, says Butler, fall back upon the absolute imperative of conscience; this at least gives us certainty, however doubtful the *utility* of virtue may be. Man is 'by nature' a law unto himself, and he would be under the same obligation to obey that law even though he were ignorant or sceptical of any authority in the universe capable of punishing violation of it.

Butler now enters upon the discussion of 'self-love and social'—the classic problem of eighteenth century ethics. There is 'a strange affectation', he says—and he is alluding to the Epicureans, to La Rochefoucauld, and above all to the inevitable Hobbes, who for more than a century after his own time represented the evil principle for all orthodox moralists—which consists in regarding the whole of human life as 'one continued exercise of self-love'. Butler distinguishes two grades of 'selfishness': (1) Cool and settled selfishness, and (2) Passionate or sensual selfishness. Only actions springing from (1) can be said to proceed from 'self-love', or to deserve the name of 'interested' actions. Particular actions, due to passion, spring not from love of self, but from love of their respective objects: wealth, honour, power, etc., and are often performed in contradiction to true self-love. Self-love in itself, and in its due degree, 'is as just and morally good as any affection whatever'. The 'interestedness' of an action is not the criterion of its moral quality, neither is its being attended with pleasure or pain; the only criterion is whether it 'becomes such creatures as we are'. We cannot even wish self-love weaker than it is, for we see it overcome continually by every whim and caprice, by inquisitiveness, love, hatred, and any 'vagrant inclination'. It is ridiculous, moreover, to call a life of self-indulgence or debauchery 'interested', for it is plainly contrary to real self-interest even in this world. In fact, in so far as self-love contains a principle of reflection or discrimination, it is a much better guide than passion; and although a life motivated by it would be neither religious nor moral (since the 'felicific calculus' is *not* the test of goodness), it were to be wished that more people would guide themselves by it rather than, as they commonly do, by mere appetite. But of course Butler does not accept the analysis of all our actions into some form of self-love. Human nature, for him, is as clearly ordered for public as for private good. There is a 'natural principle of benevolence in man', which has the same relation to society as self-love has to the individual. At this point Butler seems to resume common ground with Shaftesbury, or even with Mandeville: the social and the self-affections, he agrees, are so intimately connected, that we cannot procure self-satisfaction without having some benevolence, and conversely self-love is the great security for our correct social behaviour. Even our passions, those which are neither benevolent nor self-loving, have *de facto* (as Mandeville had said) a tendency to promote both public and private good—such is the wisdom with which Providence has designed the universe. Man is naturally united to his fellows, and the same principles which would lead him to injure society lead also to self-injury. The frantic pursuit of riches and power and honour (the current travesty of 'self-interested' action) demonstrably and admittedly fails to lead to happiness. The fact is that men are commonly as lacking in reasonable or 'cool' self-love as they are in public affection, whereas a wise following of *both* principles of their nature would, in fact, produce the same course of virtuous action. But these utilitarian reassurances come from Butler, as it were, incidentally; they are part of his eighteenth century stock-in-trade, not his own distinctive wares. We recognize him better again when he assures us that it is safer, and so more truly moral, to act from conscience, which is a settled principle, than merely from natural affection, which may or may not function steadily.

What course of life, then, does our real 'nature' suggest as proper for us? Butler admits that there is a diversity among men in respect of their 'natural sense of moral good and evil', but he thinks nevertheless that there is a standard, common to the whole human species, sufficiently fixed to enable us to discourse intelligibly about 'human nature'. The existence of an inner check can no more be questioned than the existence of eyesight, though both are liable to error. Now *religion*, indeed, requires us, not to do good when we feel so disposed, but to form our whole scheme of living upon conscience; to direct it wholly by loyalty to a categorical imperative which transcends each passing gust of passion or impulse. But can it be demonstrated, he asks, that this surrender of our lives to conscience, this living under Duty's habitual sway, is in any real sense 'living according to our Nature' (this being, it will be remembered, what he is concerned to prove)? Might it not perhaps be more 'natural' to do as others use, sometimes sporting with Amaryllis in the shade, and sometimes (perhaps) living laborious days, but in every case yielding only to whatever impulse happens at the time to be strongest: being, in fact, consistent only in inconsistency? Butler replies, that

> 'if by following nature were meant only acting as we please, it would indeed be ridiculous to speak of nature as any guide in morals.'[1]

It would, in fact, be impossible in that case to deviate from

[1] *ibid.*, p. 61.

'Nature'. The fact is, he sees, that 'Nature' is used in different senses. In one sense our 'Nature' implies the notion of 'that which is a law unto itself'; in another sense, we are 'by Nature' children of wrath. It is not this latter 'Nature' that we are to live by, but that whereby (in St Paul's words) the Gentiles 'do by nature the things contained in the law'. It is by the possession of that 'magisterial faculty', conscience, which is 'natural' to man, that he becomes a moral agent, and a law to himself. A man may yield to strong impulse, and yet be violating his proper 'Nature'. 'Suppose a man, foreseeing the danger of certain ruin, should rush into it for the sake of a present gratification'; there would then be a 'disproportion' between his action and the 'Nature' of man, and it would thus be 'unnatural' for him so to act. But since we should not call the man's behaviour 'unnatural' if, in the case mentioned, self-love had prevailed over passion, self-love must be a principle superior to passion. Passion may be contradicted without violating Nature; reasonable self-love cannot. There really is, then, such a thing as a *natural* superiority of one impulse over another, quite distinct from their degrees of strength or frequency. Still more emphatically can it be said that where impulse comes into conflict with reflection or conscience, conscience must be held to be the 'naturally' superior principle, quite apart from the strength of the impulse. The distinction is analogous to that between mere *power* and true *authority*. The very notion of 'conscience' includes the idea of its 'superintendence'. 'Had it strength, as it has right; had it power, as it had manifest authority, it would absolutely govern the world.'[1] Every subordinate impulse is a real part of our nature, but not the whole. As the ancients have said, tortures and death are not so contrary to human nature as injustice.

Butler feels that he has now proved his case, which is, that 'exclusive of Revelation' (how vital it seemed to the Hanoverian divines, even to so saintly and orthodox a

[1] *ibid.*, p. 70.

Christian as Bishop Butler, to ground their case firmly upon Nature, before appealing to Revelation!), man is demonstrably not a creature of the moment, left by his Maker to act at random. And if it be asked: even if the moral law be thus written upon our hearts, what obligation is there to obey it? Butler answers (relying implicitly on the numinous quality of the idea of Nature): 'Your obligation to obey this law is its being the law of your nature'.[1] The imperative of conscience is 'categorical'.

As we have seen, it is not Butler's purpose to justify virtue on the score of its pleasantness; yet he feels free to use that argument, when it seems desirable, in order to refute those who seek pleasure in vice. Why, for instance, should we not take the primrose path to present 'good' without regard for others? This question implies the false assumptions that our own happiness is really distinct from that of others, and that vice has no sting of its own. Actually, as we have seen, most of our enjoyments depend upon our regard for our fellows, and the states of mind associated with rage, envy, resentment, etc., do not yield greater happiness than meekness, forgiveness, good-will, nor is the satisfaction arising from riches and power greater than that arising from justice and charity. The restraints of vice are far more galling than the easy yoke of duty—which, indeed, by being deliberately worn, soon becomes a delight and not a burden. There is seldom any inconsistency between duty and even what is commonly called 'interest', still less between duty and what is really 'interest'. Self-love 'does in general perfectly coincide with virtue, and leads to one and the same course of life'. He adds that whatever exceptions there may be to this rule —and they are much fewer than is commonly imagined— 'all shall be set right at the final distribution of things'. But this consideration, again, belongs to Butler's reserve; it is not put much into front-line action, any more than the hedonic value of virtue or the equivalence of virtue and self-love. We are not to be virtuous for the sake of plea-

[1] *ibid.*, p. 78.

sure, or from the motives of self-love, even though an unerring felicific calculus, or the insight of perfect self-love, would invariably lead to actions identical with those dictated by conscience. In the *Dissertation on Virtue* he further argues (against the utilitarian position) that we must not confuse even benevolence with virtue. It is taken as agreed that we have this 'moral sense' or 'conscience', and that there is an almost universal agreement about its dictates; but the proper object of this faculty is right conduct, quite apart from all consideration of consequences, whether in terms of our own happiness or that of others. Butler means, I think, that it is neither safe nor wise for us to be utilitarians—to hold that virtue consists in actions tending to promote the 'greatest happiness' of mankind. 'Some of great and distinguished merit' (Shaftesbury?), he writes,

> 'have, I think, expressed themselves in a manner, which may occasion some danger to careless readers, of imagining the whole of virtue to consist in singly aiming, according to the best of their judgment, at promoting the happiness of mankind in the present state; and the whole of vice, in doing what they foresee, or might foresee, is likely to produce an overbalance of unhappiness in it: than which mistakes, none can be conceived more terrible.' [1]

Why is the 'greatest happiness' principle (which for good utilitarians comprised the whole of the law and the prophets) a terrible mistake? Because, in Butler's view, we simply do not possess, in our present imperfect state, sufficient clairvoyance for us to be certain about the consequences of our actions, 'nor do we know what we are about, when we endeavour to promote the good of mankind in any ways but those he [God] has directed'. Shocking actions might be performed with a view to producing an overbalance of happiness. Such ultimate objectives as the happiness of mankind are beyond our limited scope, and we may easily, in attempting to pursue them, become

[1] *ibid.*, p. 99.

moral monsters. Our safety lies in following the God-given instinct which condemns violence, injustice, and falsehood, and approves benevolence towards some (e.g. kindred, friends, or countrymen) rather than towards others; whereas with the more grandiose aims we may easily be led into perpetrating the former, and neglecting the latter. 'The happiness of the world', he concludes, 'is the concern of him who is the Lord and the proprietor of it'; our concern is only with conduct dictated by the sense of duty. Or as Dr Broad expresses it: God might be conceived to be a utilitarian 'were his moral character merely that of benevolence; yet ours is not so'. 'And though it is of course our duty', Butler adds,

> 'within the bounds of veracity and justice, to contribute to the ease, convenience and even cheerfulness and diversion of our fellow-creatures: yet, from our short view, it is greatly uncertain whether this endeavour will, in particular instances, produce an overbalance of happiness upon the whole; since so many and distant things must come into the account.'

Butler has a strong sense (akin to Burke's) of the incalculable complexity of the moral world, and a corresponding distrust of the calculating principle as a moral dynamic. We are so apt to overlook some vital term in making our equations, that our only safe course is to leave moral arithmetic alone, and keep to conscience and the sense of duty. Yet Butler lives in the eighteenth century climate, and just as true self-love is probably equivalent to virtue, though we must not be virtuous on that account, so probably dutiful conduct will in fact maximize happiness, though we must be dutiful, not for that reason, but solely out of regard for the law of our nature—and of course he would add (and does add elsewhere), out of regard for the Author of that law. In spite of Butler's decorous concealment of his religion, it may be doubted whether after all he has succeeded in building morality upon a 'natural' foundation. Or perhaps he has done so only by including a supernatural principle in the make-up of 'human nature'.

The reverence he expects us to pay to conscience (call it the 'law of our being' as he will) is of a kind that most men will only accord to something other than themselves.

> From worlds not quickened by the sun
> A portion of the gift is won.

CHAPTER VI

'Nature' in Satire

I

MANDEVILLE

TWO chief views about the moral order of the universe are to be found in the eighteenth century (often held simultaneously by the same thinkers): one, that the world is a system which automatically works together for good, and the other, that in order to secure good results we must make good efforts. Associated with the first of these, as we have seen, is the view that there is a 'natural' identity of interest between the individual and society (self-love and social are the same), so that each man in following his own interest is in fact thereby promoting that of the whole. This view, as we see particularly in Bentham, is compatible with the theory that egoism is the mainspring of human action. But on the whole the eighteenth century thought well of human nature, and it was generally believed that men were 'by nature' sociable, sympathetic, and benevolent. Good results, therefore, were to be expected from the nature of man, and as for vice (which undeniably existed), the wise ordinances of Providence could be relied upon to turn it to good ends (or at least to set matters right in the hereafter). So that even if we made no good efforts, 'good' would ultimately triumph just the same. On the whole, man's 'good nature' was supposed to be a part of the beneficent automatism of things.

Of the various writers of the time Mandeville (1670-1733) is remarkable, not so much for originality of thought, as for the new and (to his own generation) startling pattern he made out of the old materials. For, as we shall see, he took something from Hobbes and the libertines, something from Christianity, and something from eighteenth century optimism. Out of these incongruous but ready-made ingredients he constructed his celebrated *Fable of the Bees*, of which the paradoxical subtitle was 'Private Vices, Publick Benefits'. Many had urged that God and Nature knew how to evoke good from ill, to turn private vice to public advantage, but the orthodox view (as stated by Butler) was—Woe unto him through whom the scandal cometh! We must not put too great a strain upon the moral refineries of Providence; and the world would be an even better place without any vice at all, than it is with vice being constantly turned, by divine alchemy, into good. Mandeville alone had the audacity to declare that the refinery *needed* the raw material: that the public benefits existed not in spite of, but because of, the private vices. In the *Fable* itself, which is a short satire in Hudibrastic verse, Society is shown as a Bee-hive. This hive is prosperous and great as long as pride, selfishness, corruption, luxury, hypocrisy, fraud, injustice, and every conceivable vice are freely practised. One day, however, Jove 'rid the bawling Hive of fraud', with what result? Trade and the professions languished, unemployment and depopulation set in, and the few surviving bees deserted their hive for a hollow tree, where they took up their abode, 'Blest with Content and Honesty'. The moral, as Mandeville draws it, is:

> Then leave complaints: Fools only strive
> To make a Great an Honest Hive.
> T'enjoy the World's Conveniences,
> Be famed in War, yet live in Ease,
> Without great Vices, is a vain
> Eutopia seated in the Brain.
>
> Bare Virtue can't make nations live
> In Splendor.

What are we to conclude from this fable? That the bees were wise who fled from a corrupt society and sought for rural innocence in a hollow tree, forswearing splendour for the sake of virtue? Or that the 'Vice' which is so beneficial to society deserves some other name? The peculiarity of Mandeville's position is that he seems to accept neither of these alternatives. He is clearly at one with his age in desiring worldly greatness, in approving of the splendour of the hive, yet he retains a routine reverence for 'virtue' as something of a loftier order. His point is, however, that virtue is impracticable, or at any rate unpractised, and that since it is therefore to vice that we owe our benefits, it is more honest and realistic to recognize it as vice, instead of pretending that it is virtue. For what, according to Mandeville, is 'virtue'? His idea of it is as rigorous as that of Butler or Kant: it is, he says, 'every Performance, by which Man, *contrary to the impulse of Nature*, should endeavour the Benefit of others, or the Conquest of his own Passions, out of a Rational Ambition of being good'.[1] Virtue, then, is self-conquest, altruism and rational behaviour: well and good; Mandeville places himself securely on the side of the angels of ethical tradition. But then he proceeds to demonstrate that men never do, in actuality, conquer themselves in this way—never do behave altruistically or rationally. We yet enjoy many good things in civilized life; whence then can they come? They must arise from 'vice', i.e. from conduct motivated by pride, selfishness, and the rest of the deadly sins. Christian saints and moralists have taught that wealth and power are vicious, because hostile to the life of the spirit, but they have preached renunciation as the remedy. Mandeville adopts the most rigoristic definition of virtue, not in order to persuade us to renounce the world, but to encourage us to accept it and make the best of it. Virtue? Yes! admirable, of course; but it transcends human nature. We live in the splendid hive, and we wish to go on living in it; therefore, we should take an honest, scientific interest in its structure. There is much in it that is good,

[1] Kaye's edition of the *Fable*, vol. i, pp. 48-9 (*Enquiry into the Origin of Moral Virtue*). (My italics.)

but don't let us pretend that this is due to any 'virtue' of ours. Similarly, Mandeville's definition of virtue prevents him from adopting the utilitarian standpoint. To any liberal utilitarian who demands how any conduct which benefits society can be called 'vice', Mandeville replies that virtue is to be judged, not by the *consequences* of actions, but by their *motives*, and human motives are almost invariably impure. This is not to deny, of course, that it is these very 'consequences' that interest Mandeville, for his whole argument is that impure motives can and do produce beneficial results. If we should enquire further, how can private vices work together for public good? Mandeville will refer us, in quite the approved manner, to the Divine Wisdom:

> 'nothing can render the unsearchable depth of the Divine Wisdom more conspicuous, than that Man, whom Providence had designed for Society, should not only by his own Frailties and Imperfections be led into the Road to Temporal Happiness, but likewise receive, from a seeming Necessity of Natural Causes, a Tincture of that Knowledge, in which he was afterwards to be made perfect by the True Religion, to his Eternal Welfare.' [1]

It is curious that Mandeville should have adhered to his lofty notion of virtue while accepting with so good a grace the viciousness of man and its gratifying consequences; or, to put it another way, that he should have been moralist enough, after showing (with no apparent disquiet) how ubiquitous and inevitable vice is, to add the palinode 'but don't forget that it *is* vice!'. It is difficult to say exactly what his motive can have been. Sometimes, as we have seen, he uses the traditional language of religion; is it then possible that Mandeville is a true Christian satirist, who, like Machiavelli, rejected 'the myth of human goodness, which for liberal thought replaces the belief in Divine Grace'? [2] Hardly, for though he confesses that there is no health in us, he does not ask for mercy upon us miserable offenders. He rather thanks God for making sin so

[1] *ibid.*, vol. i, p. 57.

[2] T. S. Eliot, *Lancelot Andrewes*, pp. 62-4.

advantageous. Some have supposed that his satire drove in the opposite direction; that he was exposing the transcendental notion of virtue that he ostensibly accepts, by revealing its astronomical remoteness.[1] Perhaps we may suggest that his aim (it was certainly the *outcome* of his work) was to show the incompatibility between traditional moral standards and actual ways of living, and that he disliked the cant of virtue more than the reality of vice—that for him, in short, there lived more faith in honest vice than in half the moral creeds. One may add that like other satirists, he was also prepared at times to use the loftiest moral ideals purely as a standard of satirical reference, and without implicating himself with them. His main plea —and herein lies such moral strength as he has—was for honesty and realism; like Machiavelli, he thought we should learn more by looking at what men are than by enlarging upon what they should be. Here we are, honouring one set of principles and acting upon another: what is to be done? Recognize and accept the facts, and don't imagine you are practising virtue when you are really only following the promptings of your egoism, and when the real practice of virtue (however admirable in the sight of heaven) would lead to such inconvenient consequences. Mandeville belongs to our story only because he shared the eighteenth century belief in Nature—because he believed, that is to say, that you had only to accept, to let natural causes produce their natural effects, in order to arrive at a very tolerable state of affairs. To get a good society, you need only go on being as wicked as you like. But Mandeville stands queerly poised between several conflicting schools of thought; he is not of pure eighteenth century extraction. Remove his 'Hobbist' or 'cynical' view of human nature, and you get an eighteenth century *laissez-faire* liberal. Remove his complacent acceptance of the splendid hive, and you get a misanthrope or an austere Christian moralist. As it is, he remains an obstinate amalgam, irreducible to any simple formula, though

[1] Cf. Kaye's *Introduction*, *op. cit.*, vol. i, p. xlix.

made up of ingredients which could only have co-existed in his own age.

2

A NOTE ON SWIFT

'To show the incompatibility between traditional moral standards and actual ways of living' (the phrase used a few lines above)—this is of course the general aim and end of Satire, and it cannot escape notice that the age we are considering, the age of Dryden, Pope, Swift, and Voltaire, was exceptionally fertile in satiric work. Just when the metaphysicians were demonstrating that all was for the best in the best of possible worlds, a number of major writers were pointing out that a great deal of whatever was, was wrong. In Pope there is a combination of both attitudes, for the optimism of the *Essay on Man* is hardly maintained in, say, the *Dunciad*. It is evidently possible to be Pangloss in theory and Candide in practice: to believe intellectually in the Beautiful Order, or the Great Chain of Being, but at the same time to be painfully aware, in actual living, of what man has made of man. In my view it was precisely the prevalence of the belief in 'Nature', and especially in 'Nature and Reason', which made this period the golden age of satire. If all in Nature pleases, then Man will at times appear vile by contrast; if you worship 'Nature and Reason', you will be the more afflicted by human unreason; and perhaps only the effort to see man as the world's glory will reveal how far he is really its jest and riddle. An age which believes in 'Nature' must fit man somehow into the picture; it can either see man, with Shaftesbury, as naturally reasonable, sociable, and amiable, and human institutions (with Soame Jenyns) as an extension of the divine pattern, or it can see him as Yahoo rather than Houyhnhnm—deviating at every turn from Nature and Reason, and following only the devices and desires of his own corrupt heart. As we saw in Chapter I, the eighteenth century felt a deep nostalgia, not for the Eden of theology, but for the State of Nature from which man had somehow departed (though possibly the Tahitians still enjoyed it). According to venerable theory, at least as old as Aristotle, reinforced by Stoicism and Christianity, and now re-emphasized by Descartes and Locke, man's essential nature was his rational soul. The real State of Nature, then, as Locke had said, has the Law of Nature (which is the law of Reason) to govern it, and man's affairs are rightly ordered only when his institutions correspond to the true theory of human nature.

It was by standards of this kind that most of the satire of this time measured the actual. 'True Satire', Mr Middleton Murry has said, 'implies the condemnation of society by reference to an ideal'; 'the satirist', he goes on, 'is engaged in measuring the monstrous aberration from the ideal' [1]; and he contrasts the satirist with the comedian, who is merely concerned with aberrations from current social normality, and refers to no remoter standard than the accepted conventions. Conditions in the early eighteenth century were, I think, especially favourable for the satiric kind of measurement. By that time the mediaeval rack had sufficiently dislimned for the harsh outlines of the modern situation to be clearly visible. Man, hitherto the immortal soul in quest of salvation, or the rational soul in quest of virtue, was now seen to be the economic or political ego in quest of wealth, power, and position. During the seventeenth century the acquisitive urges still hid behind religious and political outworks, but by now it was too clear that what both individuals and states were really after was the material spoils of the world, now lying readier for exploitation than they had ever been for the Tamburlaines or Jews of Malta. Yet—and this is the point—yet the old standards lived on in ghostly fashion, sitting crowned upon the graves of Christianity and Humanism; it was to them that one still instinctively turned, and by them one was still, in theory, supposed to be living. Anyone, then, who still held firmly to them, and yet had the

[1] *The Problem of Style*, p. 65.

gift of seeing things as they really were, could find all the materials of satire ready to hand: the ideal and the actual in sharp juxtaposition. Such a one was Swift, who, says Mr Aldous Huxley, could never forgive man for being a vertebrate mammal as well as an immortal soul. One thinks at once of his distinction between 'real' and 'nominal' Christianity in the *Argument Against Abolishing Christianity*, or between rational man (Houyhnhnm) and brute man (Yahoo) in *Gulliver's Travels*. Swift differs from Mandeville mainly, one might say, in not being content with the 'splendid hive' as it is, and in not imagining virtue to be by definition unattainable. His satires imply a reference to a standard of Nature and Reason which is as old as creation, and is attainable, if only men would not perversely depart from it. The Houyhnhnm, it will be remembered, 'thought Nature and Reason were sufficient guides for a reasonable animal, as we pretended to be, in showing us what we ought to do, and what to avoid'.[1] But Swift's position is full of ambiguities, particularly with respect to the Christian religion. Is 'real' Christianity, for him, equivalent to Nature and Reason, as it was for many contemporary minds? Would he, like a true Christian divine, reject the splendid hive in its favour? His account of the likely effects of introducing 'real' Christianity into a modern society closely resembles Mandeville's account of the effects of introducing virtue into the hive:

> 'I hope no reader imagines me so weak to stand up in the defence of real Christianity, such as used, in primitive times (if we may believe the writers of those ages) to have an influence upon men's belief and actions: to offer at the restoring of that, would indeed be a wild project; it would be to dig up foundations: to destroy at one blow all the wit, and half the learning of the kingdom: to break the entire frame and constitution of things; to ruin trade, extinguish arts and sciences, with the professors of them; in short, to turn our courts, exchanges, and shops, into deserts; and would be full as absurd as the proposal of Horace,

[1] *Gulliver*, bk. iv, ch. 5.

> where he advises the Romans, all in a body, to leave their city, and seek a new seat in some remote part of the world, by way of cure for the corruption of their manners.'[1]

The logic of the irony in the *Argument*, in which Swift's device is to adopt the tone of the 'nominal' Christians and to defend Christianity for the wrong reasons, would seem to place him as an upholder of the 'real' or primitive Christianity. On the other hand, his writings in general show his attachment to reason and good sense, to the Anglican Church as their embodiment, and to settled and orderly government. He does not really want a revolutionary Christianity; no one hates religious enthusiasm more than he, and no one has analysed more devastatingly the sources of fanaticism ('Aeolism') and of any kind of megalomania. As a Church of England man, a friend of Revolution principles, and a statesman, he accepts the splendid hive—'our present schemes of wealth and power', with which he says real Christianity is utterly inconsistent. Both his life and his writings show that he had no wish to abandon those schemes, or to 'break the entire frame and constitution of things'. He does not believe, with Mandeville, that the hive must needs be vicious to be great; indeed, he is a satirist precisely because he feels that it should and could be directed by standards which would have been acceptable to Plato or Cicero—standards of rationality, 'nature' and civilization for which the great ancients stood, and for which the Church of England now stands. Swift was for the ancients against the moderns because he saw history not as progressive amelioration, but as a struggle, often marked by phases of disastrous failure, to maintain the values fixed for ever by antiquity. Modern philosophy, science, criticism, and politics, and much modern religion, were for him so many fantastic divagations from the plain path of Nature and Reason. The Goths of ignorance, pedantry, pride, or corruption were ever ready to swarm from their frozen North and

[1] *Argument Against Abolishing Christianity* (*ad init.*).

bury all in universal darkness, and the few friends of Nature and of civilization must be continually vigilant in their defence. The crooked designs of statesmen, the subtleties of divines and lawyers, the follies of 'projectors' and natural philosophers, the affected refinements of poets —all these must be checked by perpetual reference to the simple canons of Reason and Nature. 'God hath given the bulk of mankind a capacity to understand reason when it is fairly offered; and by reason they would easily be governed, if it were left to their choice.'[1]

A remark of Mill's about Bentham aptly describes the purport and method of Swift's satire: Bentham, he says, took his stand 'outside the received opinion' and surveyed it 'as an entire stranger to it'. Indeed it is the aim of all major satire to trick us into seeing actual and familiar conditions as if for the first time, or as though we were visitors from some Utopian planet, or from China, Persia, or any other supposed headquarters of Reason. Hence arise the classic technical devices of satire, all of which are employed by Swift. The actual may be depicted in a distorted or inverted form, so that we judge and condemn it first, and only then recognize its essential likeness to our own system (Lilliput). Or the actual may be described and explained to some person who is entirely ignorant of existing conditions, and who can therefore stand for uncorrupted Nature and Reason (the King of Brobdingnag, or—to take a modern instance—Plato, in Lowes Dickinson's *After Two Thousand Years*). The mere recital of the facts to one who is assumed to view things entirely according to true theory, produces the satiric situation. One might to-day, for example, try to expound the meaning of such terms as 'Christendom', 'Democracy', 'Peace', and the like, to a child (or might we say, to a genuine Hindoo yogi?); the result, if one were sufficiently accurate, would be satire. A variant of this method is to introduce into the actual world some unsophisticated stranger from China,

[1] *Some Free Thoughts upon the Present State of Affairs* (1714), quoted by R. Quintana, *The Mind and Art of J. Swift* (1936), *q.v.*, especially ch. iv.

Persia, Mars, etc., and to give us, through his artless comments, a glimpse of how we look to the eyes of first innocence. Or the satirist may prefer simply to depict a Utopia where all is rationally ordered, and leave us to make the required application to actuality. Swift occasionally drops into the Utopian method, as in the passage where he tells us that the Lilliputians, in choosing public officers, had 'more regard to good morals than to great abilities', since 'Providence never intended to make the management of Public affairs a mystery, to be comprehended only by a few persons of sublime genius, of which there seldom are three born in an age; but they suppose truth, justice, temperance, and the like, to be in every man's power'.[1] Swift adds, it is true, that in describing these and other Utopian regulations in Lilliput he 'would only be understood to mean the original institutions, and not the most scandalous corruptions into which these people are fallen by the degenerate nature of man'. He is thinking here of their political corruptions, for, as Sir Charles Firth has pointed out, 'as soon as Swift turns to describe the politics of Lilliput it ceases to be Utopia and becomes England itself, instead of being an example to England'.[2] It is consoling to our national pride to remember, in this connexion, that the greatest French satirist of the eighteenth century found in the same England a norm of Nature and Reason whereby to measure the aberrations of the *ancien régime* in France. It would doubtless be going too far to suggest that Voltaire's *Letters on the English Nation* (better known in the French version as *Lettres Philosophiques*) are an example of the Utopian method of satire; Voltaire's clear sight did not overlook the many deviations from reason on this side of the Channel as well, and we find them duly noted—as in his remarks on Shakespeare, and on the English temperament (its susceptibility to the effects of an east wind). But England seemed sufficiently Utopian in 1726-9 to serve his present purpose. It was a convenient method of attacking

[1] *Gulliver*, bk. i, ch. 6. [2] *Essays Historical and Literary* (1938), p. 214.

traditional theology to describe the views of an English sect (the Quakers) who seemed to have reached a religious outlook almost Chinese in its rationality. It was an equally convenient means of attacking scholasticism to describe the rise of English philosophy from Bacon to its culmination in that most modern and reasonable of philosophers, Mr Locke, and to enlarge upon the triumphs of the scientific method in Newton's work. Similarly he could contrast the commercial propensities of the English nobility (Lord Townshend's brother was a city merchant, and Lord Oxford's a 'factor' in Aleppo) with the quixotic fastidiousness of continental aristocrats, many of whom had no patrimony save their escutcheons and their pride. Voltaire was present at Newton's funeral, and was deeply impressed by this, and by other signs of the honour paid to men of genius in England. China, as is well known, served many writers of this period as a symbol of Nature and Reason, and it is made use of in this way by Voltaire also; but readers of Swift may be gratified to find that for once Voltaire had no occasion to appeal to China, since England was closer to hand.

Whatever technique the satirist uses (there are many gradations of irony, in Swift, for instance, which I am not to examine here[1]), his effort is always to strip the object satirized of the film of familiarity which normally reconciles us to it, and to make us see it as in itself it really is, as the child saw the unclothed emperor in Hans Andersen's story. This frustration of the 'stock-response' is sometimes achieved in Swift and Voltaire, for example, by a deliberate refusal to see, in some ignoble object which custom has consecrated or made symbolic, anything further than the object itself. Thus Voltaire's Quaker, who for the time being represents Reason, says of a recruiting campaign:

> 'Our God, who has commanded us to love our enemies, and to suffer without repining, would certainly not permit us to cross

[1] On Swift's irony see the excellent essay of that title by F. R. Leavis in *Determinations*.

the seas, merely because murderers cloath'd in scarlet, and wearing caps two foot high, enlist citizens by a noise made with two little sticks on an ass's skin extended.' [1]

Or Gulliver, when enlightening the King's ignorance on the advantages of gunpowder, explains

'that we often put this powder into large hollow balls of iron, and discharge them by an engine into some city we were besieging, which would rip up the pavements, tear the houses to pieces, burst and throw splinters on every side, dashing out the brains of all who came near.' [2]

Bentham, says Mill, habitually missed the truth that is in received opinions; that at any rate, I suggest, is what the satirist does and must do. He must, whether deliberately or no, miss precisely those aspects of the ignoble thing which in fact make it endurable to the non-satiric everyday eye: that is to say, he must ignore the *explanation* of the thing satirized—how it came to be, its history. It is a fact of experience that *tout comprendre c'est tout pardonner*, and the satirist *ex officio* cannot pardon, so he must decline to understand all and explain all. Satire is by nature nonconstructive, since to construct effectively—to educate, for example, to reform, or to evangelize—one must study actual situations and actual persons in their historical setting, and this kind of study destroys the satiric approach. This is not to say that satire is not or has not been often a most valuable weapon for the moralist. When the 'pardon' I have spoken of means the toleration of avoidable evil, satire has an important function. But 'pardon' is not the only or the inevitable attitude engendered by a historical study of persons and institutions; one may, if one is a moralist, an educator, an apostle or a revolutionary, desire to alter and amend things after having explained them. Satire seems to occur somewhere between acceptance and revolution, and it is not surprising, if this is so, that the early eighteenth century should have been its most

[1] *Letters on the English Nation* (1733), p. 10.
[2] *Gulliver*, bk. ii, ch. 7.

high and palmy time. Swift himself, for all his discontent (divine or pathological), was no revolutionary; his satire, as we have suggested, always refers to standards which exist ready-made, and which would become operative without need for subversive change, if only men would not perversely depart from them. To these standards, however, Yahoo man *will* not adhere, and Swift seems at last to throw up the sponge—to abandon hope of ever lessening the disparity between the ideal and the actual. Instead, he barricades himself within his ivory tower of reason, and there 'enjoys' the bitter satisfaction of knowing himself the only wise being in an insane or bestial world, or, at most, of sharing, with a few kindred spirits (Pope or Arbuthnot), his own consciousness of superiority. Other satirists—Cervantes, Fielding, Dickens—have been known to fall in love with their abstractions, and Don Quixote, Joseph Andrews, and Pickwick have emerged full-formed from the satiric shadow-world. But Swift fell more and more out of love with man, and the result—his final tragedy—was the total dissociation of Houyhnhnm from Yahoo. So remote became his ideal that he could not symbolize his disembodied rationals as men at all, but only as horses. Man delighted him not, no, nor woman neither, so he escaped into his satiric fairyland or solaced himself with the strange baby-prattle of the *Journal to Stella*.[1]

As the eighteenth century wore on, it was discovered that the 'Nature' of man was not his 'reason' at all, but his instincts, emotions, and 'sensibilities', and what was more, people began to glory in this discovery, and to regard reason itself as an aberration from 'Nature'. *Cogito ergo sum* is superseded by the *je sens, donc je suis* associated with Rousseau. Shaftesbury, Hutcheson, and Hume had prepared the way by proclaiming that our moral judgments, like our aesthetic judgments, are not the offspring of Reason at all; but proceed from an inner sentiment or

[1] On this aspect of Swift see Aldous Huxley's essay in *Do What you Will.*

feeling which is unanalysable. Burke announced that 'politics ought to be adapted, not to human reason, but to human nature, of which reason is but a part, and that by no means the greatest part'. Wesley and Whitefield range the world, converting their ten thousands, not by rational ethical suasion, but by impassioned appeals to the heart. When we reach this phase satire declines, and ceases to be the normal reaction of representative minds to existence. It survives mainly in minds (Jane Austen, Byron, Peacock, Samuel Butler, Anatole France) which retain an affinity with the early eighteenth century.

CHAPTER VII

David Hume

Defender of 'Nature' against 'Reason'

'All probable reasoning is nothing but a species of sensation. 'Tis not solely in poetry and music, we must follow our taste and sentiment, but likewise in philosophy.'

[*Treatise of Human Nature*, bk. i, pt. iii, sect. 8.]

I

METAPHYSICS: 'NATURE' AS A HABIT OF THE MIND

DAVID HUME would belong to our present story if only because he is the fine flower of the English (or shall we say the Anglo-Scottish) eighteenth century mind, but more specifically (since the present volume does not pretend to be a history of eighteenth century thought) because he can be represented as the defender of Nature against Reason.

Hume is usually, and rightly, regarded as the arch-sceptic who overturned the philosophic card-castle erected by Descartes and his successors. He did, indeed, destroy all traditional certainties: matter, the soul, God, Nature, causation, miracles; and by more rigorously applying the methods of Locke and of Berkeley he demonstrated that their philosophy led nowhere. A fresh start had to be made after his work had been done, and in approaching him we begin to cross the great intellectual watershed of the mid-century. Hume is perhaps the writer in whom the distinctive characteristics of 'our excellent and indispensable eighteenth century' are most completely expressed, and he is representative not least in this—that his function was not so much to break new ground as to break up old ground. Of his 'excellence' (as of that of his century) there can be no question; it is enough to say that he writes philosophy with an exquisite decorum which puts us all to shame. As for the 'indispensability' of the eighteenth century, it may be said that that century represented a necessary stage or climacteric in the life-cycle of Western civilization, so that a country like Russia can be diagnosed by a modern historian as one that has never had an eighteenth century. It was 'indispensable' as a period in which the dry light of reason was free to penetrate to the furthest limits of the universe, scattering the yellow-skirted fays and all the last enchantments of the Middle Ages. It was perhaps not least indispensable as a time when, as in Hume, the illumination became dark with excessive light, and reason was used to reveal the limitations of reason. Before Hume: empiricism and sensationalism; after him, the 'Copernican revolution' of Kant; before him, Nature and Reason go hand in hand; after him, Nature and Feeling. Hume was 'indispensable', if only because, by the very completeness of his destructive efficacy, he showed that man cannot live by Reason alone. But, as Professor Laing has shown,[1] Hume's thought has its more positive and constructive side, and it is this that I am mainly concerned to emphasize. Hume desired, not merely to destroy the flimsy superstructures of pure reason, but also to show (in Halévy's words) 'that it is a good thing to trust to instinct, to give oneself up to Nature, without being duped by any logical illusion'.[2]

The sub-title of Hume's *Treatise of Human Nature* (1738) is: 'An Attempt to introduce the experimental method of reasoning into Moral Subjects.' Hume thus declares himself to belong to the very tradition he did so much to undermine. The *Treatise* is one of the many con-

[1] *Hume* (Benn's 'Leaders of Philosophy' series, 1932).
[2] *Growth of Philosophic Radicalism*, p. 11.

temporary efforts to formulate a 'moral Newtonianism' (Halévy's phrase): to find, that is, a moral counterpart to gravitation, a principle which should unify the moral world as 'attraction' had unified the physical. Some thought they had found it in self-love, others in benevolence or the principle of utility (both notions appear in Hutcheson's *System of Moral Philosophy*). But the most important of these moral Newtonianisms was the principle of the Association of Ideas. The elaboration of this doctrine was mainly the work of David Hartley (*Observations on Man*, 1749; see Chapter VIII below), but Hume had already made great use of it in the *Treatise*. I propose now briefly to examine part of that work, with a view to showing its bearing on the main subject of these studies.

Hume differs from his modern philosophical predecessors in having no theological presuppositions, no *deus ex machina* in reserve, to extricate him from any speculative crux (such as the interaction of matter and mind had been to the Cartesians). He begins, where he hopes to end, with experience, what is 'given', our 'perceptions', which he divides into 'impressions' ('all our sensations, passions and emotions, as they make their first appearance in the soul') and 'ideas' ('the faint images of these in thinking and reasoning').[1] He continues with an orthodox account of 'memory' and 'imagination', contrasting the inseparable connexion of ideas in memory with the 'liberty of the imagination to transpose and change its ideas'—as in 'poems and romances', where Nature is 'totally confounded, and nothing mentioned but winged horses, fiery dragons, and monstrous giants'.[2] The incorrigibly prosaic character of the English philosophic tradition at this time comes out well here, as elsewhere in Hume, cf.:

> 'The *imagination* of man is naturally sublime, delighted with whatever is remote and extraordinary, and running, without controul, into the most distant parts of space and time in order to

[1] *Treatise*, bk. i, pt. i, sect. 1. [2] *ibid.*, bk. i, pt. i, sect. 3.

avoid the objects, which custom has rendered too familiar to it. A correct *Judgment* observes a contrary method, and avoiding all distant and high enquiries, confines itself to common life, and to such subjects as fall under daily practice and experience; leaving the more sublime topics to the embellishment of poets and orators, or to the arts of priests and politicians.' [1]

Hume's position on the eighteenth century watershed gave him no glimpse of the Çoleridgean 'Imagination', though that faculty assumes increasing importance in Hume for very different reasons, and quite otherwise conceived. Into the flux of 'ideas' the grand principle of Association introduces an order by means of the relations of Resemblance, Contiguity in Time or Place, and Cause and Effect.

> 'These are therefore the principles of union or cohesion among our simple ideas, and in the imagination supply the place of that inseparable connexion, by which they are united in the memory. Here is a kind of ATTRACTION, which in the mental world will be found to have as extraordinary effects as in the natural.' [2]

From this associative principle (whose causes 'must be resolv'd into *original* qualities of human nature, which I pretend not to explain') are derived the 'complex ideas', comprising Relations, Modes, and Substances. Here I will only quote a few characteristic pronouncements. Of 'substance', for example, we have no idea 'distinct from that of a collection of particular qualities'; and again, 'the idea of a substance [e.g. 'gold'] as well as that of a mode [e.g. 'beauty'] is nothing but a collection of simple ideas, that are united by the imagination'. In all this the influence of Berkeley is apparent, and Berkeley is expressly cited on the topic of Abstract Ideas, as 'the author of one of the greatest and most valuable discoveries that has been made of late years in the *republic of letters*'—the discovery, namely, that Abstract Ideas 'are in themselves individual, however they become general in their representation', and that in conceiving such an idea 'the image in the mind is

[1] *Enquiry Concerning Human Understanding*, sect. xii, pt. 3.
[2] *Treatise*, bk. i, pt. i, sect. 4.

only that of a particular object, tho' the application of it in our reasoning be the same, as if it were universal'.[1] 'A particular idea becomes general by being annex'd to a general term; that is, to a term, which from a customary conjunction has a relation to many other particular ideas, and readily recals them in the imagination.'

Again, the ideas of Space and Time are 'no separate or distinct ideas, but merely those of the manner or order, in which objects exist'.[2] This brings Hume to the fundamental problem of the Not-Ourselves, of External Existence: what is the relation between our ideas and 'Things'? can we know Things-in-Themselves? or what is happening when we suppose that we do? Hume replies,

> 'Let us fix our attention out of ourselves as much as possible: let us chace our imagination to the heavens, or to the utmost limits of the universe; we never really advance a step beyond ourselves, nor can conceive any kind of existence, but those perceptions, which have appear'd in that narrow compass. This is the universe of the imagination, nor have we any idea but what is there produc'd.'[3]

As for the *origin* of the impressions, this must always be 'perfectly inexplicable', and Hume characteristically rejects the three standard explanations: we cannot say, he declares, whether impressions 'arise immediately from the object, or are produc'd by the creative power of the mind, or are deriv'd from the author of our being'. But all this does not mean for Hume that all our perceptions are on a level; he assumes that there is 'Nature', a real order of existence, and that this may be either justly represented by our ideas, or else distorted. How, then, since we are irrevocably shut up within the narrow compass of our own ideas, are we to distinguish what is 'just' representation

[1] *ibid.*, bk. i, pt. i, sect. 7. I have italicized *republic of letters* for its period interest. It seems to me to indicate a view of the status of philosophic literature very different from that which now prevails.

[2] *ibid.*, bk. i, pt. ii, sect. 4. Cf. Leibniz's view: 'Space is the order of coexistence, time the order of succession, in the monad's perceptions.' (H. Wildon Carr, *Leibniz*, Benn, 1929, p. 153.)

[3] *ibid.*, bk. i, pt. ii, sect. 6.

from what is illusion, fiction, poetry, or faith? As Carr remarks in expounding Leibniz, 'the order in which we represent things must have its reason in an order which exists between the reals represented'[1]; but how, on Hume's principles, can we tell when we are representing the reals and when we are merely constructing private worlds? Hume's answer to these questions seems to be virtually an appeal to 'common-sense'. He does not in the least wish to impugn the common-sense belief in the existence of an external order—indeed, no one believed in it more firmly than he. He merely denies that this belief is founded upon reason, and that reason alone can account for it. 'Belief', he says, 'is more properly an act of the sensitive than of the cogitative part of our natures', and our belief in the order of Nature, though not capable of rational demonstration, is practically valid because it arises from 'the principles of human nature'. But the criterion between 'true' and 'false' ideas remains subjective: it consists, he tells us, in the 'superior *force*, or *vivacity*, or *firmness*, or *steadiness*'[2] of the true ideas. Indeed a 'true' idea is simply an idea having these characteristics; to 'believe' is simply to *feel* this 'vivacity'. Belief is 'something *felt* by the mind, which distinguishes the ideas of the judgment from the fictions of the imagination'; 'an idea assented to *feels* different from a fictitious idea'—and there's an end on't. Hume is here invoking the famous Principles of Constant Conjunction, Customary Connexion, and the Association of Ideas, in order to give us back the world of which his scepticism seemed likely to rob us. 'Things' may all be 'facts of mind' for all we can tell, but that daily-reiterated system of 'ideas' which we call 'the world', and which is apparently common to all sane men, controls our whole practical lives, because only by conforming to its 'laws' can we continue to exist for a single hour.

''Tis not solely in poetry and music, we must follow our taste

[1] *op. cit.*, p. 92.

[2] *Treatise*, bk. i, pt. iii, sect. 7.

> and sentiment, but likewise in philosophy. When I am convinc'd of any principle, 'tis only an idea, which strikes more strongly upon me. . . . Objects have no discoverable connexion together; nor is it from any other principle but custom operating upon the imagination, that we can draw any inference from the appearance of one to the existence of another.' [1]

When we believe in the 'order of Nature', then, we are not determined by reason, but by 'certain principles, which associate together the ideas of these objects, and unite them in the imagination'.

> 'Our reason never does, nor is it possible that it should upon any supposition, give us an assurance of the continu'd and distinct existence of body.' [2]

The common belief in such continued existence is the product of imagination, not of reason.

What we call 'causation' is a main example of these principles, for it consists in a 'vivacious' feeling arising from the customary connexion of certain ideas. One or two instances of idea 'B' following idea 'A' would not generate the idea of 'cause', but when 'B' is invariably found to follow 'A', we call 'A' the cause of 'B', though nothing has happened save that a feeling of their constant conjunction has been set up in our minds.

> 'All ideas are deriv'd from, and represent, impressions. We never have any impression, that contains any power or efficacy [e.g. 'power' of fire to burn, or of a magnet to attract]. We never therefore have any idea of power. . . .
>
> 'The several instances of resembling conjunctions leads us into the notion of power and necessity. These instances are in themselves totally distinct from each other, and have no union but in the mind, which observes them, and collects their ideas.' [3]

Hume professes to be *exposing* the arguments of 'that fantastic sect' (the total sceptics) when he proclaims that 'all our reasonings concerning causes and effects are deriv'd from nothing but custom; and that belief is more properly

[1] *ibid.*, bk. i, pt. iii, sect. 8.
[2] *ibid.*, bk. i, pt. iv, sect. 2.
[3] *ibid.*, bk. i, pt. iii, sect. 14.

an act of the sensitive, than of the cogitative part of our natures'.[1] He means, presumably, that this customary connexion in our minds, though it may refer to no corresponding external order, is yet as important for us as if it did, and that a man of correct judgment may therefore regard the vivacity of his 'beliefs' as a reliable index that they are just representations of Nature (or, if we prefer to put it so, he may excusably give the name of 'Nature' to that pattern of vivacious ideas which he shares with other reasonable individuals). Hume can pose as an anti-sceptic because it is not human reason that primarily concerns him, but human nature—of which reason is but a part, and perhaps not the greatest part. What custom has joined, let no man put asunder; and Hume has only dismantled the machine in order to put it together again, and in so doing to reveal its true workings.

It will not have escaped notice that in thus committing himself to 'imagination' Hume is (from his own point of view) entering upon dangerous ground. Is he not basing practical life upon the very faculty which, in 'poets and orators', utterly confounds Nature by changing and transposing its ideas? The reply is, I think, that he uses 'imagination' in two main senses: in one, he means what since Coleridge we generally call 'fancy' (the faculty which produces winged horses, fiery dragons, etc.); in the other, he means that mental screen whereon, *in men of correct judgment*, the customary connexions of 'just' ideas are projected. That Hume felt a little uneasy on this score can be conjectured from the sections he devotes to poetic belief and to education. He admits that 'assent', being founded on 'vivacity' of ideas, is akin to the less respectable offspring of the 'imagination': its 'whimsies and prejudices'. Wherein, then, does the force or vivacity of poetic fiction differ from that which accompanies (or *is*) true belief? All Hume can say is that they 'feel' different. Poets are 'liars by profession', and we never get from poetry that feeling of 'solidity' and 'force' which accompanies 'reason-

[1] *ibid.*, bk. i, pt. iv, sect. 1.

ings from causation'. 'Whatever emotion the poetical enthusiasm may give to the spirits, 'tis still the mere phantom of belief or persuasion'.[1] The poetic imagination could not yet seem an important mode of apprehending reality. Hume admits, too, that half the opinions that prevail among mankind are produced, not by 'reasonings from causation', but by education. But education is an 'artificial and not a natural cause', and so is not recognized by philosophers.

In what has been said I have tried to indicate what was meant by calling Hume a 'defender of Nature against Reason'. Just as in ethics and aesthetics (as we shall see in a moment) the correct standard is the approval or disapproval of average educated men, so in metaphysics Reality ('Nature') is the mental habit of *all* men—except perhaps lunatics, lovers, and poets. Poetry is a most elegant amusement, but its world is really brazen; men of sense, only, deliver a world which, if not golden, is at least inhabitable. Hume ends this part of the treatise with a most engaging and highly characteristic chapter of personal confession. After completing his sceptical round by demolishing 'the soul' and even 'personal identity', he stops, and ironically scrutinizes his own philosophizing with a levity, and a freedom from implication, which are the product both of his century and of his own tranquil temper, and which contrast significantly with the high (and '*tief*') seriousness of some of his philosophical successors. What is all this he has been saying? What is the use of all this philosophizing, which leads only to doubts and contradictions? Reason has destroyed itself: shall we then abandon it, and yield to the illusions of ordinary life? Hume is not certain what answer to give, but he knows very well what is done in practice: the dilemma is ignored. Since Reason cannot dispel the clouds, let 'Nature' break in with a dinner or a game at backgammon; and then, when the philosopher returns to his study, his speculations 'appear so cold, and strain'd,

[1] *ibid.*, bk. i, pt. iii, sect. 10.

and ridiculous',[1] that he can hardly find it in his heart to enter into them any further. Indeed, there is no particular reason why Hume or anybody else should philosophize, unless they feel a 'serious good-humour'd disposition' to do so. We ought to preserve a 'careless disposition' in our studies; and Hume goes to the length of prescribing this attitude as the cure for sceptical doubt:

> 'Carelessness and inattention alone can afford us any remedy. For this reason I rely entirely upon them; and take it for granted, whatever may be the reader's opinion at this present moment, that an hour hence he will be persuaded there is both an external and internal world.' [2]

2

ETHICS: MORALITY AS A SENTIMENT OF THE HEART

The scepticism of Hume, then, as Halévy puts it, 'can be thought, not lived'; 'reason is insignificant as compared with the instinct by which we live'.[3] Hume's remark that whenever he left his study all his doubts vanished is deservedly well known, for it is perhaps in this that he is most representative of the eighteenth century spirit in these islands: intrepidity in speculation co-existing with conservatism in practice. It is true that in his ethical as in his metaphysical enquiries Hume carries the 'experimental' method as far as it will go, but in his conclusions, as in his own life, he was no more a moral experimenter than he was a revolutionary in politics. The 'atheist Hume', whose name was a legend of horror to the orthodox, was affectionately known to his friends as 'le bon David'. After his burial it was thought desirable to place two men to guard his tomb for eight nights for fear of mob-outrage; yet Adam Smith, who knew him best, wrote of him: 'Upon the whole, I have always considered

[1] *ibid.*, bk. i, pt. iv, sect. 7. [2] *ibid.*, bk. i, pt. iv, sect. 2.
[3] *op. cit.*, p. 10.

him, both in his lifetime and since his death, as approaching as nearly to the idea of a perfectly wise and virtuous man, as perhaps the nature of human frailty will permit'. It has often been pointed out that in the France of Hume's time speculative freedom was associated with the revolutionary spirit (see Chapter IX below). Why was Hume's voice not joined with Voltaire's in the cry of *écrasez l'infâme*? Amongst the possible reasons (of which his own serene temper was one) perhaps the most important was that England had already had both its religious 'reformation' and its bourgeois revolution (though not its industrial sequel), whereas in France the forms and privileges of feudalism and of mediaeval religion had survived almost intact into the heart of the enlightenment, so that the new and the old confronted each other there with a sharpness of contrast which was blurred on this side of the Channel. Hume and those of his class could thus feel, as no bourgeois Frenchman could, that conditions in this country were on the whole favourable to the sort of lives they preferred to live and to see lived. Accordingly, the Rights of Man did not interest him, and of the various possible forms of government, he favoured benevolent despotism, as the one likely to be best administered, and to cause least disturbance. 'Absolute monarchy, therefore, is the easiest death, the true Euthanasia, of the British Constitution.'[1]

It is in his writings on morals that Hume's conformity to accepted social standards comes out most clearly. Just as in his metaphysics his scepticism is directed against the traditional bogus entities and not against common sense, so in his ethics he criticizes, not existing moral conventions, but only older ethical theories. He rejects all supernatural and metaphysical sanctions for morality, but finds all the sanctions he requires in human nature. His ethical position thus corresponds to his position in metaphysics; here again he rejects Reason in favour of Nature. Just as he had reduced the other 'Nature', the not-ourselves, to a

[1] *Essays, Moral, Political and Literary*, vii.

mental habit of our own, so now he reduces morality to sentiment. Reason is not the source of moral judgments any more than of 'belief'; it is concerned with states of affairs and affirmations of 'is' or 'is not', and no contemplation of a state of affairs as such is a moral judgment. Such a judgment only occurs when a sentiment of approval or disapproval is aroused, or in other words, when pleasure or pain are produced. We know nothing but our own minds and hearts; what can we reason but from what we know? In ethics, therefore, the proper method is to enquire into the substance of men's moral judgments, and see what they are in fact composed of. His conclusion briefly is, that they are composed of the sentiments of approbation and disapprobation. 'This is good' means 'This is approved of; this is an object of esteem'; 'This is bad' means 'This is disapproved of; this arouses aversion'. In order to discover the nature of the 'good' and the 'bad', therefore, we have not to embark upon any dialectical enquiries; we have only to collect statistics. The method was so simple that nothing, Hume believed, could have prevented mankind from hitting upon it long before, except theological and metaphysical presuppositions.

> 'So that when you pronounce any action or character to be [virtuous or] vicious, you mean nothing, but that from the constitution of your nature you have a feeling or sentiment of [approval or] blame from the contemplation of it. Vice and virtue, therefore, may be compar'd to sounds, colours, heat and cold, which, according to modern philosophy, are not qualities in objects, but perceptions in the mind: And this discovery in morals, like that other in physics, is to be regarded as a considerable advancement of the speculative sciences; tho', like that too, it has little or no influence on practice. Nothing can be more real, or concern us more, than our own sentiments of pleasure or uneasiness; and if these be favourable to virtue, and unfavourable to vice, no more can be requisite to the regulation of our conduct and behaviour.'[1]

Hume was proud of his discovery, and (rather surprisingly)

[1] *Treatise*, bk. iii, pt. i, sect. 1.

regarded his *Enquiry Concerning the Principles of Morals* (1751) as 'incomparably the best' of all his writings. Perhaps this was because his solution satisfied his deepest instincts, which were also those of his time and of his class. 'This is good' means 'This is approved', but—approved by whom? The fact that Hume does not feel called upon to raise and answer this question indicates how complete was his acceptance of current values. He is aware, indeed, that different ages and races have approved different things, but for his purpose it is sufficient to make a catalogue of the qualities approved and condemned by his own age and social group. The moral judgments of this group, he evidently feels, are sufficiently representative to be taken as those of average humanity. It is worth noting that in the Essay *Of the Standard of Taste* [1] he does examine this problem in its relation to aesthetic judgments, and the discussion is relevant, since for Hume (as for Shaftesbury) aesthetic and moral judgments are closely akin. If Hume had been pressed to declare *whose* approval determined the good, it is reasonable to suppose that he would have answered somewhat as he did to the question, whose approval determines the beautiful?

> 'Strong sense, united to delicate sentiment, improved by practice, perfected by comparison, and cleared of all prejudice, can alone entitle critics to this valuable character; and the joint verdict of such, wherever they are to be found, is the true standard of taste and beauty.'

But when actually speaking of moral judgments, he seems to take it for granted that all are good critics—that 'what is approved' means 'what all approve'.[2] This assumption, I think, indicates what may be called the social and cultural solidarity of the 'republic of letters' in the pre-revolutionary eighteenth century; it would not be available to-day for any but 'totalitarian' moralists.

[1] No. XXIII.

[2] He allows, however, that the taste for moral beauty, as for aesthetic, may be *cultivated*. (*Enquiry Concerning the Principles of Morals*, sect. i.)

Hume's emphasis on 'approbation' and 'esteem' is highly characteristic, both of himself and of his age—which, it will be recalled, was also the age of Lord Chesterfield. That he should 'please'—excite the approbation of the *beau monde*—was the height of Chesterfield's ambition for his son. And similarly with Hume, we hear little about *self*-approval, or of the morality of living for some principle in the teeth of society's disapproval. A virtuous act or character is by definition one which gives pleasure to the natural moral sense of those who contemplate it. Your virtue may be described as 'my approval of you'; my virtue is 'your approval of me'. Hume's moral world is a closed and interlocked system of mutual admiration and criticism—very like the 'society' of Chesterfield's Letters. As T. H. Green observes, 'respectability', the virtue of standing well with one's neighbours, becomes, in this kind of world, the *summum bonum*.[1]

In the *Enquiry Concerning the Principles of Morals*, pursuing his plan of collecting moral statistics, and rejecting all theories not founded upon 'fact and observation', Hume proceeds to enumerate the qualities that go to form what we call personal merit or demerit, and to indicate the common properties in each list. He decides that personal merit consists simply in the possession of qualities '*useful* or *agreeable* to the *person himself* or to *others*'.[2] Hume thus adopts a hedonistic and utilitarian standpoint. A meritorious quality is one which excites a sentiment of pleasure, but many such qualities please because of their utility. All men agree to admire the social virtues of benevolence, humanity, friendship, gratitude, public spirit, etc., and part, at least, of the merit of such virtues lies in their 'tendency to promote the interests of our species' and to 'bestow happiness on human society' ('utility' being thus readily reducible to 'conduciveness-to-happiness'). If they are exercised in such a manner as to produce pernicious instead of 'useful' consequences, we cease to approve (as,

[1] *Introduction* to bk. ii of the *Treatise*, p. 70.

[2] *Enquiry*, sect. ix, pt. 1.

e.g., in such matters as unwise alms-giving, tyrannicide, etc.). 'Justice', again, derives its merit solely from its usefulness as the foundation and support of society; this can be shown by imagining either a Golden Age in which every possible human need was satisfied, or a state of war or extreme destitution—in both of which justice would be useless, and therefore no longer a virtue. 'This truth is so natural and obvious', Hume says, that it has not escaped 'even the poets', who have depicted such conditions in their accounts of the *Saturnia regna*. This agreeable fiction of the poets (Hume adds) is analogous to the philosophical fiction of the 'state of nature', except that the latter is depicted as 'a state of mutual war and violence'.[1] Hume himself, it is interesting to find, does not believe in this 'state of nature'; actually, men are born members of a family, and the notion of justice arising there (as 'what is useful for the family') gradually expands, as family unites with family to become tribe and finally nation. At every stage 'justice' ends where the notion of 'advantage to one's own' ends. The main function of 'justice' now is the *protection of property*, and Hume emphatically denounces the sophistries of 'writers on natural law', and others, who confuse 'justice' with chimerical visions of human equality. Fanatics may have supposed that 'dominion is founded on grace', and levellers may have demanded 'an equal distribution of property', 'but the civil magistrate very justly puts these sublime theorists on the same footing with common robbers, and teaches them by the severest discipline, that a rule, which, in speculation, may seem the most advantageous to society, may yet be found, in practice, totally pernicious and destructive'. All this illustrates Hume's complete acceptance of the social order of the *ancien régime* (cf. above, pp. 119-20). Equalitarian doctrines suggested to him nothing but the excesses of

[1] Hume refers here in a footnote to Hobbes, who, he says, was not the first so to depict it, for Plato has tried to refute 'an hypothesis very like it in the 2nd, 3rd and 4th books de republica,' while Cicero (in one passage at least) assumes it to be universally acknowledged. (*Enquiry*, sect. iii, pt. 1.)

mediaeval or seventeenth century religious frenzy, and they could be confidently dismissed, together with everything Gothic, as destructive to that power and authority, and that due subordination of class to class, on which the social order depends.

Now since it is on account of their 'utility' that we approve of the above-mentioned virtues, 'utility' itself must please us. Why is this? It must be either from considerations of self-interest, or from more generous or altruistic motives; and Hume's opinion is that our approbation of the useful extends beyond ourselves, and includes the interest of others. We have within us a natural tendency to *sympathize* with the joy or sorrow of others; we are even pleased by the virtue of a magnanimous foe. This principle of human nature 'accounts in great part, for the origin of morality'. It is even the source of our enjoyment in the theatre, where we rejoice with the hero in his success, or weep with him in his adversity, while 'our breasts are affected with the liveliest resentment against the author of these calamities'. We experience pain when we hear a person stutter; and, 'so delicate is our sympathy', that it is a rule in literary criticism, that a harsh collocation of syllables is to be avoided, because of the pain it would give to anyone pronouncing it. Would any man, however selfish, 'tread as willingly upon another's gouty toes, whom he has no quarrel with, as upon the hard flint and pavement'? Hume elaborates this argument by showing that there are many qualities of which we approve simply because they are useful or agreeable to their possessors, because they conduce to his happiness, and to ours only through 'sympathy'. Such are industry, discretion, frugality, personal beauty, 'chearfulness', magnanimity, tranquillity of mind. Even poetic talent is 'a very considerable merit' of this type, and so is delicacy of taste. Lastly, of course, there are all the qualities associated with social success and the arts of pleasing: good manners (which restrain our self-love in social intercourse), wit, eloquence, modesty, decency, cleanliness, and the *je ne sais quoi, qui plaît*.

In conclusion Hume professes to be amazed that it should be necessary, 'in so late an age', to prove by lengthy argument so obvious a proposition as that Personal Merit consists in the possession of qualities either useful or agreeable to oneself or to others. 'Systems and hypotheses', or 'the delusive glosses of superstition and false religion', must have perverted our natural understandings, for so simple a truth to have escaped our notice for so long. Why do 'men of sense' everywhere despise the 'monkish virtues' of celibacy, fasting, penance, mortification, self-denial, humility, silence, solitude? Because these virtues 'serve to no manner of purpose; neither advance a man's fortune in the world, nor render him a more valuable member of society; neither qualify him for the entertainment of company, nor increase his power of self-enjoyment'. We have here, in the bland assurance with which Hume contrasts his own list of meritorious qualities with the monkish virtues, a fair illustration of the eighteenth century sense of enlightenment, and of immunity from disturbing contacts with the transcendental. Hume is troubled by no suspicion that the contrast might not, in every particular, work in favour of his own list. The social foundations of eighteenth century morality were still too secure to admit of any misgiving, and Hume can conclude his paragraph by saying that 'a gloomy, hair-brained enthusiast, after his death, may have a place in the calendar; but will scarcely ever be admitted, when alive, into intimacy and society, except by those who are as delirious and dismal as himself'.

3

RELIGION: BASED ON 'FAITH', NOT ON 'REASON'

Whitehead has described the eighteenth century as an age of reason based upon faith—the faith in question being a confidence in the stability and regularity of the universal frame of Nature. Nothing can better illustrate Hume's adherence to this faith, and its separation in his mind from his philosophical scepticism, than his celebrated Essay *Of Miracles*.[1] The very man who proved that, for all we can tell, anything may be the 'cause' of anything, was also the man who disproved the possibility of miracles because they violated the invariable laws of Nature. The customary connexion of ideas which we call 'Nature', be its metaphysical status what it may, is yet the fountain-light of all our day, and when confronted with 'arrogant bigotry and superstition' Hume appeals to 'Nature' as confidently as if no sceptical doubts had ever crossed his mind. History, both sacred and profane, teems with accounts of miracles and prodigies, and Hume flatters himself that he has discovered an argument, resembling Archbishop Tillotson's against the Real Presence, which will be an 'everlasting check to all kinds of superstitious delusion'. The Essay is so well known that it will not be necessary to discuss it in detail.

The argument hinges upon the question of belief in the truth of 'testimony'. Like all our beliefs, this one rests upon experience—our experience, in this case, that men have memories, and are on the whole veracious. But testimonies may conflict, or their authority may be rendered doubtful by the manner of their delivery. And when the 'facts' related are 'marvellous', and not corroborated by 'experience', 'the very same principle of experience, which gives us a certain degree of assurance in the testimony of witnesses, gives us also, in this case, another degree of assurance against the fact, which they endeavour to establish'. But suppose the event related is not only marvellous, but 'miraculous', and that the testimony, in and by itself, amounts to a proof. Now 'a miracle is a violation of the laws of nature', and as 'a firm and unalterable experience has established these laws', we are confronted here with proof against proof, 'of which the strongest must pre-

[1] *Enquiry Concerning Human Understanding*, sect. x.

vail'. There must, he continues, be a uniform experience against

> 'every miraculous event, otherwise the event would not merit that appellation. And as a uniform experience amounts to a proof, there is here a full and direct *proof*, from the nature of the fact, against the existence of any miracle; nor can such a proof be destroyed, or the miracle rendered credible, but by an opposite proof, which is superior.'[1]

Can a testimony ever constitute such an opposite and superior proof? No: 'there never was a miraculous event established on so full an evidence' that its falsehood would be more miraculous than the 'fact' related. We must always reject the greater of two miracles, and false evidence is never a very great miracle. 'There is not to be found,' says Hume, in a passage of unusual trenchancy,

> 'There is not to be found in all history, any miracle attested by a sufficient number of men, of such unquestioned good-sense, education, and learning, as to secure us against all delusion in themselves; of such undoubted integrity, as to place them beyond all suspicion of any design to deceive others; of such credit and reputation in the eyes of mankind, as to have a great deal to lose in case of their being detected in any falsehood; and at the same time attesting facts, performed in such a public manner, and in so celebrated a part of the world, as to render the detection unavoidable: All which circumstances are requisite to give us a full assurance in the testimony of men.'[2]

For the orthodox apologist (Paley, for instance) the apostles were precisely a 'sufficient number of men', possessing the right credentials. But to Hume, the apostolic virtues could not appear 'useful or agreeable', and those primitive enthusiasts could only figure, in his view, as members of the lower orders, uneducated and lacking 'reputation in the eyes of mankind'. Neither could Palestine, in an age whose affinity was with Athens, and Rome, and Paris, really be regarded as a 'celebrated part of the world'. The

[1] *ibid.* Works (ed. Green and Grose), vol. ii, p. 93.
[2] *ibid.*, vol. ii, pp. 94-5.

'passion of surprise and wonder' is strong in us all, and when this is reinforced by the spirit of religion, 'there is an end of common sense, and human testimony, in these circumstances, loses all pretensions to authority'. A strong presumption against miracles lies in the fact that they abound most in the beginnings of time, and amongst primitive and barbarous peoples, and tend to disappear 'as we advance nearer the enlightened ages'. Moreover, all religions abound in miracles wrought in support of their several doctrines, and as these different religions cannot all be true, the miracles are mutually destructive. Well-attested miracles are even related of eminent pagans like Vespasian, and of course they still occur in Popish countries, but we do not trouble to believe these because we do not believe in the opinions they are supposed to support. Credulity and delusion, then, are two very 'natural' things; 'and shall we' (Hume rhetorically asks), 'rather than have recourse to so natural a solution, allow of a miraculous violation of the most established laws of nature'?

The ending of the Essay is of special interest: it is one of those passages in which Hume seems to be delicately poised upon the escarpment of eighteenth century thought, and needing only a touch to topple him down the Kantian incline. Nature is a habit of the mind, morality is a sentiment of the heart, belief is a product of the imagination, not of the reason; what next? Hume has accepted all these conclusions, preferring 'nature' to reason in the last resort: will he now tell us that religion is founded upon faith, not upon reason, and urge us to render unto faith that which is faith's? This is what he actually says:

> 'I am the better pleased with the method of reasoning here delivered, as I think it may serve to confound those dangerous friends or disguised enemies to the *Christian Religion*, who have undertaken to defend it by the principles of human reason. Our most holy religion is founded on *Faith*, not on reason; and it is a sure method of exposing it to put it to such a trial as it is by no means fitted to endure.'

If we read the Pentateuch in any other way than as the word of God himself, would the falsehood of such a book be more miraculous than all the miracles it relates?

> 'So that, upon the whole, we may conclude that the *Christian Religion* not only was at first attended with miracles, but even at this day cannot be believed by any reasonable person without one. Mere reason is insufficient to convince us of its veracity: And whoever is moved by *Faith* to assent to it, is conscious of a continued miracle in his own person, which subverts all the principles of his understanding, and gives him a determination to believe what is most contrary to custom and experience.' [1]

Defenders of the faith had used these arguments before, and were soon to use them again; moreover, Hume had himself taught us that 'mere reason' was insufficient to convince us of the reality of Nature and Nature's laws. His own principles, then, would have allowed him to take the next step, and urge us, in all earnestness, to build religion, not upon reason, but upon our experience as moral beings. But, of course, that is not what Hume is doing here. However nearly he seems to approach to the edge of the slippery slope, he is, in reality, attached by tough cords to an eighteenth century base. And when he is confronted by 'religion' (just as when he leaves his study), he forgets his sceptical doubts, and becomes one of the average 'reasonable persons' of his time. 'Custom' and 'experience' were to be relied upon as long as they offered us nothing but the clear, familiar outlines of the Newtonian world and the society of the old régime; directly they seem to point towards encompassing mysteries they become suspect, and he falls back upon the much-despised 'reason' (now used in the popular sense). Belief is not reasoning, yet our beliefs must be 'reasonable', or the priests and the poets and the hare-brained enthusiasts may yet have it all their own way again. 'Nature' is only 'natural' if it is methodized in the eighteenth century taste.

[1] *ibid.*, vol. ii, pp. 107-8.

The same precarious poise is reassumed in the *Dialogues Concerning Natural Religion* and the *Natural History of Religion*. In these two important works Hume enquires into the foundations of religion in 'reason' and in 'human nature', and decides (quite correctly, as we may well think) that it is founded upon 'nature' rather than upon 'reason'. He does, it is true, allow that a refined and philosophical theism may be rationally arrived at:

> 'The whole frame of nature bespeaks an intelligent author; and no rational enquirer can, after serious reflection, suspend his belief a moment with regard to the primary principles of genuine theism and Religion.' [1]

But an honest God's the noblest work of man, and 'though I allow', says Hume, 'that the order and frame of the universe, when accurately examined, affords such an argument', he cannot suppose that a 'barbarous and necessitous animal', such as primitive man, could have formed his idea of God by contemplating 'the regular face of nature'. 'There is a great difference', he wisely remarks, 'between historical facts and speculative opinions',[2] and the actual origins of religion turn out to be much less respectable than an eighteenth century theist might have hoped. It was not by contemplating the spacious firmament on high that primitive man arrived at his notions of a divine original. He simply personified his own hopes and fears, and then proceeded to worship and placate the gods he had made in his own image. 'Even at this day', says Hume,

> 'Even at this day, and in Europe, ask any of the vulgar, why he believes in an omnipotent creator of the world; he will never mention the beauty of final causes, of which he is wholly ignorant: He will not hold out his hand, and bid you contemplate the suppleness and variety of joints in his fingers, their bending all one way, the counterpoise which they receive from the thumb, the softness and fleshy parts of the inside of his hand, with all the other circumstances, which render that member fit for the use, to

[1] *Natural History of Religion*, Introduction. [2] *ibid.*, sect. i.

> which it was destined. To these he has been long accustomed; and he beholds them with listlessness and unconcern. He will tell you of the sudden and unexpected death of such a one: The fall and bruise of such another: The excessive drought of this season: The cold and rains of another. These he ascribes to the immediate operation of providence: And such events, as, with good reasoners, are the chief difficulties in admitting a supreme intelligence, are with him the sole arguments for it.'[1]

Fear of the unknown, hope for next year's crops, dread of famine, and a sense of dependence upon blind chance—these, and not the topics of Ray, Shaftesbury, or Derham, were and are still the sources of popular religion. There are unknown causes to be placated, and naturally these are personified. 'Personifications', indeed, furnish a useful example of the kind of fictions or pseudo-statements to which Hume is always directing our attention. Their prevalence in poetry, he says, proves that they spring from a natural propensity in us; they bear witness to 'a certain tendency in the imagination, without which they could be neither beautiful nor natural'. But, of course, the personifications of poetry 'gain not on the belief' of educated men, whereas those of popular religion did and do enter into the real creed of the 'ignorant vulgar'. In the development of religion from crude polytheism to philosophic theism, a stage is reached, he grants, when men finally ascribe all power and perfection to one supreme god. They do this partly in order to flatter their deity, partly so as not to be outdone by the deities of other tribes, and partly through genuine enlightenment. But there is a perpetual tendency to fall back into idolatry, because men's 'feeble apprehensions' cannot long be kept to the contemplation of abstract Deity. Hence arise subordinate agents or mediators between God and man; these gradually become chief objects of devotion, and a new kind of idolatry begins afresh.

Hume's historical treatment of these matters is on the whole pleasantly objective. It bears witness to his own

[1] *ibid.*, sect. vi.

and the century's awakening to a realization of the importance of historical explanations. But history has seldom been without a 'purpose', and the eighteenth century wrote and read history, not so much to record and learn 'facts', as to discover the general nature of man, which had become overlaid with evil customs—in particular the errors associated with the Christian centuries.[1] There had been 'good' historical eras, such as the ages of Pericles and Augustus, or the Renaissance, and bad ones like the Dark and Middle Ages. The aim of history was to exhibit the 'universal principles' of human nature fully realized in the former, and thwarted in the latter. Moreover, the eighteenth century itself must be seen as one of the ages of enlightenment, and (as C. L. Becker has pointed out) its programme must be regarded as a phase of the endless conflict between light and darkness, and not as a local squabble between philosophers and priests. Hume, unlike the French philosophers, had no programme to advertise, no 'infâme' to destroy, but he fully shared the anti-clerical sentiments of the eighteenth century intellectuals. Priests, he wrote, 'being elevated above humanity, acquire a uniform character, which is entirely their own, and which, in my opinion, is, generally speaking, not the most amiable that is to be met with in human society'.[2] But Hume's dislike of established religion was based, more widely, upon the feeling that church-Christianity was still a force hostile to true philosophy—that it represented, in a word, all the powers of popular delusion and superstition embattled against the light. This is why, I think, in spite of his professed adherence to a refined theism, he allows a touch of animus to appear whenever he speaks of actual 'religion'. Philosophy is still in danger of being corrupted by theology. This feeling appears clearly towards the end of the *Natural History of Religion*, where he discusses the

[1] Cf. Hume's remark: 'History's chief use is only to discover the constant and universal principles of human nature' (quoted by C. L. Becker, *The Heavenly City of the Eighteenth Century Philosophers*, pp. 85 ff., *q.v.*).

[2] *Essays*, pt. i, xxi: *Of National Characters*.

relations between religion and philosophy. Where theism forms the chief principle of a popular religion, he says (characteristically disguising his reference to the present time in high generalities), philosophy is apt to be incorporated with its theology. And if the other dogmas of this system are contained in a sacred book, such as the Alcoran (useful, as ever, when the Bible is to be discreetly glanced at), or determined by a visible authority, such as the Pope (he does not say Parliament), speculative reasoners tend naturally to embrace these dogmas, which have been instilled into them from their earliest childhood. In time, however, the friendly partnership between speculation and orthodoxy becomes impossible, for philosophy finds itself 'perverted to serve the purposes of superstition'. Now all popular theology, he goes on,

> 'has a kind of appetite for absurdity and contradiction. If that theology went not beyond reason and common sense, her doctrines would appear too easy and familiar. Amazement must of necessity be raised: Mystery affected: Darkness and obscurity sought after: And a foundation of merit afforded to the devout votaries, who desire an opportunity of subduing their rebellious reason, by the belief of the most unintelligible sophisms.' [1]

We know how, some hundred years before, Sir Thomas Browne had rejoiced in the wingy mysteries of divinity, and subdued his rebellious reason with Tertullian's *certum est quia impossibile est*, and a comparison between the celebrated passage in the *Religio Medici* and this of Hume's affords a measure of the change which those hundred years have produced in the intellectual climate. Hume, like most of his contemporaries, had a distaste for mystery, and realizing that existing religion is founded upon mystery, he rejects it with repugnance. But the queerness of his position is revealed again in the *Dialogues Concerning Natural Religion*, where the sceptical Philo (who surely represents *part* of Hume's own mind) is made to show that though even philosophic theism has no sure foundation in reason,

[1] *Natural History of Religion*, sect. xi.

yet 'the cause or causes of order in the universe probably bear some remote analogy to human intelligence'. And what is still more remarkable, Philo adds that 'the most natural sentiment which a well-disposed mind will feel' when confronted with this vague and vestigial theism is

> 'a longing desire and expectation, that heaven would be pleased to dissipate, at least to alleviate this profound ignorance, by affording some particular revelation to mankind, and making discoveries of the nature, attributes, and operations of the divine object of our faith.' [1]

Once again Hume seems to be balancing upon the edge of the escarpment. Religion is irrational, theism is permissible only in utter attenuation: oh for a revelation! but not, if you please, the one we are supposed to have had already.

[1] *op. cit., ad fin.*

CHAPTER VIII

David Hartley and Nature's Education

he of mortal kind
Wisest, he first who marked the ideal tribes
Up the fine fibres through the sentient brain.
[Coleridge, *Religious Musings*, 368.]

IN 1796 Coleridge's eldest child was born at Clevedon, and in naming him 'David Hartley' he expressed the hope that if he grew to manhood 'his head will be convinced of, and his heart saturated with, the truths so ably supported by that great master of Christian philosophy'.[1] David Hartley, who preceded Coleridge at Jesus College, Cambridge, by some three-quarters of a century, had been intended for the Church, but, having had scruples on the subject of eternal punishment, had taken up medicine instead. Throughout his *Observations on Man* (1749) there is to be found a characteristic blend—rare even in England after the eighteenth century, and by that time virtually extinct in France—of scientific ardour with religious certainty. Hartley was a man of unusual originality and penetration, and he writes with the zest of one who knows he is engaged in pioneering work, but who feels, at the same time, that he is building up morality and religion on unshakable foundations. In this respect Hartley is clearly in the apostolical succession of English physico-theologians from Bacon, through Boyle, Locke, and Newton, to Joseph Priestley. In eighteenth century France, although English scientific and deistic thought had been a major emancipating influence, the enlightened philosophers found themselves, for the most part, militant enemies of religion. That peculiarly English phenomenon, the holy alliance between science and religion, persisted (in spite of Hume)

[1] *Letters of S. T. Coleridge* (ed. E. H. Coleridge, 1895), vol. i, p. 169.

till near the close of the century. It is Hartley's distinction that he evolves his religion, not from the starry heavens, but from a study of human psychology. Hartley was both necessitarian and Christian, materialist and religious, and as this was approximately Coleridge's position in 1796 one can understand the reverence Hartley inspired in him.[1] For our present purposes he is of importance chiefly because he showed how Nature builds up for us 'the being that we are', from sensation, through imagination to reflexion, and because he is therefore a spiritual forerunner of Wordsworth.[2]

As we have seen, there existed in the eighteenth century a widespread desire to equate the moral with the physical world: to see in it an order comparable with the order of Nature. Newton's principle of gravitation had bound together all physical bodies into a harmonious unity; could not some principle be found which should unite moral phenomena into an analogous synthesis? Sometimes it seemed that the principle of self-love was the true moral counterpart of gravitation; sometimes, that it was the principle of universal benevolence. But, as we saw in the last chapter,[3] the most important of these varieties of moral gravitation was the principle of the Association of Ideas. It is for the elaboration of this doctrine that Hartley is chiefly remembered, but Hume (as we saw) had already made great use of it in his *Treatise*. For Hume the whole order of Nature, with its so-called laws of causation, is itself a bundle of ideas connected together in our minds by customary association. Hartley, on the other hand, uses the principle to explain not only the mechanism of all our mental processes, but also the evolution of our moral characters from childhood to manhood, and the development of the moral sense out of simple sensation.

[1] Cf. *Religious Musings* (written 1794), footnote to l. 42—'see this *demonstrated* by Hartley'.

[2] The question of Wordsworth's affinities with Hartley has been elaborately investigated by A. Beatty, *Wordsworth, his Doctrine and Art in their Historical Relations* (Madison, 1927).

[3] Cf. above, p. 112.

Hartley takes as his starting-point certain suggestions of Newton, Locke, and the Rev. John Gay. Newton furnished him with the doctrine of vibrations: Locke and Gay with the first hints towards an associationist psychology. In the Preface to the first edition of the *Principia* Newton had said:

> 'I offer this work as the mathematical principles of philosophy, for the whole burden of philosophy seems to consist in this—from the phenomena of motions to demonstrate the other phenomena. . . . I wish we could derive the rest of the phenomena of Nature by the same kind of reasoning from mechanical principles, for I am induced by many reasons to suspect that they may all depend upon certain forces by which the particles of bodies, by some causes hitherto unknown, are either mutually impelled towards one another, and cohere in regular figures, or are repelled and recede from one another.'[1]

And at the end of the *Opticks* he had declared that to demonstrate how the properties and actions of all things follow from two or three principles of motion 'would be a very great step in Philosophy', adding that

> 'if natural Philosophy in all its Parts, by pursuing this Method, shall at length be perfected, the Bounds of Moral Philosophy will also be enlarged. For so far as we can know by natural Philosophy what is the first Cause, what Power he has over us, what benefits we receive from him, so far our Duty towards him, as well as that towards one another, will appear to us by the Light of Nature.'[2]

There is no need to re-emphasize the all-importance of the mechanical world-picture in the eighteenth century, but it is interesting to observe the tone in which Newton is introduced to eighteenth century readers by a Plumian Professor at Cambridge[3] in 1713. In his Preface to the second edition of the *Principia* the Professor first demonstrates the superiority of the Newtonian philosophy to that of the

[1] Motte's (1729) translation, ed. Cajoli (California, 1934).
[2] *Opticks*, bk. iii, pt. 1, qu. 31 (1st ed., 1704; reprint, ed. E. T. Whittaker, 1931).
[3] Roger Cotes.

peripatetics ('that useless medley of words'), and to that of Descartes, whose 'vortices' are disproved by the behaviour of comets. He then proclaims its religious tendency in the following terms:

'Fair and equal judges will therefore give sentence in favour of this most excellent method of philosophy, which is founded on experiments and observations. And it can hardly be said or imagined, what light, what splendor hath accrued to that method from this admirable work of our illustrious author, whose happy and sublime genius, resolving the most difficult problems, and reaching to discoveries of which the mind of man was thought incapable before, is deservedly admired by all those who are somewhat more than superficially versed in these matters. The gates are now set open, and by the passage he has revealed we may freely enter into the knowledge of the hidden secrets and wonders of natural things.... Therefore we may now more clearly behold the beauties of Nature, and entertain ourselves with the delightful contemplation; and, which is the best and most valuable fruit of philosophy, be thence incited the more profoundly to reverence and adore the great Maker and Lord of all. . . . Newton's distinguished work will be the safest protection against the attacks of atheists, and nowhere more surely than from this quiver can one draw forth missiles against the band of godless men.' [1]

No wonder, then, that Hartley, 'that great master of Christian philosophy', could take his cue from Newton. For had not that sublime genius predicted, not only that the mechanical principles would prove the key to unlock mysteries yet unexplained, but that such further discoveries would lead us back towards heaven? One further illustration may serve to illustrate the prevalence, during our period, of this religiose attitude towards Nature, and towards Newton—the authorized interpreter of her laws to man: this is taken from a popular exposition of Newtonianism which appeared in 1775:

'Our views of Nature, however imperfect, serve to represent to us, in the most sensible manner, that mighty power which pre-

[1] *op. cit.*, p. xxxii.

vails throughout, acting with a force and efficacy that appears to suffer no diminution from the greatest distances of space or intervals of time; and that wisdom which we see equally displayed in the exquisite structure and just motions of the greatest and subtilest parts. These, with the perfect goodness, by which they are evidently directed, constitute the supreme object of the speculations of a philosopher; who, while he contemplates and admires so excellent a system, cannot but be himself excited and animated to correspond with the general harmony of Nature.'[1]

From Locke and John Gay, on the other hand, Hartley learned of the influence of Association over our opinions and affections. His indebtedness to Gay, which he expressly acknowledges in the Preface to the *Observations on Man*, can be briefly illustrated. The Rev. John Gay had composed a *Dissertation Concerning the Fundamental Principles of Virtue or Morality*, which had been prefixed by Bishop Law to his translation of King's *Essay on the Origin of Evil*. In that Preface Hartley read, amongst other things, that 'though Happiness, private Happiness, is the proper and ultimate end of all our Actions whatever', yet the particular means of happiness we adopt are often connected with the main end only by Association. These means of happiness Gay calls Resting Places, or acquired principles of action. We first connect the idea of pleasure with certain objects, and then 'those things and Pleasure are so ty'd together and associated in our Minds, that one cannot present itself but the other will also occur. And the Association remains even after that which at first gave them the Connection is quite forgot' (as with money, knowledge, fame, and so on). Further, says Gay, 'it is necessary in order to solve the principal Actions of human life to suppose a *Moral Sense* . . . and also public Affections; but I deny that this Moral Sense, or these public Affections, are innate, or *implanted* in us: they are acquired either from our own *Observation* or the *Imitation* of others'.[2]

[1] Colin Maclaurin, *An Account of Sir I. Newton's Philosophical Discoveries* (quoted by C. L. Becker in *The Heavenly City of the Eighteenth Century Philosophers* (Yale, 1932), pp. 62-3).

[2] Gay's *Dissertation*, sect. iv (from Law's translation of King, 1732 ed.).

We shall see how Hartley combined and elaborated these suggestions.

The first part of the *Observations on Man* need not detain us long. It consists of an elaborate description (admittedly conjectural) of the mechanism of sensation, and may be said to develop, in much greater detail, the views of Hobbes on this subject. The white medullary substance of the brain, he says, is 'the immediate Instrument of Sensation'; it is also the 'immediate Instrument, by which Ideas are presented to the Mind: or in other words, whatever Changes are made in this Substance, corresponding Changes are made in our Ideas, and vice versa' (Propositions I and II). The minute particles of this substance receive, and can reproduce, vibrations from sensible objects. 'Sensory Vibrations, by being often repeated, beget in the medullary Substance of the Brain, a Disposition to diminutive Vibrations, which may also be called Vibratiuncles and Miniatures, corresponding to themselves respectively' (Prop. IX). Further

> 'Any Sensations, A, B, C, etc., by being associated with one another a sufficient Number of Times, get such a power over the corresponding Ideas a, b, c, etc., that any one of the Sensations A, when impressed alone, shall be able to excite in the Mind b, c, etc., the Ideas of the rest.' [Prop. X.]

Simple Ideas 'run into complex ones' by means of Association, and when this occurs, 'we are to suppose that the simple miniature Vibrations corresponding to those simple Ideas run, in like manner, into a complex miniature Vibration, corresponding to the resulting complex Idea' (Prop. XIII); he thinks, moreover, that 'some of the complex Vibrations attending upon complex Ideas . . . may be as vivid as any of the sensory Vibrations excited by the direct Action of Objects' (Prop. XIV).

Hartley strongly suspects that the workings of the 'mind' can be truly pictured in some such mechanical fashion, and he explains each of the senses in turn according to the hypothesis of vibrations and vibratiuncles. But, unlike Hobbes, or even Locke, he will not commit himself to the view that 'Matter can be endued with the Power of Sensation'.[1] He postulates, instead, a parallelism between brain and 'mind', whereby the vibrations and the sensations 'attend upon' each other, whatever may be the connexion between them. All he asserts is that whatever changes are made in the brain-substance, corresponding changes are made in our ideas, and vice versa; he claims, moreover, that this theory, like the 'pre-established harmony' of Leibniz or the 'occasionalism' of Malebranche (to both of which, he believes, his own system bears a near relation [2]), avoids the difficulty of having to 'explain' the connexion. But, unlike some philosophers, Hartley can be critically watchful of his own pet theory. Like Dr Richards with his system of mental magnetic-needles, Hartley admits, for instance, that the whole doctrine of vibrations may be fictitious. Nevertheless it may be a useful myth, if it helps to provide a scientific method of approach to psychology (cf. 'Principles which, though fictitious, are, at least, clear and intelligible', p. 109). Where any kind of explanation is probably mythical, it only concerns us to have a good myth rather than a bad one. So he conjectures that Propositions I and II (quoted above) may be 'true, in a very useful practical Sense, yet they are not so in an ultimate and precise one'. He is also clear-sighted enough to perceive that the doctrine of the Association of Ideas may stand, even if the Vibrations have to be abandoned.[3] Is not its truth presupposed in all that ancients and moderns alike have taught us about Custom, Habit, and Education?

How then does Hartley build up his moral superstructure on the basis of association? His fundamental

[1] *Observations on Man* (1749), vol. i, p. 33. [2] *ibid.*, vol. i, p. 111.

[3] 'The Doctrine of Association may be laid down as a certain Foundation, and a Clue to direct our future Inquiries, whatever becomes of that of Vibrations' (*ibid.*, vol. i, p. 72).

doctrine, as expressed by J. S. Mill, is 'the formation of all human character by circumstances, through the universal principle of Association, and the consequent unlimited possibility of improving the moral and intellectual condition of mankind by education.'[1] Hartley is an optimist of the progressive and perfectibilist type: 'Association has a Tendency to reduce the State of those who have eaten of the Tree of the Knowledge of Good and Evil, back again to a paradisiacal one'.[2] How can this be? It is because, in the first place, we are all similar, and all exposed to the gentle and irremissive action of the mighty sum of things, so that in the end our 'particular differences' will be smoothed away, and 'if one be happy, all must'. That happiness is the final end, and not misery, follows, for Hartley, first from his conception of the world as a Providentially designed 'system of benevolence',[3] and secondly from his own special view of the workings of the association-principle. 'Some degree of spirituality', he writes, 'is the necessary Consequence of passing through life. The sensible Pleasures and Pains must be transferred by Association more and more every Day, upon things that afford neither sensible Pleasure nor sensible Pain in themselves, and so beget the intellectual Pleasures and Pains.'[4] Hartley, following the Rev. John Gay, taught that

> 'Our Passions or Affections can be no more than Aggregates of simple Ideas united by Association.'[5]

The moral sense is not inborn, but 'factitious'—that is, acquired through the association of pleasurable sensations with certain objects. We can, of course, associate pleasure with the wrong objects, but the world was in fact designed by Providence as a system of benevolence, so that ideally, or under a proper educational regimen, our characters are built up for us by what Wordsworth calls 'the powers that

[1] *Autobiography*, p. 91 ('World's Classics' ed.).
[2] Hartley, *op. cit.*, pp. 82-3.
[3] *ibid.*, vol. ii, p. 245
[4] *ibid.*, vol. i, p. 82.
[5] *ibid.*, vol. i, p. 368.

of themselves our minds impress', and we need only cultivate 'wise passiveness' in order to proceed from childhood, through youth, to the 'years that bring the philosophic mind'.

1. We begin, then, with Sensation, and proceed, by associating pleasure with ever loftier and wider objects, until we reach the stage when God is All in All:

> 'Since God is the source of all Good, and consequently must at last appear to be so, i.e. be associated with all our Pleasures, it seems to follow . . . that the Idea of God, and of the Ways by which his Goodness and Happiness are made manifest, must, at last, take place of, and absorb other Ideas, and He himself become, according to the Language of the Scriptures, All in All.' [1]

The human individual, then, may be regarded as a sort of refinery in which the loftiest spirituality is being mechanically distilled out of sense. But only, of course, as long as our days are indeed bound each to each by natural piety: only as long as our minds are in what Wordsworth has called 'a healthy state of association'. Only then is the benevolent scheme of Providence being realized according to its own intention. The development may be deflected or arrested, and the child may be father of a monster instead of a man. In such cases, when a faulty education has produced a Peter Bell, or the 'young man' of the *Letter to 'The Friend'* (1809-10), the only course for the sufferer is to be 'remanded to Nature', to 'go back, as occasion will permit, to Nature and to solitude', and to 'measure back the track of life he has trod'.[2] Similarly Hartley tells us that

> 'It is of the utmost Consequence to Morality and Religion,

[1] *ibid.*, vol. i, p. 114. This is one of the passages referred to by Coleridge in the footnote to *Religious Musings*. Cf. his

> ' Till by exclusive consciousness of God
> All self-annihilated it shall make
> God its Identity: God all in all!
> We and our Father one!' [*R.M.*, 42.]

[2] Wordsworth's phrases: *Letter to 'The Friend'*, Dec. 1809-Jan. 1810.

that the Affections and Passions should be analysed into their simple compounding Parts, by reversing the Steps of the Associations which concur to form them. For thus we may learn how to cherish and improve good ones, check and root out such as are mischievous and immoral, and how to suit our Manner of Life, in some tolerable Measure, to our intellectual and religious Wants.'[1]

Just so Peter Bell, after the terrors of his night's adventure have turned him 'adrift into the past', sits deeply musing,

> As if his mind were sinking deep
> Through years that have been long asleep,[2]

and at last awakens to the new life breathed into him by Nature. Just so Wordsworth himself, after the French episode and the temptation in the Godwinian wilderness, sank back upon himself and upon his past, and fetched 'invigorating thoughts from former years'. So build we up the being that we are.

Hartley reminds us, in his second volume, that the Pleasures of Sense, though they are the foundation of the whole pyramid of association, must not be made an immediate end throughout life. To attempt this is to defeat oneself, for experience teaches that 'he who would obtain the Maximum of the sensible Pleasures, even those of Taste, must not give himself up to them; but restrain them, and make them subject to Benevolence, Piety, and the Moral Sense'. It is also to defeat Providence, which intends the great business and purport of this present life to be

> 'the Transformation of Sensuality into Spirituality, by associating the sensible Pleasures, and their Traces, with proper foreign Objects, and so forming Motives to beneficent Actions, and diffusing them over the whole general Course of our Existence.'[3]

---

[1] *Observations on Man*, vol. i, p. 81.
[2] l. 1093.
[3] *Observations on Man*, vol. ii, p. 214.

2. Next after Sensation comes Imagination:

> 'The Recurrence of Ideas, especially visible and audible ones, in a vivid manner, but without any regard to the Order observed in past Facts, is ascribed to the Power of Imagination or Fancy.'[1]

(Coleridge, it will be observed, did not learn from Hartley to desynonymize Fancy and Imagination. Hartley's description of 'Imagination or Fancy', indeed, resembles Coleridge's definition of 'Fancy', as 'a mode of memory emancipated from the order of time and space'.[2]) The pleasures of the Imagination are the first category of the intellectual pleasures, pleasures which are not 'original', but deducible from the sensible ones by association. For instance, our delight in the Beauty of Nature (the first kind of imaginative pleasure he considers) is built out of such original elements as delight in tastes, colours, smells of flowers and fruit, warmth and coolness, country sports and pastimes, together with the healthfulness, tranquillity, and innocence of the country contrasted with the offensiveness, dangers, and corruptions of cities. Thus, in vacant or in pensive mood, or amidst the dreary intercourse of daily life, there may come gleams like the flashing of a shield, and spots of time may be recalled, whereby the mind is nourished and invisibly repaired.[3] Hartley has this important point to add here, that the pleasures of Theopathy (sense of union with God), that is, one of the last to be generated, can be and often are transferred to Nature:

> 'Those persons who have already formed high Ideas of the Power, Knowledge, and Goodness of the Author of Nature . . . generally feel the exalted Pleasures of Devotion upon every View and Contemplation of his Works.'[4]

However, Hartley observes of the Pleasures of the Imagination in general, that 'from the Nature of our Frame' they must necessarily decline in intensity after youth,

[1] *ibid.*, vol. i, p. 383.
[2] *Biog. Lit.*, ch. xiii, *ad fin.*
[3] For this composite Wordsworthian sentence no apologies are proffered.
[4] *Observations on Man*, vol. i, p. 420.

yielding place to more exalted and purer pleasures. How much of all this teaching not only influenced Wordsworth, but actually accounts in advance for some of the peculiarities of his development as a poet, is an interesting topic for reflection.[1]

Another section of the Pleasures of the Imagination is concerned with Poetry and the Arts, and here Hartley anticipates Peacock's view of poetry as the 'mental rattle' for the infancy of society, to be discarded, along with other childish things, in maturity. As imaginative pleasures are proper mainly to the period of youth, so the arts are proper to the 'early ages of the world'.

> '... if we consider Mankind as one great Individual, advancing in Age perpetually, it seems natural to expect, that in the Infancy of Knowledge, in the early Ages of the World, the Taste of Mankind would turn much upon the Pleasures of this Class.' [2]

The arts give pleasure largely in virtue of a principle which was to be invoked by a series of later critics and aestheticians, including Wordsworth and Coleridge—the principle of uniformity in variety. Hartley's scientific realism as an associationist is seen in his not scrupling to reckon social snobbery, also, amongst the sources of our pleasure in the arts; we associate music and painting, in particular, with High Rank. But there must always be great divergencies in 'taste', and the preferences of no age, nation, or class should be set up as the criterion of excellence:

> 'The only Things that can be set up as natural Criterions here seem to be Uniformity with Variety, Usefulness in general, and the particular subserviency of this or that artificial Beauty to improve the Mind, so as to make it suit best with our present Circumstances and future Expectations.' [3]

But Hartley adopts, in the end, a Platonico-religious attitude towards the arts. The pleasures of the imagination

[1] See Beatty, *op. cit.*, especially ch. vi.
[2] *Observations on Man*, vol. i, p. 431.
[3] *ibid.*, vol. i, p. 442.

must not be made a lifelong pursuit, if only because they 'come to their Height early in Life, and decline in old Age'.[1] If we do not some day sing our Ode to Duty, if years do not at last bring the philosophic mind, the benign workings of Association are somehow being hindered.

> 'The Pleasures of the Imagination are the next remove above the sensible ones, and have, in their proper Place and Degree, a great Efficacy in improving and perfecting our Natures. They are to Men in the early Part of their adult Age, what Playthings are to Children; they teach them a love for Regularity, Exactness, Truth, Simplicity; they lead them to the knowledge of many important Truths relating to themselves, the external World, and its Author; they habituate to invent, and reason by Analogy and Induction; and when the social, moral, and religious Affections begin to be generated in us, we may make a much quicker Progress towards the Perfection of our Natures by having a due Stock, and no more than a due Stock, of Knowledge in natural and artificial Things, of a relish for natural and artificial Beauty.' [2]

As Plato had taught, the love of beautiful things and persons is important at the beginning of the soul's education, to allure it on its upward path, but in due course we must bid these joys farewell and pass them for a nobler life. All earthly beauty fades; our hopes are with infinitude, and only there. Moreover, Hartley shares with Plato and the Puritans other grounds for condemning the pursuit of the 'polite arts'; it is evident, he says, 'that most kinds of Music, Painting, and Poetry, have close connexions with Vice'. They 'cannot be enjoyed without *evil Communications*, and Concurrence in the Pagan Shew and Pomp of the World', and they 'introduce a Frame of Mind, quite opposite to that of Devotion, and earnest Concern for our own and others' future Welfare'. Indeed, 'the polite Arts are scarce to be allowed, except when consecrated to religious Purposes'.[3] It is highly significant, however, that all this censure is reserved mainly for *artificial* beauty; the

[1] *ibid.*, vol. ii, p. 244.
[2] *ibid.*, vol. ii, p. 244.
[3] *ibid.*, vol. ii, pp. 253-4.

Beauties of Nature, as the handiwork of God, are of a nobler kind:

> 'they lead to Humility, Devotion, and the Study of the Ways of Providence. We ought therefore much rather to apply ourselves to the Contemplation of natural than of artificial Beauty.'[1]

The critics, down at least to Dryden and Pope, had held that the poets can offer beauty 'as perfectly, and more delightfully than Nature'; Nature's world is brazen, poetry alone delivers a golden. But we are now in the age of physico-theology, when, as we have seen, religious emotions formerly attached to super-nature are being transferred more and more to 'Nature'. And half a century later, the associationist poet gives thanks to the Spirit of the Universe for linking up his early passions and affections

> Not with the mean and vulgar works of man,
> But with high objects, with enduring things—
> With life and nature—purifying thus
> The elements of feeling and of thought.[2]

3. Next come the Pleasures and Pains of Ambition. These are Hume's social reactions: they are the pleasures and pains arising from the approbation and disapprobation of others. By association we come to seek whatever produces the former and to avoid what produces the latter. Here the automatic generation of virtue is illustrated, for men's very pride and vanity, for example, will lead them to seek the praise of humility.

4. Self-Interest. The same principle is exemplified still more strikingly under this heading. There is, first, 'gross self-interest'; then, 'refined self-interest' (as when friendship and even 'devotion' are cultivated for the sake of their

[1] *ibid.*, vol. ii, p. 249.
[2] *The Prelude*, bk. i, 408. (Cf. what was said above, p. 40, on Wilkins and Derham.)

attendant pleasures); and lastly, 'rational self-interest', which merges with the 'abstract Desire of Happiness'. Hartley is confident that the first should evolve naturally into the last in the course of life's probation. We learn by checks and disappointments where to seek our lasting satisfactions, and are eventually impelled to 'resign all to God':

> 'It appears . . . that all Aggregates of Pleasure . . . must, from the Mechanism and Necessity of our Natures, and of the world that surrounds us, be made at last to centre and rest upon Him who is the inexhaustible Fountain of all Power, Knowledge, Goodness, Majesty, Glory, Property, etc. So that even Avarice and Ambition are, in their respective Ways, carrying on the benevolent Designs of Him who is *All in All*. And the same thing may be hoped of every other Passion and Pursuit. One may hope, that they all agree and unite in leading to ultimate Happiness and Perfection.'[1]

Thus all things work together for good under the kindly superintendence of the laws of Association.

5. Sympathy. Compassion, Mercy, and Sociability are generated by association in early life. The selfish ingredient in these impulses is gradually eliminated, and we have thus a proof, says Hartley, 'from the Doctrine of Association, that there is, and must be, such a Thing as pure disinterested Benevolence'.[2] The pleasures of Sympathy, unlike those of Sense, Imagination, and the rest, are not transitory; moreover, they turn us from children of wrath into inheritors of the glorious liberty of the Sons of God.

6. Theopathy. Love of God may, at first, contain elements of self-interest, but 'after all the several Sources of the Love of God have coalesced together, this Affection becomes as disinterested as any other'.

[1] *Observations on Man*, vol. i, p. 463. [2] *ibid.*, vol. i, p. 474.

7. Lastly comes the Moral Sense, not, as with Shaftesbury or Hutcheson, an innate faculty, but the resultant and complex of all the preceding. At this stage

> 'the reiterated Impressions of those Associations will at last make Duty itself a Pleasure, and convert Sin into a Pain, giving a Lustre and Deformity respectively to all their Appellations; and that without any express Recollection of the Hopes and Fears of another World.'

The moral sense, regarded as the final outcome of Nature's holy plan,

> 'employs the Force and Authority of the whole Nature of Man against any particular Part of it, that rebels against the Determinations and Commands of the Conscience or Moral Judgment.'

Arrived at this point, a man may love or hate 'merely because he ought'.[1] As against the 'moral sense' school, then, or those who base moral judgments on rational insight into the relations of things, Hartley favours the 'Deduction of all our moral Judgments, Approbations, and Disapprobations, from Association alone'.

It may suggest itself that, in spite of Hartley's religiosity, we have here a philosophy which looks back to Hobbes and forward to Godwin. For it appears to be, on the one hand, materialist, mechanistic, and necessitarian, and on the other hand perfectibilist. In the Preface Hartley confesses that he is a necessitarian, explaining that he did not realize that Associationism implied 'Necessity' until several years after he had begun his enquiries, and that he had only admitted it at last with the 'greatest reluctance'. He would never commit himself to frank materialism, or to any of the accepted hypotheses which tried to account for the union of soul and body:

> 'it is all one to the Purpose of the foregoing Theory, whether the Motions in the medullary Substance be the physical Cause of the Sensations, according to the System of the Schools; or the occasional Cause, according to Malebranche; or only an Adjunct,

---

[1] *ibid.*, vol. i, pp. 497-8.

according to Leibnitz. However, this is not supposing Matter to be endued with Sensation, or any way explaining what the Soul is; but only taking its Existence and Connexion with the bodily Organs in the most simple Case, for granted, in order to make farther Inquiries.'[1]

His own theory, he feels, will stand firm whatever metaphysical basis we care to assume. But on the necessitarian issue he tries to take a firm line: the moral sense is 'generated necessarily and mechanically',[2] he tells us. Are we then, we may ask, simply to fold our hands in wise passiveness and let our affections gently lead us on, until, after a sufficient interval of moral *laissez-faire*, we awake to find ourselves complete theopaths? There is, it appears to me, the usual fundamental confusion in this part of Hartley's teaching—a confusion which is seen in all the necessitarian moralists of the time: in Holbach, for instance, and again in Godwin later. The very people who, as necessitarians, loudly proclaim that men's characters are the product of circumstances, are also the people who, as moralists and educators, are most anxious to control and alter circumstances so as to produce the right kind of character. Hartley's second volume, dealing with religion and the Rule of Life, is full of 'oughts' and 'shoulds', whereas in the first part, where he is showing the inevitability of our progress towards perfection, 'is' tends to predominate. The doctrine of mechanism, he says (anticipating Godwin),

> 'has a Tendency to make us labour more earnestly with ourselves and others, particularly Children, from the greater Certainty attending all Endeavours that operate in a mechanical way.'[3]

In other words, if we want to produce better behaviour, if we want the laws of association to exert their maximum influence for good, we must see to it that they have free play, or rather we must *arrange* the circumstances so as to

[1] *ibid.*, vol. i, p. 511.
[2] *ibid.*, vol. i, p. 504.
[3] *ibid.*, vol. i, p. 510.

secure for these laws the attainment of their own end. But what are 'we' in this proposition? The theory seems to me to reintroduce free-will by imputing to us the power of originating such arrangements, whereas Hartley has expressly disallowed any power in us to begin motion. According to his associationism, we are passive all along the line; as he has said, the moral sense 'is' generated in us mechanically. Yet he goes on to describe the transformation of sensuality into spirituality as the great business of life: we 'must' not rest content with the pleasures of the senses or of the imagination; we 'ought' never to be satisfied until 'we arrive at perfect Self-annihilation, and the pure Love of God'.[1] Why this severe, this earnest air? one may be inclined to ask. The answer seems to be that with one part of his mind Hartley assumes that we are capable of altering the circumstances out of which character is formed. We may agree that a man would not be 'free' to do either A or B if the previous circumstances were the same in both cases, but to grasp the full implications of this we must exhaust all the circumstances. And the chief of them is the state of mind of the agent. X's state of mind, let us say, produces A, Y's produces B, all other circumstances being assumed to be identical. Why is this? Perhaps because X has disciplined himself to respond in that way to the stimuli which, from Y, produce B. This does not overthrow necessity, perhaps, but it suggests that there may be different levels of necessity, and that man is 'free' to place himself upon one or other of these levels. There may be deliberation in face of A or B: which law shall I identify myself with? After the decision, the action follows 'necessarily'. The two halves of Hartley's doctrine, then—*laissez-faire* on the one hand, and conscious effort towards perfection on the other—do not seem to me to hang together. His confusion is highly characteristic of the materialist position in the eighteenth century, in which man appears simultaneously as the product and the changer of circumstances, though there is no

[1] *ibid.*, vol. ii, p. 282.

theoretic acceptance of this paradox as yet. All one can expect the eighteenth century materialists to do is, first to compound the mind out of the senses, and character out of circumstances—and then, as moralists and world-changers, to insist on our pressing forward towards perfection. In Godwin, I think, it is the changing which occupies most of the picture; in Hartley, on the whole, it is the passivity. Hartley's significant contribution is his joining up a materialist psychology, not with a Hobbist pessimism, but with the optimistic theism of his century, to yield a confident faith in the necessity of progress towards perfection. He thus contributed to the stream of tendency which flowed into the nineteenth century as philosophic radicalism, and also as Wordsworthian naturalism.

CHAPTER IX

Holbach's Système de la Nature (1770)

'Ceux qui connoîtront la vaste chaîne des maux que les systèmes erronés de la superstition ont produits sur la terre, reconnoîtront l'importance de leur opposer des systèmes plus vrais, puisés dans la nature, fondés sur l'expérience.'

[*Système de la Nature*, vol i, p. 225.]

IN the course of his celebrated work, the *Système de la Nature*, Holbach himself points out that in countries like England, and the other Protestant lands, where toleration exists, there are plenty of Deists and infidels, but very few atheists. As he is passionately proclaiming the necessity of atheism as a means to the attainment of the liberties partially realized in England, he has to explain this circumstance. It is due (as suggested above) to this: that the English have already had their bourgeois reformation and revolution, and have thus reached a degree of tolerance, whereas in France, feudalism and superstition still flourish side by side with the *philosophes*. In France the enlightened are impelled by oppression to 'cite the Divinity itself to the bar of reason'; the more fortunate English, on the other hand, can rest content with merely having rejected the grosser superstitions. The work of Holbach (and the other Encyclopédistes) is of peculiar importance to our present studies, if only because in it we can see the 'Nature'-philosophy of the century working itself out to its ultimate conclusions,and touched to revolutionary issues. Hume philosophizes boldly in the study, but becomes conventional again in ethics and politics; Hartley and Priestley, in English fashion, manage to be Christians of sorts as well as materialists and necessitarians. With Holbach and Helvétius (to mention no others) 'Nature' is seen no longer as a christianized demiurge, working obediently under heavenly auspices, but as a defiant Titaness who would dethrone the established gods and overturn all earthly altars and thrones, the symbols of priestcraft and tyranny. It is worth while to turn our attention to such writers, so as to observe what 'Nature' can mean when divested of religious associations, and when used as a slogan of revolution. Moreover, by the middle of the eighteenth century, after the passing of Newton, Locke, and the deists, it was no longer England but France which was conducting the main speculative attack—and this because, for reasons already hinted at, the *philosophes* were compelled to be world-changers rather than world-explainers. The familiar Marxian phrases serve to suggest what is indeed the fact, that very many of the characteristics of modern revolutionary theory are to be found already in the French materialists of the eighteenth century. The divergencies are, of course, equally unmistakable, and have often been pointed out: that the eighteenth century materialists were metaphysical rather than historical or dialectical, bourgeois and not proletarian in affinity and outlook, and so forth. It is also sometimes maintained that the eighteenth century lacked a comprehensive theory of the inter-relations of man and Nature, that it saw them merely as unrelated opposites, and civilization as 'artificial', because diverging from a fixed 'Nature'. As we shall see, this is only partially true of Holbach, who in moments of insight saw through this false antithesis of 'natural' and 'artificial', and could declare (for example) that 'l'art n'est que la Nature agissante à l'aide des instruments qu'elle a faits'.[1] More habitually, however, Holbach falls into the typical confusion of the century. His book opens with the assertion that man is part of Nature, that he is a purely physical being, that his moral nature is part of his physical nature, that he is part of the chain of causation; yet in the same breath he declares that all our misfortunes are due to our neglecting and departing from Nature, and the rest of the book is one

[1] *Système de la Nature* (1780 ed.), vol. i, p. 3.

long lament over man's perversions of Nature's holy plan. How comes it, then, that Nature engenders such 'unnatural' offspring? Or if all is 'Nature', and there is nothing unnatural, is all our unhappiness 'natural'? The reason why Holbach cannot admit this is that, after all, he is a man of the eighteenth century, and therefore he cannot help thinking in terms of an unspoilt Nature which he worships, and an erring humanity which he condemns. Our errors *cannot* be 'natural', are not what Nature intended; yet there is nothing which Nature has not produced, nothing which does not fall within the 'domain of causality'. For these contradictions two typically eighteenth century mental habits are chiefly responsible: first (one which we have previously noticed), that of honouring Nature with a reverence which, in spite of professed atheism, is in fact religious or transferred from religion, and secondly, that of taking too abstract a view of human institutions, so that they appear, not as the result of historical growth, but as mere departures from a fixed norm of Nature and Reason.

With these considerations in mind we can now examine Holbach at closer range. He began by writing Encyclopedia articles on minerals and kindred subjects, and ended as a moralist and sociologist. In this development he was representative of his age, which was increasingly trying to use science as a foundation for a new and better social order. It was, he believed, because man had disdained to learn from Nature and experience, that he had fallen into slavery and superstition, and remained in so protracted an infancy. 'Faute de connoître la nature, il se forma des Dieux'. Now the universe, says Holbach, consists solely of matter and movement; but matter should not be thought of as 'inert' by definition, and consequently motionless until impelled from without. Nor is matter simply homogeneous 'body', variously modified or configured. Matter is eternally in motion: this is its nature or essence (Holbach refers here to Toland's *Letters to*

Serena, where the same doctrine was maintained), and it is heterogeneous in texture.

> 'If, by "Nature", we understand a mass of dead material, devoid of all properties and entirely passive, we shall doubtless be compelled to search outside this Nature for the principle of its movements. But if by Nature we understand that which it really is, a whole of which the various parts have various properties, behave in accordance with these properties, and are in a state of perpetual interaction upon each other—then we shall have no need to have recourse to supernatural forces in order to account for the objects and the phenomena that we see.' [1]

So, he concludes (boldly making choice of the most congenial doctrine),

> 'let us be content to say that matter has always existed, that it moves in virtue of its own essence, and that all the phenomena of Nature are due to the different movements of the various kinds of matter of which Nature consists.' [2]

Nature is a realm of complete determinism; it knows no 'order' and 'disorder'. We call 'disorder' what disturbs or afflicts us, but all is in truth 'order', in the sense that all occurs by fixed causation; order is just simply 'what happens'. Man, as we have seen, is part of this order; how does he fit into it? All things are trying to be themselves; man seeks his own happiness. In Nature the principles of attraction and repulsion rule supreme; in man, desire and aversion; in Nature, the laws of inertia or of conservation; in man, self-love. Man is, at every moment of his existence, a passive instrument in the hands of destiny. Yet, finding that he was able to 'act', he imagined that he possessed within himself a motive principle independent of the rest of Nature, and from this error sprang all the false doctrines about the soul and its immortality. The 'soul' is in truth the body in its aspects of thinking, feeling, and willing. Rather than assert, with the Christians and the Cartesians, an unbridgeable dualism of mind and matter, would it not be more natural simply to

[1] *ibid.*, vol. i, p. 24. (For convenience I have translated some of the longer extracts.)

[2] *ibid.*, vol. i, p. 31.

say: As man, who is material, can think, therefore matter is capable of thought? Holbach continues by giving the Hobbist account of sensation, reflexion, memory, and imagination. We cannot inspect the inner mechanism of the material soul, but then neither do we know the mechanism of gravity or repulsion; and we only land ourselves in worse difficulties by imagining the soul to be an ineffable entity. Since the soul is a function of the body, the way to the soul lies through the body, and medicine is the true key to morality. Morality and politics therefore stand to gain from materialism advantages such as 'spiritualism' can never offer, and such as it prevents us from even dreaming of. Let us therefore aim at improving men's material environment, and we shall soon find their morals improving. You will always get vicious 'souls' as long as the bodies they inhabit are miserable. Men are 'by nature' neither good nor evil; Nature makes them simply machines, some more and some less energetic, for the attainment of happiness. If they are wicked it is because they are made so; at present government, education, public opinion, and religion all conspire to corrupt humanity. The distinctions between good and bad, vice and virtue, are not founded upon human conventions, still less upon the supposed will of a supernatural being, but upon the eternal and invariable relations between human beings in society. Virtue is all that is truly and constantly useful to society. Our 'duties' are the means without which we cannot arrive at our ends, and 'moral obligation' is the necessity of employing the means proper to make happy those with whom we live, so that they in turn may make us happy. It is our own greatest interest to be virtuous; this is the true foundation of morality, and would be recognized as such in a properly ordered state. The purpose of Law is to prevent individuals from seeking their private good at the expense of the whole, and 'politics' ought to be

> 'the art of regulating the passions of men, and directing them

> towards the good of society. . . . They are commonly so corrupt, only because they are not founded upon nature, expediency and the general utility, but on the passions, caprices and particular utility of those who govern society.' [1]

Holbach adds some declamation, much in the manner of the modern materialists, against the doctrine of a future life—that mirage which blinds men to the real and remediable evils of the present life. Having acknowledged that *post mortem nihil est*, we can then concentrate our laws and our educational system upon the task of making it men's interest and happiness to be virtuous here and now.

Holbach's main attack on religion is developed in his second volume, and we must especially attend to his arguments here because 'Nature', for him, derives its special significance from its supposed opposition to super-nature, and it is by exposing religion that he hopes to persuade us to come forth into the light of things, and let Nature be our teacher. Religion, he proclaims, is to be condemned on three main counts: it offers a wrong basis for morality, its teachings are contrary to scientific truth, and it is the mainstay of a corrupt political and social order. He follows Hobbes in ascribing its origin to primeval fear of the unknown; it has always been, he says,

> 'a system of conduct invented by imagination and ignorance in order to conciliate the unknown powers to which Nature was thought to be subjected. Some irascible and placable divinity was always at the bottom of it, and it was on this puerile and absurd notion that the priesthood founded its rights, its temples, its altars, its wealth, its authority and its dogmas. On such crude foundations rest all the religious systems of the world; invented originally by savages, they still have the power to control the fate of the most civilized nations.' [2]

To-day, religion has become

> 'the art of intoxicating men with enthusiasm, so as to divert their attention from the evils with which their rulers load them here on

---

[1] *ibid.*, vol. i, p. 141.   [2] *ibid.*, vol. ii, p. 15.

earth. . . . They are made to hope that if they agree to being unhappy in this world, they will be happier in the next.'[1]

It is injurious to morality, since whoever discovers the falsity of the alleged religious foundations of ethics will naturally suppose that the morality is as chimerical as the religion. That is why

'the words *infidel* and *libertine* have become synonyms. There would be no such disadvantage if a natural morality were taught, instead of a theological. Instead of prohibiting debauchery, crime and vice, because God and religion forbid them, we ought to say that all excess is harmful to man's conservation, makes him despicable in the eyes of society, is forbidden by reason, which wants each man to conserve himself, and is forbidden by nature, which wants him to work for his lasting happiness.'[2]

Ignorance begets gods; enlightenment destroys them. Their persistence in an age of enlightenment, 'in which natural law had provided a more satisfactory explanation of natural phenomena', is due entirely to the sinister influence of the clergy. *Tantum religio potuit suadere malorum*; and he who should now succeed in destroying the notion of 'God' would be the greatest friend of man.

Next, Holbach inserts an interesting section on Samuel Clarke's *Treatise on the Being and Attributes of God* (1704), a standard work of orthodox apologetic to which allusion has been made above (pp. 59-60). Holbach treats Clarke rather as Marx afterwards treated Hegel; all that Clarke says of 'God', he assures us, may truly be said, and intelligibly said, of 'Matter' or 'Nature'. Attributed to 'God', such properties as eternity, infinity, uniqueness, etc., are incomprehensible. The habit of so speaking merely sets up a fictitious being abstracted from Nature, whereas it is precisely to 'matter' that we ought to attribute such properties. Of matter, indeed, we can also say that its essence (the thing-in-itself) is incomprehensible, but then we do know its '*écorce*', and are affected by it

[1] *Christianisme Dévoilé*, quoted by Wickwar, *Baron d'Holbach* (1935), p. 129.
[2] Wickwar, *op. cit.*, p. 127.

every moment of our lives. Of incomprehensible non-matter we know just nothing, and we may therefore regard it *as* nothing. Movement is as much a necessary attribute of matter as extension or figure, so why should we seek for a 'motor' outside Nature? For Holbach, the impulse to seek some supernatural first cause is the last infirmity of noble mind, and he remarks that even the great, the immortal Newton, as soon as he leaves geometry and physics, becomes a child. As for Descartes' 'ontological' argument, this would equally prove the existence of hippogriffs. 'Nature', then, is all and produces all. Nor does this mean that effects are produced 'by chance', for Nature acts invariably by fixed laws. It does mean, however, that we must base our lives on 'experience', and fear no ghosts. Holbach accepts quite cheerfully the idea that matter, existing from eternity, having certain properties and subject to certain laws, could spontaneously generate such a system as our universe. He condemns 'Spinozistic' pantheism, but it may well seem that his own 'Matter', having so many wonderful 'attributes' and 'potentialities' and 'principles' within it, becomes, after all, something tolerably godlike before he has finished with it. 'It is of the essence' of a seed to grow: it is its 'nature' so to do: this is Holbach's constant refrain, and this is the kind of statement which evidently satisfies him. Why, you ask, does Nature exist? To what end? Where the dogmatic schoolman had pointed to God, the eighteenth century atheist points to Nature itself; Nature is its own end—it has no other aim but to exist, to act, to preserve its own 'ensemble'. In distinguishing 'God' from 'Nature', the 'soul' from the body, 'life' from the living organism, and so forth, men are making the same inveterate mistake all the time. Nor is this merely a metaphysical error having no importance for conduct, since in addressing themselves to a fictitious Deity men have come to expect everything from Him, and have ceased to rely upon Nature and their own activity. We *must* teach men that beyond Nature there is nothing, and that 'science' alone (i.e. knowledge of Nature applied to the conduct of man in society) can make them happy. When Holbach says of men: 'il leur faut du mystère pour remuer leur imagination',[1] he is complaining of a weakness in them, not stating an inescapable psychological fact. He goes on, in the usual eighteenth century way, to blame the priests, in whose 'interest' it is to maintain the mysteries:

> 'a religion which was clear, intelligible and without mystery would not seem particularly divine to the ordinary man, and would be of little use to the priests.'[2]

'Natural' religion, though certainly preferable to the priestly variety, has equally precarious foundations. Those who imagine they see God in 'Nature' are deceived, for they see only a corner of the universal picture, not the ensemble. Moreover, so-called 'natural' religion has an inevitable tendency to degenerate into 'superstition'. The spectacle of the actual world is so impossible to harmonize with mere theism, that the theist is bound to fall back successively upon all the reveries of theology. Was not Jesus a theist? and yet has not the religion he founded become the most noxious superstition in the world?

> 'It is thus evident that the deists or theists have no real ground for distinguishing themselves from the superstitious, and that it is impossible to fix the line of demarcation which separates them from the most credulous men.'[3]

(One remembers that it came to be said of Voltaire, 'Voltaire est bigot, il est déiste'.) 'The moment a man can admit the God of theology, there is no longer anything else in religion that he cannot admit'[4]; indeed the religious are really more logical than the 'enlightened' theists. The acuteness of these latter observations will not have concealed from the reader the typical confusion into which Holbach has fallen in speaking of the 'spectacle of the actual world'. When he is refuting theism he makes the

[1] *Système de la Nature*, vol. ii, p. 185.
[2] *ibid.*, vol. ii, p. 185.
[3] *ibid.*, vol. ii, p. 225.
[4] *ibid.*, vol. ii, p. 227.

very worst of that spectacle, and finds it irreconcilable with the notion of an omnipotent and benevolent creator. The creator of such a world could only be regarded as a *moral* being by deliberately averting one's eyes from the facts, and arbitrarily attributing to him a number of human qualities. Yet we have only to call the 'actual world' *Nature*, and Holbach's tone changes to one of semi-religious exaltation. What would be odious as divine purpose becomes admirable as natural law. We have already noticed the further difficulties which spring from trying to combine vehement disapproval of the status quo with theoretical approval of all that 'Nature' has produced. 'Nature', he writes (and he might equally have said 'the founder of Christianity'),

> 'bids man be sociable, to love his fellows, to be just, peaceful, indulgent, beneficent, to make or leave his associates happy':

—whereas 'religion'

> 'counsels him to flee society, to detach himself from all creatures, to hate them when their imagination furnishes them with dreams different from his own, to break, in the name of his God, all the most sacred links, to torment, to afflict, to persecute, to massacre those who refuse to be mad in his fashion.'[1]

'Nature' bids men be self-reliant, and conquer removable evils by mastering the natural laws; 'religion' diverts them from this, their true end, by bidding them turn their gaze towards heaven. Holbach appends here one of those footnotes which are sometimes more graphic than his text:

> 'In 1725, the city of Paris was afflicted by a famine which was considered likely to cause a popular rising, so they brought down the casket of St Geneviève, patron and tutelary goddess of the Parisians, and carried it round in procession in order to end this calamity, which was caused by monopolies in which the mistress of the first minister of those days was interested.'[2]

'The priests have good reason to be the enemies of science,

[1] *ibid.*, vol. ii, p. 277. [2] *ibid.*, vol. ii, p. 289.

for the progress of light will put an end, sooner or later, to the ideas of superstition.'

What, finally, is to be said of this atheism of whose necessity Holbach is so firmly persuaded? Will it, as is often suggested, produce moral monsters? No: it is superstition that releases all the evil passions, while atheism, by confining our views to this life, promotes the social virtues. Holbach admits that a man *may* embrace atheism because he wrongly thinks it will enable him to drink on and defy the parson; there are admittedly vicious men who will attack the gods because they think them enemies of their passions. The good man attacks them because he finds them enemies of virtue. Atheism will not make a good man bad, or a bad man good, but if an atheist chances to be a wicked man he can at least not pretend that his misdeeds are authorized by God. An atheist who reasons aright will probably be good, and meanwhile let us remember those illustrious 'atheists' who have been peaceable and studious men: Epicurus, Lucretius, Bodin, Spinoza. 'Hobbes did not cause bloodshed in England, where in his lifetime religious fanaticism put a king to death on the scaffold.'[1] Atheism is not a creed for 'the people', so we need not fear its political consequences. But Holbach has been accusing 'religion' of baffling 'the people' with its subtleties, while 'Nature' is clear and plain to all. Is religion, then, perhaps, 'useful' even if false? No! Holbach will not have this either, for there is always most vice where there is most superstition. He avoids this difficulty by saying that we cannot convert a whole people at once to atheism; an enlightened author writes and works for posterity and for the human race, and not merely for his own times or his actual fellow-countrymen, for whom his doctrine is too advanced. Let it not be supposed, in spite of the great Lord Bacon, that deeper thinking will bring posterity back to religion; what more often happens is that shallow thinkers arrive at seeing the absurdities of religion, but, through being unaccustomed

[1] *ibid.*, vol. ii, p. 354.

to meditation, are plunged by further thought back into the theological labyrinth.

In the final chapters Holbach's tone becomes more and more exalted: 'chaleur', 'attendrissement', and 'sentiment' infuse the style increasingly, and finally there is a hymn or prayer to Nature, from which it seems evident that he has not outgrown all religious sentiment, but rather transferred it to another divinity. I shall quote the passage in the original, in order to convey its quality more precisely:

> 'O Nature! souveraine de tous les êtres! et vous ses filles adorables vertu, raison, vérité! soyez à jamais nos seules Divinités; c'est à vous que sont dus l'encens et les hommages de la terre. Montre-nous donc, ô nature! ce que l'homme doit faire pour obtenir le bonheur que tu lui fais désirer.... Inspirez du courage à l'être intelligent; donnez-lui de l'énergie; qu'il ose enfin s'aimer, s'estimer, sentir sa dignité; qu'il ose s'affranchir, qu'il soit heureux et libre, qu'il ne soit jamais l'esclave que de vos loix; qu'il perfectionne son sort; qu'il chérisse ses semblables; qu'il jouisse lui-même, qu'il fasse jouir les autres.' [1]

This was the book which Goethe, recalling his youthful revulsion from the spirit of eighteenth century France, described as 'so gloomy, so Cimmerian, so deathlike, that we found it difficult to endure its presence, and shuddered at it as at a spectre'.[2] There was, indeed, one 'Romantic' poet—the one in whom the spirit of the eighteenth century philosophers most clearly survives, though imaginatively transfigured—who read it with enthusiasm in his youth. In his notes to *Queen Mab*, Shelley quotes from the *Système de la Nature* two passages, one demonstrating the rigid necessity controlling all seemingly 'chance' phenomena in Nature, and the other exposing the origin, and denouncing the inadequacy, of the popular notion of God. But ten years later (1822) he wrote that the doctrines of the French materialists 'are as false as they

[1] *ibid.*, vol. ii, p. 415.

[2] *Poetry and Truth* (Bohn ed., translation by Miss M. Steele Smith), vol. ii, p. 38.

are pernicious; but still they are better than Christianity, inasmuch as anarchy is better than despotism'. Shelley never lost the passion for human improvement which ennobled eighteenth century materialism, but his repudiation of that philosophy is typical of the spiritual reaction which accompanied, and largely produced, the best poetry of the next era. We shall see something analogous in Wordsworth's rejection of Godwin, and in the modifications which Godwin himself—the chief English exponent of Holbach's ideas—afterwards introduced into his original system.

CHAPTER X

Joseph Priestley and the Socinian Moonlight

'Socinianism, moonlight; methodism, a stove. O for some sun to unite heat and light!' [Coleridge, *Anima Poetae.*]

COMING back to England, we encounter once again in Priestley, the follower of Hartley, what I called above that typically English phenomenon of the period, 'the holy alliance between science and religion'. Priestley belongs to the present story, not so much as the chief apostle of modern Unitarianism but as the last representative of the fusion of two main currents in English life and thought: the mechanical philosophy and the traditional spirit of Protestant Dissent. It does not enter into my present scheme to speak of the Methodist stove, but without some reference to the Socinian moonlight our picture of natural religion in the eighteenth century would be incomplete. We have spoken of the Deists and the physico-theologians, and it is needless to repeat how widespread was the belief, amongst the educated in this century, in the validity, if not the all-sufficiency, of 'natural' religion. But with the Deists 'Nature' came before 'religion', whereas with Priestley, physicist and chemist as he was, it was the reverse. In approaching Priestley we enter (to repeat the insolent phrase) 'the Protestant underworld', and indeed, for the student of life and thought, his voluminous works are mainly important because they show how the mind of English Dissent matured into an autumn inflorescence in the chilly climate of eighteenth century rationalism. In the seventeenth century, before the coming of toleration, the Church was often more 'liberal' in doctrine than the sects, but now that toleration had reduced the theological temperature and diminished the need for credal rigidity, the Establishment necessarily remained nominally orthodox, while the sects were free to follow the contemporary stream of tendency towards a more and more explicit liberalism. In orthodox quarters theology could not develop in genuine harmony with the spirit of the age; it remained, perforce, a Gothic shrine in a Palladian basilica. The Dissenters of this century, on the other hand, were men who had accepted the political and social disabilities of nonconformity, and had therefore nothing to lose in following, wherever it led, what seemed to them to be the light of truth. It is for such reasons that Priestley can illustrate, more completely than Horsley or Paley, the last developments of religious thought within the limits of the 'Nature'-philosophy of the century.

In the variety and scope of his interests Priestley recalls the Renaissance rather than the age of specialization. In the histories of science he figures as the distinguished discoverer of oxygen (though he persisted in regarding the new gas as 'dephlogisticated air'), nitric and nitrous oxide, and the absorption of carbon dioxide ('fixed air') by chlorophyll in sunlight. He was made a Fellow of the Royal Society for his *History of Electricity*, and became the honoured friend or acquaintance of many of the most eminent scientists and philosophers of the time, both in England and France, consorting in London with men like Franklin, Pringle and Price, in Paris with Lavoisier, Morellet, Turgot, and the Encyclopédistes, or at Birmingham with Erasmus Darwin, Day, Edgeworth and the other members of the Lunar Society. Before the Birmingham riots his collection of 'philosophical instruments' was one of the best in the world. But Priestley's science, though he revelled with boyish ingenuousness in his experiments, was always a side-interest. Religion was the core of his life, and the propagation of what he believed to be true Christianity was the main object of his labours. His miscellaneous works, which extend to upwards of twenty volumes, include writings on Church History (e.g. the *History of the Corruptions of Christianity*, 1782, and the *History of Early Opinions Concerning Jesus Christ*, 1786),

Metaphysics (*Disquisitions Relating to Matter and Spirit*, 1777), Politics (*Essay on the First Principles of Government*, 1768), together with Lectures on History, two works on English Grammar, and innumerable tracts, treatises, and letters on moral, political, and theological subjects. Bentham acknowledged his indebtedness to Priestley's *Essay on Government* for suggesting to him the 'greatest happiness principle'. And all the while, except for his period of seven years as librarian and secretary to Lord Shelburne, and his last years of retirement in America, Priestley was actively engaged as minister of religion or schoolmaster, or both at once. Priestley's incessant transitions between religion and philosophy, and his diffuse productivity as a writer, suggest, what is indeed the fact, that his mind was comprehensive rather than profound. He does not qualify for the first rank in any one field, except perhaps in 'pneumatic chemistry', and even here his results were correctly interpreted not by himself but by Lavoisier. But through this very versatility his work becomes interesting as a compendium of contemporary notions, and it would be hard to find a better representative of what was admirable in the mind and spirit of the late eighteenth century. Though his style lacks distinction, his transparent candour, the noble singleness of his aim, and the innocence of his life, compel admiration. Priestley was one of those who have believed that Truth was attainable, that it should be unceasingly pursued, that it need only be declared to be acknowledged, and that its promulgation must make for the glory of God and the relief of man's estate. Like Hartley, Priestley believed in progress and perfectibility, and he never doubted that a dawn, in which it would be bliss to be alive, was even then breaking upon his own generation. This confidence gives a characteristic buoyancy, and, the modern reader may feel, a certain pathos, to the tone of all his writings. 'The morning is opening upon us,' he writes in 1782, 'and we cannot doubt but that the light will increase, and extend itself more and more unto the perfect day. Happy are they who contribute to diffuse the pure light of this everlasting gospel.'[1] This was written of religious enlightenment, but for him all truth had religious value, and he worked at his philosophical instruments in the same spirit. In the Preface to his first volume on Air he says that scientific experiment reminds him of 'Pope's description of travelling among the Alps, with this difference, that here there is not only a *succession*, but an *increase* of new objects and difficulties', for 'the works of God are, like himself, infinite and inexhaustible'.[2] The progress of scientific knowledge, he continues, will put an end

> 'to all undue and usurped authority in the business of *religion*, as well as of *science*; and all the efforts of the interested friends of corrupt establishments of all kinds will be ineffectual for their support in this enlightened age; though, by retarding their downfall, they may make the final ruin of them more complete and glorious. It was ill policy in Leo the X to patronize polite literature. He was cherishing an enemy in disguise. And the English hierarchy (if there be any thing unsound in its constitution) has equal reason to tremble even at an air pump, or an electrical machine.'[3]

Priestley's visit to Paris in 1774 has a certain symbolic value, for it illustrates with special clearness the contrast referred to above, between the outlook of English and French philosophers at the time. Priestley, the Yorkshire Nonconformist, at the table of Holbach and of Turgot!—this is indeed a juxtaposition for the historical imagination to dwell upon. Priestley had been forewarned, so that it was the *philosophes*, and not he, who received the shock. 'As I was sufficiently apprised of the fact', he writes in his *Memoirs*,

> 'I did not wonder, as I otherwise should have done, to find all the philosophical persons to whom I was introduced at Paris, unbelievers in Christianity, and even professed atheists. As I

[1] *History of the Corruptions of Christianity*: Works (ed. Rutt), vol. v, p. 4.
[2] Quoted by Anne Holt, *Joseph Priestley*, p. 97.
[3] *ibid.*, p. 98.

> chose on all occasions to appear as a Christian, I was told by some of them that I was the only person they had ever met with, of whose understanding they had any opinion, who professed to believe Christianity. But on interrogating them on the subject, I soon found that they had given no proper attention to it, and did not really know what Christianity was.'[1]

When he was dining with Turgot, M. de Chastellux told him that

> 'the two gentlemen opposite me were the Bishop of Aix and the Archbishop of Toulouse, "but", said he, "they are no more believers than you or I". I assured him that I was a believer; but he would not believe me; and Le Roi, the philosopher, told me that I was the only man of sense he knew that was a Christian.'[2]

In England, Priestley's more normal avocation was to defend 'Christianity' against the 'Christians', and it is a queer spectacle to find him championing it against the infidel with arguments which the orthodox would have condemned as heretical. However, there were infidels at home as well as at the 'Café de l'Europe', and Priestley, always ready to fight on two fronts alternately, hoped to 'combat their prejudices with some advantage' also. He deals with Gibbon as he did with the philosophical persons in Paris; Gibbon does not know what Christianity itself really is—he only knows what for too many centuries, alas! it has unfortunately seemed to be.

> 'I can truly say that the greatest satisfaction I receive from the success of my philosophical pursuits arises from the weight it may give to my attempts to defend Christianity, and to free it from those corruptions which prevent its reception with philosophical and thinking persons, whose influence with the vulgar and unthinking is very great.'[3]

His advantage, then, in tackling Gibbon, is that he is not obliged, like the orthodox apologist, to defend the 'superstitious' outworks of Christianity. He grants freely

[1] *Memoirs* (Centenary ed.), p. 48.
[2] *Early Life of S. Rogers*, p. 266, quoted by A. Holt, *op. cit.*, p. 94.
[3] *Memoirs*, p. 49.

that no historical evidence and no miracles could prove such doctrines as the incarnation, the atonement, or the Trinity:

> 'They are things that no miracles can prove. As soon should I propose to him the belief of Mahomet's journey to the third heavens, and all his conversations with God while a pitcher of water was falling, or the doctrine of transubstantiation, neither of which are more absurd, and both of them are much more innocent.'[1]

Mr Gibbon should learn to distinguish between Christianity and its corruptions:

> 'Hitherto he seems to have been acquainted with nothing but the corrupt establishments of what is very improperly called Christianity; whereas it is incumbent upon him to read and study the New Testament for himself. . . . Had Mr Gibbon lived in France, Spain or Italy, he might, with the same reason, have ranked the doctrine of transubstantiation, and the worship of saints and angels, among the essentials of Christianity, as the doctrines of the Trinity and of atonement.'[2]

What, then, in Priestley's view, was this 'genuine and rational' Christianity, which needed rescuing from the pseudo-Christians and recommending to the unbelievers? In order to answer this question I propose first to refer briefly to Priestley's metaphysical views and then to give an outline of the development of his religious beliefs, a development which is sufficiently representative to be of general interest.

2

MATTER AND SPIRIT

We may illustrate Priestley's metaphysical position from his *Disquisitions Relating to Matter and Spirit* and *The Doctrine of Philosophical Necessity Illustrated* (1777), both

[1] *History of the Corruptions*: Works, vol. v, p. 492.
[2] *ibid.*, vol. v, p. 493.

composed at Calne while he was in the service of Lord Shelburne. Priestley had read Hartley as a youth, and had been so deeply impressed by him that in 1775 he republished the *Observations on Man*, omitting, however, most of the anatomical as well as the theological matter. He did this because, like Hartley himself, he believed that the theory of the association of ideas would stand firm in isolation, and he was anxious to promote its acceptance. In producing this edition, Priestley became an important link in the transmission of Hartley's ideas to the nineteenth century. In one of the Three Dissertations prefixed to this work, Priestley had 'expressed some doubt of the immateriality of the sentient principle in man; and the outcry that was made on what I casually expressed on that subject can hardly be imagined. In all the newspapers, and most of the periodical publications, I was represented as an unbeliever in revelation, and no better than an Atheist'.[1] It was mainly to clarify his position on these issues that he wrote his *Disquisitions* two years later.

The main purpose of the *Disquisitions* was to combine a thorough-going materialist theory of man with what Priestley understood by 'genuine' Christianity. In reading it, especially after reading Holbach, one may share the astonishment of M. de Chastellux that such seeming incompatibles should be found thus conjoined. Priestley goes further than Hartley, indeed he is at one with Holbach, in accepting the full doctrine of the materiality of man. But he would not be Priestley if he did not profess also to be aiming, throughout, at 'the firm establishment of the system of *pure Revelation*, in opposition to that of a vain and absurd *philosophy*'. In order to attain his end he sees that he must remove from 'matter' the odium attaching to it from its supposed sluggishness, solidity, and the like. Once this is done, the distinction between matter and 'spirit' ceases to be important, and 'matter' will no longer seem incompatible with 'thought' or 'sensation'. It was with the inertness and impenetrability of matter

[1] *Memoirs*, p. 52.

that sensation and thought were always held to be irreconcilable; but matter is neither inert nor impenetrable. It is not inert, for powers of attraction and repulsion are inherent in it, and are the true causes of its so-called 'solidity' and 'resistance'. Priestley claims, then, that his kind of materialism is one from which 'the reproach of matter is wiped off'.[1] He proceeds boldly to deny the existence of a separate immaterial 'soul', and to accept all (or all but one) of the implications of this denial. Thought and sensation are never found but in connexion with an organized system of matter. The brain is the seat of thought, and there is no recorded instance of thought surviving the destruction of the brain. This system avoids all the difficulties (which Priestley rehearses) arising out of the Cartesian dualism of mind and body. It is a gross error, he agrees, to suppose that 'the vibrations of the brain are themselves the perceptions'. The correct view is that 'the brain, besides its vibrating power, has superadded to it a percipient or sentient power, likewise'; and he reproves Locke for seeing this possibility and yet clinging to an immaterial soul. Locke should have had the courage or consistency to declare for a full materialism.

Why, one may ask, should this Christian philosopher have been so zealous to destroy the soul, hitherto the corner-stone of the religious fabric? Once again we must remember that Priestley's characteristic method of defending 'Christianity' was to expose and remove its 'corruptions', which for him included nearly everything considered by the orthodox to be of its very essence. The notion of the soul as a substance distinct from the body, he continues, was 'part of the system of heathenism, and was from thence introduced into Christianity which has derived the greatest part of its corruptions from this source'.[2] This thought, which, as we shall see, he developed more fully in his later writings on the history of Christian corruptions, furnishes the main clue to his advocacy of

[1] *Disquisitions* (1777 ed.), p. 109. [2] *ibid.*, p. 31.

materialism. He hoped that materialism, when properly defined and understood, so far from leading to the atheism of a Holbach, would enable him to rescue Christianity from all the accretions which, as a Unitarian, he wished to be rid of, and especially the doctrine of the pre-existence of Christ the demiurge. Further, 'the common opinion of the soul of man surviving the body was (as will be shown) introduced in Christianity from the Oriental and Greek philosophy, which in many respects exceedingly altered and debased the true Christian system'.[1] Priestley was a mortalist of the same type as Milton; at death we die wholly. But here again we must note the eclecticism of Priestley's thought; in spite of all his heresies he always deferred to Scripture as he understood it, and the general resurrection at the Last Day was one of the teachings which he took to be incontestably scriptural. Hobbes and Milton had already used the Resurrection for the same purpose; both they, and Priestley after them, found that by removing immortality to this safe and miraculous distance they could combine materialism with the faith. What rises again must have died, and what has died is the whole man. What has decomposed may be recomposed by the being who first composed it, and this will probably be effected, not by a miracle, but by some natural law unknown to us. This doctrine, he claims, frees us from many of the traditional difficulties; we are dispensed, for instance, from enquiring when, exactly, the soul enters the body, or whether there are unbodied souls waiting their turn for incarnation, or whether the animals will rise again at the Last Day (many of them deserve it, he quaintly adds, after all they have undergone in this life). Priestley, whose constant use of the historical method is one of his claims to distinction, does not leave his subject without offering a historical sketch of the origin and growth of opinions about the soul and the state of the dead. 'Immateriality' in the strict sense is a *modern* notion: 'It is no article of faith that I am oppugning, but really an upstart

[1] *ibid.*, p. 156.

thing, and a nonentity.' He sums up in a passage which may deserve full quotation:

> 'The modern idea of an immaterial *being* is by no means the same thing that was so denominated by the ancients; it being well known to the learned . . . that what the ancients meant by an immaterial being, was only a *finer kind* of what we should now call matter; something like air or *breath*, which first supplied a name for the *soul*, or else like *fire* or *flame*, which was probably suggested by the *warmth* of the living body. Consequently the ancients did not exclude from mind the property of *extension*, and *local presence*. It had, in their idea, some common properties with matter, was capable of being united to it, of acting and being acted upon by it, and of moving from place to place along with it.
>
> 'But it was justly considered by the moderns, that such an immaterial substance as this was, in fact, no immaterial substance at all, but a material one; it being the opinion of all modern philosophers (though it was unknown to the ancients) that all matter is ultimately the same thing, all kinds of bodies differing from one another only in the *size* or *arrangement* of their ultimate particles, or atoms. It was therefore seen, that if the powers of sensation or thought could belong to such a material substance as the ancients had denominated an immaterial one . . . it might be imparted to the very grossest matter; . . . and therefore that the *soul* and *body*, being in reality the same kind of substance, must die together.
>
> 'To avoid this conclusion, of which divines entertained a very unreasonable dread, they refined upon the former notion of spirit, excluding from it every property which it held in common with matter; making it, in the strict metaphysical sense of the term, an *immaterial thing*, without extension, that is, occupying no portion of space and therefore bearing no relation to it; and consequently incapable of motion from one place to another, etc.' [1]

The Scriptures, Priestley finds it possible to say, do not teach the doctrine of a separable soul. His materialism is on all grounds unassailable, because it is not unscriptural, because his 'matter' is 'as immaterial as any one could wish for', and because it leaves untouched the true foundations of religious faith. No proofs of man's materiality

[1] *ibid.*, p. 222.

can be applied to God, whose 'essence' must remain unknown to us. Meanwhile the evidences for God's existence and power stand firm:

> 'I have all the foundation that the nature of things admits of for a firm belief in a first, eternal, unchangeable and intelligent cause of all things; and I have all the proof that can be given of his almighty power, infinite goodness, and constant providence. And this system of *natural religion* affords all the foundation that can be had in support of revealed religion, the history of which is contained in the books of scripture, which I most cordially and thankfully receive.'[1]

2

THE DOCTRINE OF PHILOSOPHIC NECESSITY

In *The Doctrine of Philosophic Necessity Illustrated* (1777) Priestley again enlarges upon Hartley. He writes of Necessity in a rapturous tone, referring, in his Dedication to Dr John Jebb, to 'these great and just views of the glorious system to which we belong'. It may seem strange, though it is an evident characteristic of this period, that belief in Necessity should have been part of the creed of those who were the most ardent exponents of political, intellectual, and religious Liberty. To accept Necessity meant to accept the scientific view of the universe; it meant the acceptance of those unalterable laws which preserve the stars from wrong, and the rejection of superstition and the supernatural. It was therefore indispensable to all who entertained 'enlightened and just' views of Nature. Priestley, like Hartley before him and Godwin after him, knows how to turn his Necessity to glorious gain, though, again like them, he may not always seem quite consistent in his attempt to make a virtue of it.

In denying what he calls 'philosophical liberty' Priestley is simply denying the possibility of arbitrary caprice, or

[1] *ibid.*, p. 152.

'chance' decisions. We cannot act without 'motive'. Identical causes must always produce identical effects; placed in the same circumstances (including my state of mind, outlook, etc.) I must always act in the same manner. A 'good' man is one who is determined by 'good' motives; a bad man, one who is determined by bad motives. Like the other necessitarians, he tries to 'have it both ways': a farmer who through fatalism is neglectful of his labours, is told that if he is fated to eat he is also fated to plough and to sow. Yet one of the advantages of Necessitarianism is said to be that it produces resignation, since whatever is, is right:

> 'So long as we can practically believe that there is but *one will* in the whole universe, that this one will, exclusive of all *Chance*, or the interference of any other will, disposes of all things, even to their minutest circumstances, and always for the best of purposes, it is impossible but that we must rejoice in, and be thankful for, all events, without distinction.'[1]

It is interesting to find Priestley comparing this philosophic creed of his manhood with the Calvinism in which he had been brought up. Necessity, he would persuade us, makes for morality where Calvinism undermines it, since Necessity represents all our actions as due to ourselves (i.e. our susceptibility to 'motives'), while Calvinism removes all into the hands of God. He seems in fact to be using, in criticism of predestination, the very arguments usually brought against Necessitarianism. Under Calvinism, he says in effect, you cannot urge anyone to turn from his wickedness and live: under Necessity you can and must. Why? Because men's conduct follows necessarily from their motives, and you can supply them, by persuasion, with ever better and better motives. His emphasis is thus placed not on the passive or submissive aspect of the doctrine—though he will sometimes use this as the chief consolation of philosophy—but on the active, scientific manipulation of circumstances so as to produce

[1] *Philosophical Necessity* (1777), Dedication, p. xii.

'improvement'. Some might argue that precisely herein—that we *can* change circumstances as well as merely react mechanically to them—lies our 'freedom'; but for Priestley (in this context) freedom only meant caprice, whim, action arbitrarily disjoined from causation. I think that Priestley underestimates, in his theory, the possibility of change or rebirth, though his argument implies its importance. Doubtless an avaricious or selfish man will always behave avariciously or selfishly, provided that his disposition and environment remain constant; but if and when he turns from the unrighteousness that he has committed, what has happened? The same stimuli now produce opposite results, because his state of mind has altered. For Priestley this would mean, I suppose, that another set of motives has now increased in strength, so that a new type of behaviour is necessarily produced. But this is just what distinguishes man from a billiard-ball: the latter responds unvaryingly to the same forces, whereas man may be 'converted'. This, it might be argued, is an account of man's 'freedom': not that he can will things 'arbitrarily', but that he can submit himself to higher and higher types of 'necessity'—his highest 'freedom' consisting, shall we say, in the most complete submission to moral law, Nature, or, if the phrase of Hartley be preferred, to God as All in All. Hartley seemed to teach that the mere passage through life must needs generate godliness, but he, like Priestley and the other perfectibilist necessitarians (and like ourselves), knew that this is not so, but that we must take thought, and exert ourselves continually, to approach perfection. Priestley seems to feel that he has dodged the difficulty when he writes:

> 'With respect to the temper and disposition of mind, considered in a *moral respect*, a man has, certainly, more encouragement to take pains to improve it, when he is sensible that, according to the settled constitution, and established laws of nature, it depends *entirely upon himself* whether it be improved or not.' [1]

---

[1] *ibid.*, p. 97.

But what he further subjoins on the subject of Calvinism is also, I think, applicable to Necessitarianism:

> 'I cannot, however, conclude this section without acknowledging . . . that though I consider the proper Calvinistic system as a most *gloomy* one, and particularly unfavourable to virtue, it is only so when *consistently pursued*, and when every part equally impresses the mind. But this is never, in fact, the case with any system. If there be in our minds a *prevalence of good principles* and good dispositions, we naturally turn our eyes from everything in our respective systems that, even by a just construction, is unfavourable to virtue and goodness, and we reflect with pleasure, and act upon, those parts of them only that have a good tendency.'[1]

For Priestley and those like him, 'Necessity' had come to be associated with Truth and Enlightenment, just as Calvinism was associated with Error and Superstition, and he could accordingly turn his eyes from everything in his own system that might seem 'unfavourable to virtue', while remaining alive to the same dangers in the teaching of others.

3

PRIESTLEY'S RELIGIOUS OUTLOOK

'I think', says Coleridge in the *Table Talk*, 'Priestley must be considered the author of the modern Unitarianism', and this is broadly true, if, by emphasizing the word 'modern', we understand Coleridge to have intended to distinguish Unitarianism as an English nonconformist sect from the Unitarianism of Socinus, or of Christ and the Apostles (who according to Priestley were the first Unitarians). But Priestley in his development from Calvinism to Unitarianism merely illustrates in epitome what was going on widely amongst the dissenting congregations in the eighteenth century. By 'dissenting congregations' is chiefly meant the worshippers—Presbyterian,

[1] *ibid.*, pp. 161-2.

Independent, and Baptist—in the thousand (or thereabouts) meeting-houses which were built during the thirty years following the Toleration Act. These congregations, it must be emphasized, were originally quite orthodox in doctrine—often, indeed, more strictly orthodox than the Church which had produced Arminians and Latitudinarians, and which now countenanced Dr Samuel Clarke. They remained separate from the Church either because they objected to the principle of a State Establishment, or because they disapproved of certain rites and ceremonies contained in the Prayer-Book. But, as suggested above, these dissenters, having no social or political persuasives to orthodoxy (they were disqualified for all public preferment, and for graduating at Oxford and Cambridge), were exposed in a unique degree to the contemporary winds of doctrine, and, most of their chapels having been founded on the principle of the 'open Trust' (they were licensed simply 'for the worship of Almighty God', or 'for the purpose of divine worship'), there was nothing to prevent them from becoming, as many of them did, more and more 'liberal'. Nor is this surprising, for these people, the descendants of the Puritans, were naturally disposed to welcome whatever made for 'liberty' in every sphere, and in religion, now that the battle for toleration was at least partly won, 'liberty' necessarily meant the ever-increasing rationalization of belief. Dissent was traditionally based on Scripture rather than on creed, and the Scriptures—that is to say, a whole body of literature—could be made to harmonize, much more readily than the creeds, with the intellectual predispositions of the eighteenth century. Methodism and the Evangelical movement, which really belong to the reaction against all that the eighteenth century stood for, checked the progress of 'rational' dissent; but before their impact was fully felt many of the congregations had 'lapsed' through Arianism into Unitarianism. The Unitarianism of the last quarter of the eighteenth century, indeed, came very close to the Deism of the earlier decades; it differed mainly in origin and organization. Deism was largely the perquisite of 'gentlemen', Unitarianism was bourgeois. Deism was professed by isolated free-thinkers, while the Unitarian Congregation, having evolved by imperceptible stages from the older forms of dissent, retained a strong group-consciousness as a religious fellowship. 'The generation of the modern worldly Dissenter was thus', says Coleridge, 'Presbyterian, Arian, Socinian, and last Unitarian'.[1] No one, especially after reading Professor Tawney's *Religion and the Rise of Capitalism*, need deny that Puritanism could and did generate, or degenerate into, worldliness, losing its original religious impulse and forgetting good works in its passion for (financially profitable) hard work. But Protestant Dissent was not the only form of religion which became worldly in the eighteenth century, and it was unfair of Coleridge to imply that the Unitarian was the worldliest of the series. Perhaps his remark is connected with his having professed Unitarianism himself as a young man, and then, as he puts it, to his having 'gone much further than the Unitarians, and so having come round to the other side'.[2] At any rate, it can be truthfully affirmed of men like Priestley and Lindsey that, so far from being worldly-wise, they were prepared to sacrifice everything dear for the sake of what they deemed to be 'truth'. The epithet 'worldly' seems more applicable to those who would have loved the same 'truth' just as much, had they not loved 'honour' more. The Unitarianism of Priestley and Lindsey must seem cold to those who seek in religion for colour, and symbol, and ecstasy, but in its combination of 'moonlight'-illumination with religious conviction it remains one of the most characteristic, and not the least admirable, of the products of the English eighteenth century.

Priestley, son of a Yorkshire cloth-dresser of the Independent persuasion, was brought up, he tells us,[3] 'with sentiments of piety, but without bigotry'. His aunt, Mrs

[1] *Table Talk* (Oxford ed.), p. 311. [2] *ibid.*, p. 308.
[3] In his *Memoirs*, from which ensuing phrases are quoted.

Keighley, who was responsible for his education, was 'truly Calvinistic in principle, but was far from confining salvation to those who thought as she did on religious subjects. Being left in good circumstances, her home was the resort of all the Dissenting ministers in the neighbourhood without distinction, and those who were the most obnoxious on account of their heresy were almost as welcome to her, if she thought them good and hónest men . . ., as any others'. With Mr Walker, one of the most heretical of these (that is to say, a 'rational Christian'), who was also an excellent classical scholar, Priestley struck up a lasting friendship, receiving from him frequent letters in the Latin language, and a legacy of £200 when he died. As a child he was of sickly constitution, and happening at this time to read some 'books of *experiences*', he fell into great distress of mind, to which in later life he always looked back with horror. Though he retained, from these Bunyanesque agonies, 'a deep reverence for divine things', the recollection of them gave him 'a peculiar sense of the value of rational principles in religion', and of the importance of always inculcating 'just views of things, assuring ourselves that proper feelings and right conduct will be the consequence of them'. Mainly as a result of his ill-health, he made extraordinary progress at his books, and before going to the 'Academy' he had acquired—partly at home and partly at various schools, but also from certain learned Dissenting ministers—'a pretty good knowledge' of Greek, Latin, Hebrew, French, Italian, 'High Dutch', Chaldee and Syriac, geometry and algebra; and he had also read some philosophy and logic. Before he left home he had already shown 'heretical' tendencies, and was refused admittance as a communicant in his congregation because he was unsound on the subject of the sin of Adam. In spite of his early unorthodoxies and his later changes of opinion he always acknowledged a great debt to his early religious training, and the picture he draws of the life of his congregation may usefully remind us how vigorously the business of religion was still attended to, in the heart of the 'age of reason', in Dissenting circles quite untouched by Methodism. There were catechizings, almost daily meetings of some part of the congregation, and great strictness in the keeping of the Lord's Day. 'No victuals were dressed on that day in any family. No member of it was permitted to walk out for recreation, but the whole of the day was spent at the public meeting, or at home in reading, meditation, and prayer.' Priestley was himself so serious-minded that he had 'a great aversion to plays and romances', and once seeing his brother Timothy 'reading a book of Knight-errantry' he snatched it out of his hands with great indignation and threw it away. (The unfortunate Timothy afterwards became, 'if possible, more serious than I had been', and 'after an imperfect education'—as Priestley writes, perhaps not without fraternal malice—'took up the profession of a minister among the Independents'.) Priestley left home for the 'Academy' an Arminian, but he had as yet 'by no means rejected the doctrine of the Trinity or that of the Atonement'.

The Dissenting 'Academies', it has been said, 'were the greatest schools of their day. During a period when the grammar schools slept and the Universities were sterile', they were 'thoroughly alive and active'. At a time when, according to Gibbon, the Oxford dons had absolved their consciences from the toil of reading, thinking, writing, and teaching, 'while their dull and deep potations increased the intemperance of youth', and when unreformed Cambridge, according to Chesterfield, was 'sunk in the lowest obscurity', these Academies were the real centres of higher education in England. They were open to all, without oath or subscription, and Anglicans as well as Dissenters attended them. The Daventry Academy, to which Priestley went in 1752, was the successor to the Northampton Academy in which Philip Doddridge, the most celebrated of the eighteenth century tutors, had taught and ministered from 1729 to 1751. Like the congregations, these Colleges were evolving with the times towards theological liberty. Doddridge himself was orthodox, but his daughter could say of him that 'the orthodoxy my father taught his children was charity', and he himself declared that he loved and honoured 'every benevolent and useful man in society', 'whether he be or be not a Christian'.[1] 'In my time', says Priestley, 'the academy was in a state peculiarly favourable to the serious pursuit of truth, as the students were about equally divided upon every question of much importance.... Our tutors also were of different opinions, Dr Ashworth [Doddridge's successor] taking the orthodox side of every question, and Mr Clark, the sub-tutor, that of heresy, though always with the greatest modesty.' Here Priestley first came under the influence of Hartley, to whom he ascribes a decisive and beneficial influence upon his whole future development. The *Observations on Man*, he declares,

> 'established me in the belief of the doctrine of Necessity, which I first learned from Collins; it greatly improved that disposition to piety which I brought to the Academy, and freed it from the rigour with which it had been tinctured. Indeed, I do not know whether the consideration of Dr Hartley's theory contributes more to enlighten the mind or improve the heart: it effects both in so supereminent a degree.'

In spite of the freedom of discussion here encouraged, 'the extreme of heresy among us was Arianism', and Priestley left Daventry with a 'more or less qualified' belief in the Atonement.

It is not to our purpose to follow Priestley's subsequent career in any detail, but merely to indicate some significant points in the development of his views. At Needham Market, where he conducted his first ministry for three years, he became convinced, after 'much pains and thought', of the falsity of the doctrine of the Atonement, and his examination of St Paul's epistles satisfied him

[1] The foregoing references are quoted by Gow, *The Unitarians* (1928), ch. x, *q.v.*

that the apostle's reasoning 'was in many places far from being conclusive'. He had not yet studied the Socinian doctrine, but his Arianism was enough to antagonize his flock, and he removed to Nantwich. Here he ran a school as well as a chapel, and earned enough to purchase his first 'philosophical instruments'. In 1760 Priestley was appointed tutor in languages at the famous Warrington Academy, under the principalship of Dr Aikin, the father of Mrs Barbauld. Here he was once again in congenial society; the tutors were all Arians and Necessitarians, and not even some 'obscure notions' of Dr Aikin's on the subject of Atonement could disturb their unanimity. It was while here, too, that he was introduced to Price and Franklin in London, wrote his *History of Electricity*, and became a Fellow of the Royal Society. The next stage in Priestley's theological progress was reached during his ministry at the Mill Hill chapel, Leeds, where he succeeded the Rev. Thomas Walker in 1767. Here, by reading Lardner's *Letter on the Logos*, he became 'what is called a Socinian', which may be taken to mean, in the eighteenth century, a Unitarian—one who holds that God is the only proper object of worship, and who rejects the Trinitarian doctrine of Christ's divinity, and the Arian doctrine of his pre-existence. The chief events of this period were Priestley's efforts to reanimate the waning zeal of his flock, and the attempt—significant of the times, though of course unsuccessful—by Archdeacon Blackburne, the Rev. Theophilus Lindsey (Priestley's close friend), and other Anglican clergymen, to obtain legal relief from subscription to articles in which they had ceased to believe. The main outcome of the movement was the secession of Lindsey, and his establishment of the first avowedly Unitarian chapel, in Essex Street, Strand. Of Lindsey, Priestley speaks with the warmest affection. 'To his society', he says, 'I owe much of my zeal for the doctrine of the divine unity, for which he made so great sacrifices, and in the defence of which he so much distinguished himself, so as to occasion a new era in the history of religion in this country.'

The seven years following Priestley's ministry at Leeds was the period (1773-80) of his employment with Shelburne, to which reference has already been made. It was devoted mainly to scientific and philosophical work. At this time, during the winter he spent in London, he improved his acquaintance with Benjamin Franklin. He much regretted that Franklin, with his good character and great influence, should have been an unbeliever, and he recommended him some good reading on the evidences of Christianity (selected portions of Hartley, and his own *Institutes of Natural and Revealed Religion*). But the American war intervened, and Franklin ceased to have leisure enough to be converted.

Next followed what he calls 'the happiest event of my life', his settlement in Birmingham as minister of the New Meeting. This was 'highly favourable to every object I had in view, philosophical or theological'. Here he had the society of scientific friends, including James Watt the inventor, Withering the botanist, Erasmus Darwin, and the other members of the Lunar Society; and he had, moreover, the 'most liberal' congregation in England. Soon after he settled in Birmingham he wrote his *History of the Corruptions of Christianity* (1782), a work which is sufficiently representative of his mature outlook, and of which I propose, therefore, to give a brief account.

As we have seen, the 'corruptions' of Christianity included, for Priestley, most of what had been considered its fundamental doctrines: the Trinity, the Miraculous Conception, Original Sin, Predestination, the Atonement, the plenary inspiration of Scripture. In the Preface he explains, as no doubt he did to M. de Chastellux and M. Le Roi, and as he did at the conclusion of the book to Mr Gibbon, that it is only these corruptions that prevent the universal acceptance of Christianity; that the corruptions occasion justifiable indifference in those who are not Christians, and righteous indignation in those who are; and that the only course now is to preserve Christianity by exposing the falsehood of 'what has so long passed for Christianity' and demonstrating 'what is truly so'. The argument has a familiar ring: it had been used by the Protestant reformers, by Herbert of Cherbury, by the Cambridge Platonists, by Blount and Locke and Toland, and it was to be used again by Matthew Arnold and by some 'modern churchmen' of the latter days. Coming from Priestley, however, it has a peculiar force, for Priestley was a pastor of acknowledged zeal and purity of life, and could by no means be accused of merely critical or destructive intentions. He speaks, too, for liberalism at its most hopeful and heroic phase, when revolutionary possibilities were opening on all sides, and human nature seemed about to be born anew. Something of the rapture of those expansive days sounds through Priestley's otherwise humdrum prose from time to time, as when in his dedicatory address to Lindsey he exclaims: 'The gross darkness of that night which has for many centuries obscured our holy religion, we may clearly see, is past; the morning is opening upon us. . . .'

Priestley's method is a version of the 'primitivism' so often found in the ethical and political theory of the century. He treats all the corruptions historically, and tries to demonstrate that each is a 'departure from the original scheme', Scripture—in this context—playing the part of 'Nature'. Although he rejected the 'plenary inspiration', he still belongs to the 'Scriptural' phase of liberal religious thought; to impugn a doctrine it is still necessary, or sufficient, for him to prove that it is 'no where laid down, or asserted, in the Scriptures'. Good sense and a 'just view of things' are, to be sure, his real standards, but Scripture, often admittedly in natural harmony with these standards, must be made to corroborate them, if necessary by force. The Atonement, for example, is 'unscriptural'. In the first part of the book he gives a historical account (afterwards expanded in another work) of the growth of opinions concerning Jesus Christ. The apostles and the earliest Christians were Unitarians: Christ was, as in Acts ii. 22, 'a man approved by God, by wonders and signs which God did by him', or as in 1 Timothy ii. 5, 'There is one God, and one mediator between God and men, the man Christ Jesus'. Priestley cites Athanasius as saying that the Jews were so firmly persuaded that their Messiah was to be human, that 'the apostles were obliged to use great caution in divulging the doctrine of the proper divinity of Christ'. He goes on: 'but what the apostles did not teach, I think we should be cautious how we believe. The apostles were never backward to combat other Jewish prejudices, and certainly would have opposed this opinion of theirs, if it had been an error.'[1] How, then, has Jesus come to be equated with 'the supreme eternal God, the maker of heaven and earth, and of all things visible and invisible'? The divinizing of Jesus was due to the desire of the 'philosophizing Christians', who were recommending the faith to the Gentiles, to overcome the stumbling-block of the Cross; their object was 'to make the religion of Christ more reputable, by adding to the dignity of our Lord's person'. 'The doctrine of the separate divinity of Christ was at first nothing more than a personification of a divine attribute'—the Logos, or divine Reason. We return to the question posed earlier in this chapter: What, then, did Priestley conceive 'genuine' (which for him is equivalent to 'original') Christianity to have been? He has stated his view of Christianity, in another work, as follows:

'Christianity is less to be considered as a system of opinions, than a rule of life. But of what significance is a rule if it be not complied with? All the doctrines of Christianity have for their object Christian morals, which are none other than the well-known duties of life, and the advantage we derive from this religion is that the principles of it assist us in maintaining that steady regard to the providence of God and to a future state, which facilitates and ensures the practice of those duties, inspiring greater piety towards God, greater benevolence to man, and that heavenly-

[1] *History of the Corruptions*: Works, vol. v, p. 19.

mindedness which raises the heart and the affections above those mean and low pursuits which are the source of almost all vices.'[1]

'The great object of the mission and death of Christ', he says in the work we are considering, was 'to give the fullest proof of a future life of retribution, in order to supply the strongest motives to virtue'.[2] In spite of his materialism and mortalism Priestley believed, as we have seen, in the final resurrection, and he also retained from traditional doctrine the belief in the miracles and the resurrection of Christ. Christ being wholly man, his life and death are to be regarded as examples for us, and his resurrection as a type or earnest of that of all men. Priestley's views are so completely summarized in the General Conclusion, Part I, 'Containing Considerations addressed to Unbelievers, and especially to Mr Gibbon', that I venture to quote from this section at some length:

'To consider the system (if it may be called a system) of Christianity *a priori*, one would think it very little liable to corruption, or abuse. The great outline of it is, that the Universal Parent of Mankind commissioned Jesus Christ to invite men to the practice of virtue, by the assurance of his mercy to the penitent, and of his purpose to raise to immortal life and happiness all the virtuous and good, but to inflict an adequate punishment on the wicked. In proof of this he wrought many miracles, and after a public execution he rose again from the dead. He also directed that proselytes to his religion should be admitted by *baptism*, and that his disciples should eat bread and drink wine in commemoration of his death.

'Here is nothing that any person could imagine would lead to much subtle speculation, at least such as could excite much animosity. . . . And a person unacquainted with the state of things at the time of its promulgation would look in vain for any probable source of the monstrous corruptions and abuses which crept into the system afterwards. . . .

'In reality, however, the causes of the succeeding corruptions

---

[1] Quoted from *The Evidences of Revealed Religion* by W. Lloyd, *Protestant Dissent and English Unitarianism* (1899), p. 184.

[2] *History of the Corruptions*: Works, vol. v, p. 103.

did then exist; and accordingly, without any thing more than their natural operation, all the abuses rose to their full height; and what is more wonderful still, *by the operation of natural causes also, without any miraculous interposition of Providence, we see the abuses gradually corrected, and Christianity recovering its primitive beauty and glory.*[1]

'The causes of the corruptions were almost wholly contained in the established opinions of the heathen world, and especially the philosophical part of it; so that when those Heathens embraced Christianity, they mixed their former tenets and prejudices with it. Also, both Jews and Heathens were so much scandalized at the idea of being the disciples of a man who had been crucified as a common malefactor that Christians in general were sufficiently disposed to adopt any opinion that would most effectually wipe away this reproach.

'The opinion of the mental faculties of man belonging to a substance distinct from his body, or brain, and of this invisible spiritual part, or *soul*, being capable of subsisting before and after its union to the body, which had taken the deepest root in all the schools of philosophy, was wonderfully calculated to answer this purpose. For by this means Christians were enabled to give to the soul of Christ what rank they pleased in the heavenly regions before his incarnation. . . .

'The abuses of the positive institutions of Christianity, monstrous as they were, naturally arose from the opinion of the purifying and sanctifying virtue of rites and ceremonies, which was the very basis of all the worship of the Heathens. . . . We likewise see the rudiments of all the monkish austerities in the opinions and practices of the Heathens, who thought to purify and exalt the soul by macerating and mortifying the body.' [2]

It is noteworthy that Priestley can accept the historical miracles, while rejecting the doctrinal mysteries, of Christianity. He urges Gibbon to consider that Christianity would not have spread as it did if it had not been 'true', and if the miracles had not proved it beyond dispute. If the Gospel history had been untrue, the total subversion of paganism by Christianity would have been more extraordinary than that history itself. 'In short, the question

[1] My italics.

[2] *History of the Corruptions*: Works, vol. v, pp. 480-1.

is, whether Mr Gibbon or myself, believe in more numerous, more extraordinary, or more useless miracles.'

Such, then, was the faith of a representative English 'rational Dissenter' at the time of the outbreak of the French Revolution. In his *Memoirs*, writing in 1787, four years before the 'Church and King' riots in Birmingham, he records his gratitude for having lived 'in an age and country in which I have been at full liberty both to investigate, and by preaching and writing to propagate, religious truth'. The story of those riots is well known, and need not be recounted in any detail here. It was one of the disgraceful episodes of that period of panic and reaction, which for a time curtailed the 'liberty' in which Priestley had been 'singularly happy', and which had been one of the glories of eighteenth century England. He records the event with no elaboration in his *Memoirs*:

> '. . . on occasion of the celebration of the anniversary of the French Revolution, on July 14, 1791, by several of my friends, but with which I had little to do, a mob, encouraged by some persons in power, first burned the Meeting-house in which I preached, then another Meeting-house in the town, and then my dwelling-house, demolishing my library, apparatus, and, as far as they could, every thing belonging to me.'

Three years following this 'effervescence of the public mind', as Pitt euphemistically called it, Priestley set sail for America (April 7, 1794), in the expectation of joining the 'large settlement for the friends of liberty in general, near the head of the Susquehanna', which had been projected by Thomas Cooper and Priestley's son. Exactly one day before Priestley's embarkation S. T. Coleridge secured his discharge from the army, and two months later he was eagerly scheming with Southey and others for the establishment of Pantisocracy on the banks of the same delightful river, which was recommended to him for 'its excessive Beauty, and its security from hostile Indians'.[1]

[1] Letter to Southey, Sept. 6, 1794 (quoted by L. Hanson, *Life of S. T. Coleridge* (1938), p. 52).

Priestley was at this time, next to Hartley, the special Christian hero of Coleridge, and evidently the emigration of the 'patriot, saint and sage', driven with vain hate from his loved native land by 'Statesmen bloodstained and priests idolatrous',[1] gave added zest to the pantisocratic dream. In view of the tone of Coleridge's later references to Priestley the following sonnet, composed in December 1794, is of some significance. It illustrates not only the quality of Coleridge's poetry before his intimacy with Wordsworth, but also the completeness with which Priestley then personified his religious, political, and intellectual ideals:

> Though rous'd by that dark Vizir Riot rude
> Have driven our PRIESTLEY o'er the Ocean swell;
> Though Superstition and her wolfish brood
> Bay his mild radiance, impotent and fell;
> Calm in his halls of brightness he shall dwell!
> For lo! RELIGION at his strong behest
> Starts with mild anger from the Papal spell,
> And flings to Earth her tinsel-glittering vest,
> Her mitred State and cumbrous Pomp unholy;
> And JUSTICE wakes to bid th'Oppressor wail
> Insulting aye the wrongs of patient Folly;
> And from her dark retreat by Wisdom won
> Meek NATURE slowly lifts her matron veil
> To smile with fondness on her gazing Son!

4

POLITICS AND HISTORY

(I)

It will be appropriate to consider now, in conclusion, Priestley's *Essay on the First Principles of Government, and on the Nature of Political, Civil and Religious Liberty* (1768), and his *Lectures on History* (1788). We enter here the eighteenth century stream of liberal political thinking; in

[1] The phrases are from S. T. Coleridge's tribute to Priestley, *Religious Musings* (Dec. 1794), 371.

the immediate background are Locke, Russell, and Sidney, and in the far distance, Harmodius and Aristogiton. Hartley is also there, to supply the psychological basis for perfectibility—a theme on which Priestley writes with more than his accustomed hopefulness. Physical pains and pleasures are transformed by association into intellectual ones, and man attains to larger and larger views, at length approaching the angels in scope, and even dimly glimpsing the divine standpoint from which all partial evil is universal good. Meanwhile

> 'The great instrument in the hand of divine providence, of this progress of society towards improvement, is *society*, and consequently government.' [1]

The economic basis is provided by the principle—on which Adam Smith was so shortly (1776) to enlarge authoritatively—of the division of labour, whereby progress is immensely accelerated. In the same way

> 'all knowledge will be subdivided and extended; and *knowledge*, as Lord Bacon observes, being *power*, the human powers will, in fact, be increased; nature, including both its materials, and its laws, will be more at our command; men will make their situation in this world abundantly more easy and comfortable; they will probably prolong their existence in it, and will grow daily more happy, each in himself, and more able (and, I believe, more disposed) to communicate happiness to others. Thus, *whatever was the beginning of this world, the end will be glorious and paradisaical, beyond what our imaginations can now conceive.*'

Priestley's paradise, it will be observed, lies in the future, not in any antique golden age or state of Nature, and the contemplation of that prospect, he tells us, 'always makes me happy'. It is a Baconian paradise, based on command over Nature, that he here expects, not the Kingdom of God anticipated by Milton in *Of Reformation in England*,[2]

[1] *Essay on Government* (1768), p. 6.

[2] 'When thou, the eternal and shortly expected King . . . shalt put an end to all earthly tyrannies, proclaiming thy universal and mild monarchy through heaven and earth.' (Prose Works, Bohn ed. vol. ii, p. 419.)

yet there is an affinity between these two religious libertarians, and not least in that they both lived to witness, with unconquerable mind, the shattering of their immediate hopes. In our own bad days it is perhaps the 'happiness' of these men, rather than their disappointment, which leaves us mourning.

Priestley distinguishes between 'political' and 'civil' liberty: 'political' liberty is the possession of a voice in the government, or a vote; 'civil', 'the power over their own actions, which the members of the state reserve to themselves, and which their officers must not infringe'. His thesis on political liberty is an expansion of Locke's defence of revolution. Governments exist for the promotion of general utility; where this utility is not being enjoyed, the 'people' must resume their 'natural' liberties and punish or remove their 'servants'. In a large and complex state like ours there is little danger of oft-repeated rebellion on these principles. Priestley is surprised that the utilitarian doctrine should have been so largely overlooked—the principle, that is, that

> 'The good and happiness of the members, that is the majority of the members of any state, is the great standard by which every thing relating to that state must finally be determined. . . .
>
> 'Virtue and right conduct consist in those affections and actions which terminate in the public good; justice and veracity, for instance, having nothing intrinsically excellent in them, separate from their relation to the happiness of mankind;' and the whole system of right to power, property and everything else in society, must be regulated by the same consideration: the decisive question, when any of these subjects are examined being; what is it that the good of the community requires?' [1]

It is, of course, bourgeois 'liberty' that Priestley wants; the good of the community does not and cannot require perfect political liberty in England. None but 'persons of considerable fortune', or those with the best education, are eligible for the highest offices, and 'dependents' should

[1] *ibid.*, vol. ii, pp. 17-19.

not have a vote in the election of the chief magistrates. On the other hand, when and if the risk of attempting a revolution is less than existing evils and oppressions,

> 'in the name of God, I ask, what principles are those, which ought to restrain an injured and insulted people from asserting their natural rights?'

He has a suitable reply for the rich prelate who urges that 'the powers that be are ordained of God':

> 'It is a sufficient answer to such an absurd quotation as this, that, for the same reason, the powers which *will be* will be ordained of God also.'[1]

'No man can be supposed to resign his natural liberty, but on conditions', and these conditions are violated 'whenever the plain and obvious ends of government are not answered'.

On 'civil liberty' Priestley expresses the doctrines of what became orthodox liberal individualism. A sense of political and civil liberty gives a man a 'constant feeling of his own power and importance; and is the foundation of his indulging in a free, bold, and manly turn of thinking, unrestrained by the most distant idea of control'. The government ought never to interfere, 'without the greatest caution, in things that do not immediately affect the lives, liberty or property of the members of the community'. For example, Priestley is opposed, on libertarian grounds, to public education. Here is one important sphere in which the public good can only be secured by *leaving things to nature*, that is, to individual action and initiative. He sees clearly that public education might be perverted to produce a totalitarian uniformity; 'one method of education', as he says, 'would only produce one kind of men; but the great excellence of human nature consists in the variety of which it is capable'. The argument of Mill *On Liberty* is anticipated here, and where

[1] *ibid.*, vol. ii, p. 27.

Priestley insists on the importance of diversity for the vigorous intellectual life of a nation; the Dissenters, for instance, are valuable in this way to the Establishment itself. 'Is it not universally considered as an advantage to England, that it contains so great a variety of original characters?' The argument is clearly the counterpart, as it is the near contemporary, of that of Quesnay and Adam Smith in the economic sphere.

In the section on Religious Liberty and Toleration we reach the heart of Priestley's thought, and touch the true mainspring of his libertarian ardour. Applying the utilitarian test, he first shows that the happiest countries have been those in which there was least religious intolerance and interference. Flanders was ruined by Philip II, and France by the Revocation of the Edict of Nantes; whereas Holland and England have prospered, and Pennsylvania has flourished better than less tolerant states. As for the extravagances of zeal, or of popery, it is 'absolutely chimerical' to fear them 'in this enlightened age'. He would not propose to abolish 'establishments' all at once, but he would recommend reducing the Thirty-Nine Articles by thirty-eight to begin with, and completing the toleration which is at present only partial. He reminds us that 'it is not the law, but the mildness of the administration and the spirit of the times, to which we are indebted for our present liberties', and urges that Dissenters should be capable of civil office. The thought of a potentially 'enlightened' France disturbs him (as it had disturbed Brown of the *Estimate*); we must look to our laurels, for if France should begin to reform herself, she would do it much more thoroughly than we did.

Lastly, in the section 'Of the Progress of Civil Societies to a State of greater Perfection, showing that it is retarded by Encroachments on Civil and Religious Liberty', he generalizes his theme and proclaims once again the gospel of perfectibility:

'As all things (and particularly whatever depends upon science) have of late years been in a quicker progress towards perfection than ever; we may safely conclude the same with respect to any political state now in being. . . .'[1]

'This seems to be the time, when the minds of men are opening to large and generous views of things.'[2]

Priestley's assumption that Providence is leading us slowly but inevitably to happiness along the path of progress gives him complete assurance in enunciating the *laissez-faire* faith in its most general form:

'It is an universal maxim, that the more liberty is given to every thing which is in a state of growth, the more perfect it will become.'[3]

Let us then keep things moving! Establishments tend to an unhealthy fixity. If even Locke, or Clarke, or Hoadly, had drawn up a creed only half a century ago, how unsatisfactory would it now seem! 'The hand of power . . . on the side of any set of principles cannot but be a suspicious circumstance.' The question of relief from 'subscription' being then much in the air, it is natural to find Priestley referring, near the end, to those clergymen

'who may have some reluctance to subscribe what they do not believe, and who may feel, notwithstanding every evasion to which they can have recourse, that a church preferment is dearly bought at the expense of a solemn falsehood.'[4]

The true course for such was to do what Theophilus Lindsey did a few years later (1773)—to sacrifice worldly advantage for the sake of conviction:

'A number of spirited and conscientious men, openly refusing to enter into the church, or throwing up the livings which they hold upon those iniquitous and enslaving terms . . . would rouse the attention of the temporal heads of our spiritual church.'

---

[1] *ibid.*, vol. ii, p. 131.
[2] *ibid.*, vol. ii, p. 188.
[3] *ibid.*, vol. ii, p. 137.
[4] *ibid.*, vol. ii, p. 185.

(2)

Priestley's *Lectures on History and General Policy* were composed for delivery at the Warrington Academy, but they were not published until 1788, by which time he had considerably enlarged and altered them. He introduced these lectures on history, political theory, and economics, he tells us, because he considered the existing curriculum defective:

> 'though most of our pupils were young men designed for situations in civil and active life, every article in the plan of their education was adapted to the learned professions.'

As a recent biographer has remarked, he reformed the curriculum of the Warrington Academy sixty years before the foundation of a Chair of Economics at Oxford, and more than a hundred years before history became a separate school.[1]

History in the eighteenth century (as in some other centuries) was in general written and read with a purpose, and Priestley as a historian has several axes to grind. He regarded history as edifying, educative, and encouraging. It was the assembling of the evidences, not this time of Christianity, but of Providence; the arrangement of past events to illustrate Priestley's view of the world. He would not have disagreed, perhaps, with Hume's remark that 'history's chief use is only to discover the constant and universal principles of human nature',[2] but he would add that it teaches us to see the past and the present as stages in a glorious scheme of amelioration. He had read *The Decline and Fall*, but the Roman Empire was not everything, and even Gibbon, whose great work has been described as 'a memorial oration', could 'acquiesce in the pleasing conclusion that every age of the world has increased, and still increases, the real wealth, the happiness,

[1] A. Holt, *Life of Priestley* (Oxford, 1931), p. 30.

[2] Cf. above, p. 133, n. 1.

the knowledge and perhaps the virtue of the human race'.[1] If Gibbon could still believe this after describing 'the triumph of barbarism and religion', and without Priestley's religious grounds for hope, it is not surprising that Priestley could advise his student to 'attend to every advantage which the present age enjoys above ancient times, and see whether he cannot perceive marks of things being in a progress towards a state of greater perfection'.[2] History, like Nature, is a mighty maze, but not without a plan;

> 'it is, in reality, an exhibition of the ways of God, and jointly with the works of nature (which at first sight, present a prospect equally confused and perplexed) leads us to the knowledge of his perfections, and his will.'

History is useful, also, because it furnishes the data for political science; like the other sciences, that of government has now a vast stock of facts to work upon; in history, as in a laboratory, various forms and theories of government have been tested, 'and the new governments in North America are so many *new experiments*, of which political philosophers cannot fail to make the greatest use'. Through the historical process of trial and error, 'the only proper object of government, *the happiness of the people*, is now almost universally seen, and alone attended to'. The period of history which delights him most, and on which he enlarges most lovingly, is naturally the Renaissance (he still uses the old term, the 'revival of letters') and the succeeding centuries. This was the era which saw the breaking of 'the prodigious power of the pope', the rise of manufactures, the perfecting of the arts of life, and the increase of politeness and of humanity, to such a degree that 'this part of the world is now a paradise in comparison with what it was'. In English history the revolution of 1688 was the most important event: 'a revolution so remarkable, and attended with such happy conse-

[1] Quoted by Bury, *The Idea of Progress*, p. 222.
[2] *Lectures on History* (1788), p. 531.

quences, has perhaps no parallel in the history of the world'; and

'... little did the Greeks and Romans imagine that the *Divisi toto orbe Brittani* . . . would ever make the figure they do now, and go so infinitely beyond whatever they had attained to in respect of science, commerce, riches, power, and I may add, happiness.' [1]

This decided preference for 'modern' over 'ancient' is revealed also in Priestley's emphatic rejection of the popular 'primitivism' of the period, according to which civilization is a degeneration from an age of gold, or a departure from Nature's holy plan:

'Idleness, treachery and cruelty are predominant in all uncivilized countries; notwithstanding the boasts which the poets make of the *golden age* of mankind ...' [2]

and he agrees with Voltaire that, despite the vices of civilized countries, no one would 'think his life and property so secure in the hands of a Moor, or a Tartar, as in those of a French or English gentleman'. Between delivering and publishing these lectures Priestley had read Adam Smith, and he now presents the case for economic as well as moral individualism. He quotes Adam Smith to the effect that 'it is the highest impertinence and presumption in kings, and ministers, to pretend to watch over the œconomy of private people'.[3] If goods can be imported more cheaply than they can be made at home, this is an indication that we had better not engage in that particular manufacture. In the absence of all 'artificial' restrictions the only advantage will be on the side of industry and ingenuity, 'and no man, or nation, ought to wish it to be anywhere else'. Under the beneficent sway of Nature, wealth will increase and be diffused through 'the lower ranks of society'. Wealth and innocent luxury (i.e. love of refinement and ornament) are not intrinsically

[1] *ibid.*, p. 270.
[2] *ibid.*, p. 324.
[3] *ibid.*, p. 372.

bad; education and enlightenment will teach the wealthy how to use their riches 'for the good of the whole'. Millionaires are, in fact, Nature's elect—those to whom obedience to natural law has opened the earthly paradise:

> 'Men of wealth and influence, who act upon the principles of virtue, and religion, and conscientiously make their power subservient to the good of their country, are the men who are the greatest honour to human nature, and the greatest blessing to human societies.' [1]

If only we will allow free scope to 'this natural course of things', commerce will bring international peace, and 'the world would in time recover its pristine paradisal state' (an allusion, presumably, to Eden, since Priestley has rejected the poetic age of gold). 'In time'—but how long must we wait for this happy consummation?

And here Priestley remembers the spectre of War. How will this buoyant progressivist deal with that? We must especially hope, he says, that 'societies, fully instructed by experience, will with the utmost care avoid the ruinous expences and devastation of *war*, which may dissipate in one year more than they can accumulate in a hundred'. He notes, further, the hypocrisy of the war-making powers:

> 'To see the spirit of benevolence, tenderness, equity and honour, that appears in all our declarations of war, and the manifestos which are published upon entering an enemy's country, a common reader would think that the princes of Europe were more than men; but then he would be surprised that when all princes entertained those excellent pacific sentiments, they should be obliged to have recourse to sanguinary methods in order to terminate their differences. He would think that when all parties concerned were so happily disposed, they would bear everything from one another, rather than go to war.' [2]

Alas for progress and perfectibility! the 'common reader' of to-day has the same cause for 'surprise' as Priestley in 1788, and much more for despair. Never, perhaps, has

[1] *ibid.*, p. 423. [2] *ibid.*, p. 253.

the prophecy of a good and wise man been more hideously falsified than this of Priestley's:

> 'As the world advances in civilization, *and national animosity abates, war becomes less distressing to peaceable individuals who do not bear arms.*'[1]

5

Priestley spent the last ten years of his life in America, and though for a time he was suspected both on religious and political grounds (Pickering, Secretary of State under Adams, wanted to deport him under the Aliens Act), those years were on the whole spent in the happy pursuit of his old activities. He was welcomed by various learned societies, and offered the Professorship of Chemistry in the University of Pennsylvania. He was disappointed in his hopes of becoming the 'apostle of rational religion in the New World',[2] but in the spring of 1796 he was able to deliver, in the new church of the Universalists at Philadelphia, a series of discourses on the Evidences of Christianity which were attended by a large and appreciative audience, including Adams and many members of both Houses of Congress; and from this a Unitarian Society took its rise. But it was Jefferson's election to the Presidency that brought Priestley at last the peace he had come in search of. Under Jefferson's administration, he writes to Dr Logan: 'I now, for the first time in my life (and I shall soon enter my 70th year), find myself in any degree of favour with the government of the country in which I have lived, and I hope I shall die in the same pleasing situation'.[3] His wish was granted, and in 1804 he died peacefully, where he had lived, at Northumberland, on the banks of that Susquehanna River of which Coleridge and the Pantisocrats had only dreamed.

[1] *ibid.*, p. 499. (My italics.)
[2] A. Holt, *op. cit.*, p. 187.
[3] A. Holt, *op. cit.*, p. 205.

CHAPTER XI

'Nature' in Revolution and Reaction

I. WILLIAM GODWIN

I

WE are now to consider some of the manifestations of the Idea of Nature in the complicated period of Revolution and Reaction through which the eighteenth century passed into the nineteenth. Throughout that turbulent time 'Nature' remained the dominant concept—indeed in all the phases of 'romantic' philosophy and poetry it attained an unexampled authority—but never, perhaps, were its many meanings, particularly its two fundamental senses, more confusingly intertwined. Rousseau, prophet of revolution, was afterwards appealed to by the reactionaries; the Revolution was made in the name of Nature, Burke attacked it in the name of Nature, and *in eodem nomine* Tom Paine, Mary Wollstonecraft, and Godwin replied to Burke. Wordsworth and Coleridge saw Nature symbolized first in revolutionary France, and then in reactionary England; and Wordsworth's best 'Nature'-poetry arose from his rejection of the Nature-philosophy of the Jacobins and of Godwin. Perhaps the safest clue through this labyrinth is to bear in mind what I have just called the two fundamental senses of 'Nature': we may call them the 'historical' and the 'philosophical'. In the 'historical' sense Nature means 'things as they now are or have become', *natura naturata*; in the other sense, 'things as they may become', *natura naturans*. But there are further sources of confusion. The 'nature' of anything may be conceived either as its 'original' state when fresh from the hands of God and before it has acquired any 'artificial' accretions, or as its final state, when it has attained the fullest development of which it is capable, and realized most perfectly its own inner principle. All depends upon whether 'Nature' is regarded as a fixed state or as a dynamic process, as something already realized or something 'evermore about to be'. Now it is possible to be 'progressive' and yet to be also a 'primitivist'; one may be eager for reform, and yet believe, as to some extent Rousseau seems to have done, that the true reforms are those which will lead back to some earlier, simpler, and happier mode of existence. Thus 'philosophical' naturalism becomes 'historical' (in quite another sense) if, in your view of 'what things might become', you contemplate a return to a lost paradise. Again, you may believe, like Burke, that 'Nature' is best expressed in 'things as they are', that is, in what history has actually produced, and yet not be merely conservative; for if Nature has produced the present, it will also produce the future. And on the other hand, you may be an ardent perfectibilist, like Priestley, and yet believe that the best way to attain perfection is to 'let be', to let Nature pursue its own beneficent course. *Laissez-faire* without the belief in perfectibility yields the conservatism of Burke or of the later Wordsworth; with that belief, it produces the liberalism of Priestley and the nineteenth century—though even from this standpoint you might have first to remove obstacles in order that Nature might function freely. Lastly—and this is the creed of revolution—one might treat Nature as dross to be moulded in our own likeness; we must *alter* rather than explain, and *make* the future instead of letting be, writing justice, equality, and brotherhood where history has only left a record of crimes and follies. Man is Nature's growing point; it is in him that Nature can be most clearly seen as *naturans*; and all that he fashions according to reason will then be most 'natural'. As Holbach said, 'l'art n'est que la Nature agissante à l'aide des instruments qu'elle a faits'.[1] Yet it was precisely men like Holbach and (as we shall see) his follower

[1] Cf. above, p. 156.

Godwin who were most anxious to represent man as part of the mechanism of Nature, and human character as the product of environment. Moreover, these were also the men who regarded most of what 'Nature' had actually produced (existing institutions) as 'unnatural'. Dizzied by these contradictions, we seem to understand how it was that at one time Wordsworth was ready to 'yield up moral questions in despair'. John Morley has said that Burke was of that class of minds which prefers 'that which has grown' to 'that which is made', and perhaps this distinction may help us in classifying the doctrines of our period. Our problem turns upon the degree of human participation which is supposed to be needed to produce the best world. Burke, or the 'Tory' Wordsworth, desires the minimum of this; Nature (history) produces what is best (most natural), and our part is to realize the complexity of things, explaining where we can, and reverencing where we cannot. The Liberal (Priestley or Adam Smith) wants us to leave Nature to itself, but first to remove the 'artificial' restrictions with which wicked men have somehow hampered it. The Revolutionary wants the maximum of human action to fashion all things fair: 'Nature' left to itself produces jungles and slums; if we want better conditions we must make them ourselves. This view was implicit in Holbach and the Jacobin philosophy generally, but the eighteenth century reverence for Nature prevented it from reaching full theoretic development until the time of Marx.

Another broad distinction may perhaps be made at this point: 'Nature' may be conceived rationally or emotionally. Indeed the history of the idea in the eighteenth century can be described in the most general terms as its development from a rational into an emotional principle. Nature and Reason are normally associated in the earlier part of the century, Nature and Feeling in the later. This change is associated with the growth of the cult of sensibility, the substitution of 'je sens, donc je suis' for 'cogito, ergo sum', the increasing value attributed to impulse and spontaneity, and the decreasing importance attached to pure reason. It is also peculiarly associated with the name of Rousseau—the Rousseau of the *Confessions*, the *Nouvelle Héloïse*, and the Vicaire Savoyard, and also the Rousseau who, in Morley's phrase, converted the blank practice of the political *philosophes* into a deadly affair of ball and shell. Rousseau was a romantic, but even in Hume, that pure product of the century, we have seen 'Nature', as 'Feeling', exalted in the place of Reason. This is a familiar symptom of the great reaction against the eighteenth century and all its works, which marks the end of our present enquiries. But we must not be misled by our own generalizations; nothing, in this period, is clear and simple. For instance, 'Nature and Reason' continued their partnership long after the cult of sensibility began, and the revolutionary struggle was carried on in the joint name of both. And Godwin, whom we shall presently be considering, was the man who, in the very dawn of romanticism, made the most determined effort to

> abstract the hopes of Man
> Out of his feelings

and to make 'our Reason's naked self' the object of his fervour.[1] The great traditions overlap, and the authentic voice of the eighteenth century is still heard, not only throughout the 'romantic' era in Godwin, but far into the nineteenth century in J. S. Mill and others. Nevertheless the generalizations hold good in some degree; the emotional temperature, even in the rationalists, was much higher in the latter than in the earlier part of the century. This heightening of tone can be felt in all the writings of the age (down to its epitaphs); it imparts a certain vehemence and incandescence to the entirely colourless prose of Godwin. Amongst the causes of this change, political emotion must, I think, be counted high. The peace of the Augustans was over, and great issues, fraught with untold possibilities for good or ill, were once more

[1] *The Prelude*, bk. xi, 224, 234.

dignifying the political scene. The rights and dignity of man, the nobleness of life and the Roman virtues were in the minds and mouths of many:

O times,
In which the meagre, stale, forbidding ways
Of custom, law, and statute, took at once
The attraction of a country in romance!
When Reason seemed the most to assert her rights
When most intent on making of herself
A prime enchantress—to assist the work
Which then was going forward in her name![1]

Europe at that time was thrilled with joy,
France standing on the top of golden hours,
And human nature seeming born again.[2]

'The Germano-Coleridgean doctrine', wrote J. S. Mill, '[as opposed to that of Hartley and Bentham] expresses the revolt of the human mind against the philosophy of the eighteenth century.' Where the eighteenth century was innovative, he goes on to say, the nineteenth was conservative; where the eighteenth was infidel, the nineteenth was religious; the eighteenth 'abstract and metaphysical', the nineteenth 'concrete and historical'; the eighteenth prosaic, the nineteenth poetical. The raising of the emotional temperature, to which I have referred, can be connected with this transition, in the region of politics, from 'abstract' to 'concrete'; for now, what had been merely a theory or a philosophic dream was to be realized in actuality, and men

Were called upon to exercise their skill
Not in Utopia,—subterranean fields,—
Or some secreted island, Heaven knows where!
But in the very world, which is the world
Of all of us,—the place where, in the end,
We find our happiness, or not at all![3]

The same transition, which is parallel to the movement from 'rational' to 'emotional', can be seen in the develop-

[1] *ibid.*, bk. xi, 109. [2] *ibid.*, bk. vi, 339.
[3] *ibid.*, bk. xi, 139.

ment of the idea of 'Nature', and in the contrast between the 'Nature'-poetry of Pope or Thomson and that of Wordsworth. Thomson can observe finely, but his Nature-worship has the 'spectral' [1] quality of eighteenth century deism; the deity he celebrates is the First Cause, the Supreme Being of the natural philosophers:

> Hail! Source of Being! Universal Soul
> Of Heaven and Earth! Essential Presence, hail!
> To Thee I bend the knee; to Thee my thoughts,
> Continual, climb; who, with a master hand,
> Hast the great whole into perfection touch'd.
> By thee the various vegetative tribes, etc.[2]

Compare this with

> I held unconscious intercourse with beauty
> Old as creation, drinking in a pure
> Organic pleasure from the silver wreaths
> Of curling mist, or from the level plain
> Of waters coloured by impending clouds.[3]

or

> To every natural form, rock, fruit, or flower,
> Even the loose stones that cover the high-way,
> I gave a moral life: I saw them feel,
> Or linked them to some feeling: the great mass
> Lay bedded in a quickening soul, and all
> That I beheld respired with inward meaning.[4]

The second-hand quality of the feeling in Thomson can be felt in the rhetorical rumble and the pseudo-Miltonics; the 'great whole' is an idea (and a currently accepted idea) rather than 'a feeling and a love'. In Wordsworth's slow pace, his references to particular objects, and even in his prosaisms, we are apprised of direct dealings between the poet and things themselves. His observation is the basis of his deism, whereas with Thomson they are in essence unconnected. It is a commonplace that in nineteenth century literature 'Nature' typically refers to particular scenes,

[1] Dr Inge's word.
[2] *The Seasons*: 'Spring'.
[3] *The Prelude*, bk. i, 562.
[4] *ibid.*, bk. iii, 127.

places, and objects, or 'the country' (especially picturesque country), and no longer so much to a great abstraction, or to the 'general properties and large appearances' of Dr Johnson. But the transition from 'abstract' to 'concrete', conceived by Mill as the overthrow of the Locke-Hartley tradition by the 'Germano-Coleridgean doctrine', is best expressed in the actual development of such men as Wordsworth, Coleridge, Southey, and even Godwin himself, men who lived through the revolutionary era and epitomized its successive phases. In England, emotional naturalism turned almost inevitably into Toryism, or something akin to it. Wordsworth's development illustrates this principle with peculiar clearness. Greeting the early days of the Revolution with a purely emotional dilation, as if France had suddenly achieved the spontaneity and joyous instinctiveness of his own childhood days—

> . . . the events
> Seemed nothing out of nature's certain course,
> A gift that was come rather late than soon [1]—

he came later to feel that it was the 'meddling intellect', not Nature, which was directing the course of events. So, after a short but harrowing temptation in the wilderness of Godwinism, he made the vital transition of his life, and relapsed upon the 'cool flowery lap of Earth'. The Revolution had been *made* by Man, not evolved by Nature. Once he had convinced himself that, owing to the nature of our being, radical alteration of the status quo and the worship of naked Reason were more likely to lead into the desert than into the Promised Land, then how infinitely preferable seemed things as they are to things as they may be made, the feelings to the reason, instinctive living to thinking, children and rustics to philosophers, one impulse from a vernal wood to all the sages, England to France, the Lake District to the rest of England!

> Be thankful, thou, for though unholy deeds
> Ravage the world, tranquillity is here! [2]

[1] *The Prelude*, bk. ix, 246. [2] Sonnet, *Clouds lingering yet* (1807).

An odd circumstance, which well illustrates the complexity of these times, is that Godwin himself, who for Wordsworth and his contemporaries represented the worship of 'naked Reason' in its extremest form, had rejected or greatly modified his own 'Godwinism' by 1798, the year in which Wordsworth published his anti-Godwinian *Lyrical Ballads*.

2

If Mill was right in calling the eighteenth century 'innovative, infidel, abstract, metaphysical, and prosaic', then Godwin, though he lived until 1836, must be its living embodiment, for he had all these characteristics in a high degree. Like Mill, who also possessed them (though the nineteenth century sea-change later affected him much more profoundly), Godwin seems never to have been a child. 'I remember, when I was a very little boy', he writes, 'saying to myself, "What shall I do, when I have read through all the books that there are in the world?"' Intellect was strongly developed in him from the outset, at the expense of bodily health, imagination, and feeling. There are interesting parallels between his story and Priestley's, for he too came of Dissenting stock. His father and grandfather were both Nonconformist ministers, and Godwin himself, as is not always remembered, was a minister for several years, and published a volume of sermons. In the words of one of his biographers, he was 'the perfect flower of a stock devoted for many generations to nonconformity and moral inculcation';[1] he 'reminded those who knew him', says Hazlitt, 'of the metaphysician engrafted on the Dissenting Minister'.[2] Unlike Priestley, he 'succumbed' to the philosophic influences which Priestley combated, but, even in his infidel later life, nonconformity and moral inculcation remained the very stuff of his being. It is significant that 'Godwinism', or the

[1] Ford K. Brown, *Life of W. Godwin* (1926), p. 3.
[2] *Spirit of the Age*, William Godwin, *ad fin.*

worship of naked Reason, which for a short time so dazzled the generation of Wordsworth, Coleridge, Hazlitt, and the rest, and later the youthful Shelley, was one of the forms into which eighteenth century rational Dissent was capable of evolving. The peculiar missionary fervour of *Political Justice* is more explicable when we remember its religious pedigree. Priestley stopped short at Unitarianism, while Godwin followed Holbach into atheism, but this divergence seems less important than the heritage which they received in common from the Dissenting tradition. In both, Calvinism passed naturally into Necessitarianism; and in his passion for reforming the world the atheist even exceeded the believer—for Priestley's main concern was rather with the exposure of error.

Several of Godwin's later characteristics were manifested at an early age, particularly his vanity and self-confidence, and his exclusive absorption in intellectual concerns. 'All my amusements were sedentary; I had scarcely any pleasure but in reading.' There is an illustration of his self-dramatizing vanity, which somehow falls short of the Miltonic standard, in the following anecdote from his autobiography. At the age of thirteen or fourteen he went one day alone to the Assizes, and placed himself immediately next to the Bench:

> 'As I stayed some hours, I at one time relieved my posture by leaning my elbow on the corner of the cushion placed before his lordship. On one occasion, probably when he was going to address the jury, he laid his hand gently on my elbow and removed it. On this occasion I recollect having silently remarked, if his lordship knew what the lad beside him will perhaps one day become, I am not so sure that he would have removed my elbow.'[1]

Godwin was never merely an intellectual machine; other essential ingredients in his make-up, without which *Political Justice* and *Caleb Williams* would not hold their actual place in literature, were 'sensibility' and 'enthusiasm'

[1] Quoted by F. K. Brown, *op. cit.*, p. 9.

—both secular derivatives, perhaps, from the Puritan source:

> 'He read "with the greatest transports" the early volumes (in English) of Rollin's *Ancient History*. "Few bosoms ever beat with greater ardour than mine did while perusing the story of the grand struggle of the Greeks for independence against the assaults of the Persian despot, and this scene awakened a passion in my soul which will never cease but with life."'[1]

The special mark of Godwin's best writing is its blend of abstract, intellectualized diction with an almost frantic 'intensity' of feeling. At its worst, as sometimes in *Fleetwood*, for instance, this degenerates into hysteria, but at its best it yields the capital melodrama of *Caleb Williams* —a book which, whatever its defects, still reads like a work composed under an afflatus or imaginative 'possession'.

Under the influence of a schoolmaster Godwin adopted Sandemanianism, a variety of Calvinism in which some of the principles of *Political Justice* seem foreshadowed—as, for example, that political methods of reform are vain compared with the dissemination of the spirit of Christ ('benevolence' and 'justice' in Godwin), and that as there is no New Testament sanction for the accumulation of wealth, each man must consider his property to be at the disposal of the needy. Godwin was always ready to lend, but it is too well known how many other men's property he came later to consider to be at his own disposal. After five years at the Dissenting Academy at Hoxton, where he was taught by Dr Kippis (pupil of Doddridge and friend of Priestley), and where he managed to retain his Sandemanianism in spite of Arian and Socinian influences (though he seems already to have doubted 'the being of a God'), he entered the ministry (1778). While ministering to a congregation at Stowmarket he read Holbach and Helvétius, and within five years he had left the ministry for good, though he found a temporary resting-place in

[1] *ibid.*, p. 8.

the Socinianism which satisfied Priestley for life. An abortive scheme for starting a 'seminary' at Epsom resulted only in a Prospectus, consisting largely of excerpts from Rousseau and Holbach, but looking forward so clearly to *Political Justice* that a few quotations may be of interest:

> 'The state of society is incontestably artificial; the power of one man over another must be always derived from convention, or from conquest; by nature we are equal. The necessary consequence is, that government must always depend upon the opinion of the governed. Let the most oppressed people under heaven once change their mode of thinking, and they are free.'

'Government and education are therefore "the two principal objects of human power", and of the two, education is the more important.'

> 'Government is very limited in its powers of making men either virtuous or happy; it is only in the infancy of society that it can do anything considerable; in its maturity it can only direct a few of our outward actions.' [1]

His final transition to complete 'unbelief', which occurred in 1787, is partly attributable to his friendship with Thomas Holcroft, whose vigorous personality seems at this time to have galvanized the more placid temper of Godwin into unwonted activity:

> 'My mind, though fraught with sensibility, and occasionally ardent and enthusiastic, is perhaps in its genuine habits too tranquil and unimpassioned for successful composition, and stands greatly in need for stimulus and excitement. I am deeply indebted in this point to Holcroft.' [2]

The French Revolution, which began when he was thirty-three years old, soon provided him with more 'stimulus and excitement', and, though he always hated mob violence, his 'heart beat high with great swelling sentiments

[1] Quoted, *ibid.*, p. 17. [2] *ibid.*, p. 26.

of Liberty'. The idea of *Political Justice* was conceived in May 1791, after the appearance of Burke's *Reflexions*, Mary Wollstonecraft's *Vindication of the Rights of Men* and Tom Paine's *Rights of Man*; at the time, that is, when the 'friends of liberty' began to be aware of the onset of panic and reaction.

In the Preface to the first edition (January 1793), he declared that it was twelve years since he had become 'satisfied that monarchy was a species of government unavoidably corrupt', and that he owed this conviction to the political writings of Swift, to Holbach, Helvétius, and Rousseau, and to the Latin historians. Long before publication, therefore, he had been forming his main ideas on justice, the rights of man, the omnipotence of opinion, gratitude, promises and the rest, but 'of the desirableness of a government in the utmost degree simple he was not made fully aware, but by ideas suggested by the French Revolution. To the same event he owes the determination of mind which gave existence to this work.'[1] But though occasioned by the French Revolution, the book is so far from being an incitement to further revolution that it has 'for one of its express objects the dissuading from tumult and violence'. It is meant to be an appeal, beyond prejudice and turmoil, to the immutable principles of justice and reason, and is addressed to 'men of study and reflection'. 'He conceived politics', he says (writing of himself in the third person), 'to be the proper vehicle of a liberal morality', and was accordingly

> 'desirous of producing a work from the perusal of which no man should rise, without being strengthened in habits of sincerity, fortitude and justice.'[2]

The book is being published, he knows, at a singularly inauspicious moment, when the public is panic-struck, and a project may be actually on foot for 'suppressing the activity of mind' altogether. 'All the prejudices of the

[1] *Political Justice* (2nd ed., 1796), pp. ix-x.
[2] *ibid.*, pp. vi-vii.

human mind are in arms' against the doctrines he is about to deliver, and even an unguarded word may be punished. Godwin evidently relished his own Roman virtue; it is known, however, that Mr Pitt thought a book published at three guineas a copy not worth suppressing.

3

Godwin is largely known to literary students to-day as a malign influence upon Wordsworth or as the source of most of Shelley's ideas. He appears in the literary histories and text-books mainly as a 'crank', and his doctrines are described by Mr Garrod, for example, as 'poisonous nonsense'. Those who so regard him are usually spokesmen of the 'Nature-and-Feeling' phase of romanticism, and they have at any rate this justification for their attitude, that much good poetry, especially Wordsworth's, was written in revolt against Godwin and all that he stood for. Yet Godwin is worth considering for his own sake, and perhaps still more as a representative figure: as the writer who enunciated the extreme conclusions of eighteenth century rationalism at the very moment of incipient reaction, and who thereby, in his own life-story and in his influence upon his contemporaries, acquired a certain symbolic importance. The reasons for his rapid eclipse may appear as we proceed, but for the moment we may support ourselves with the comment of Hazlitt (whose essay on Godwin in *The Spirit of the Age* is still the fairest and most discerning summary I know of):

> 'Captain Parry would be thought to have rendered a service to navigation and his country, no less by proving that there is no North-West Passage, than if he had ascertained that there is one: so Mr Godwin has rendered an essential service to moral science, by attempting (in vain) to pass the Arctic Circle and Frozen Regions, where the understanding is no longer warmed by the affections, nor fanned by the breeze of fancy.'

He enjoyed the respect of many of his distinguished contemporaries, and Wordsworth, in the very passage where he relates his rejection of 'Godwinism', adds:

> *yet* I feel [i.e. about ten years later]
> (Sustained by worthier as by wiser thoughts)
> The aspiration, nor shall ever cease to feel it.[1]

A more ordinary, and therefore more representative contemporary, Crabb Robinson, wrote of *Political Justice*: 'It made me feel more generously. I had never felt before, nor, I am afraid, have I ever since felt so strongly, the duty of not living to oneself, but of having for one's sole object the good of the community.' What was the 'aspiration' spoken of by Wordsworth? We find in Godwin so much that has become familiar in the course of our discussions, that a brief account of his main notions should suffice. There is, to begin with, a full acceptance of mechanical materialism and its moral counterpart, Necessitarianism, the whole being touched to revolutionary (not insurrectionary) issues by an unbounded faith in perfectibility. True to the Locke-Hartley tradition, he begins with the sheet of white paper: the moral character of man is built up out of sensations, by association. But if 'the Characters of Men originate in External Circumstances', then the nature of those circumstances becomes a matter of vital importance. Of those circumstances, physical influences (climate, etc.) are negligible in comparison with 'moral' causes, and chief among moral causes are education and government. Now 'perfectibility', as we have seen, is a deduction from the white-paper theory; anything or everything can be inscribed by moral agencies upon the blank sheet:

> 'Perfectibility is one of the most unequivocal characteristics of the human species.' [2]

> 'Man, considered in himself, is merely a being capable of impression, a recipient of perceptions. What is there in this abstract character that precludes him from advancement?' [3]

---

[1] *The Prelude*, bk. xi, 255. [2] *Political Justice* (1st ed.), bk. i, ch. 2.
[3] *ibid.*, bk. v, ch. 8 (vol. ii, p. 452).

Why, then, is man so little advanced? Why does he languish under wars, tyrannies, superstitions, penal codes? It is because 'of all modes of operating upon mind, government is the most considerable', and governments, unfortunately, are powerful for evil only, and powerless for good. Government, he writes (doubtless with Burke's *Reflexions* in mind),

> 'gives substance and permanence to our errors. It reverses the genuine propensities of mind, and instead of suffering us to look forward, teaches us to look backward for perfection. It prompts us to seek the public welfare, not in innovation and improvement, but in a timid reverence for the decisions of our ancestors, as if it were the nature of mind always to degenerate, never to advance.' [1]

'It may reasonably be doubted whether error could ever be formidable or long-lived if government did not lend it support.' Now, must we accept this state of affairs as unalterable? No! it is precisely because moral causes are all-important that we may work and hope for amelioration. If government operates upon mind, mind is first the foundation of government, or, as Godwin puts it, government is founded upon 'opinion' alone. Change the 'opinion', therefore, and the government will vanish like smoke. Slavery exists, not because certain climates or national characters favour it, but because it is the interest of tyrants to prevent their subjects from seeing the obvious advantages of freedom.

> 'In reality the chains fall off of themselves, when the magic of opinion is dissolved.' [2]

The real enemies of liberty in any country are 'those higher orders who profit by a contrary system'. We are all deluded by the spells and charms of ancient imposture; the age of chivalry, alas! is very far from being gone.

> 'There is a perpetual struggle between the genuine sentiments of understanding, which tell us that all this is imposition, and the

[1] *ibid.*, bk. i, ch. 4 (vol. i, p. 31).
[2] *ibid.*, bk. i, ch. 7 (vol. i, p. 64).

imperious voice of government, which bids us reverence and obey.'[1]

The present systems, gilded though they are by 'impudent mysticism', are simply devices for perpetuating inequality, slavery, and every kind of imperfection, whereas the natural propensity of mind is to advance. Nothing stands in the way of emancipation except the enchantments of despotism, which persuade us that the existing system is 'too sacred to be looked into'. But all this will be changed in the twinkling of an eye; when the fated hour arrives,

> 'when the true crisis shall come, not a sword will need to be drawn, not a finger to be lifted up,'[2]

and Jupiter will simply fall from his throne. But, in spite of Necessitarianism, we are not to await this crisis with folded hands; in the meantime we are to prepare for it—how? The true technique for the overthrow of Jupiter is to awaken men's minds by argument and persuasion. The present order exhibits a perpetual spectacle of unreason and injustice; very well, show men the possibility of another kind of spectacle, and they will welcome it with rapture. 'It is the inalienable tendency of positive institution, to retain that with which it is conversant for ever in the same state'; while, on the other hand, 'it is one of the most unquestionable properties of mind to be susceptible of perpetual improvement'. Therefore,

> 'let truth be incessantly studied, illustrated and propagated, and the effect is inevitable.'[3]

Let us meanwhile, however, 'attempt no abrupt changes', but 'calmly wait until the harvest of opinion is ripe'. Though the change, when it comes, will be sudden, the preliminaries must be gradual:

> 'The error lies, not in tolerating the worst forms of govern-

---

[1] *ibid.*, bk. v, ch. 5 (vol. ii, p. 418).
[2] *ibid.*, bk. iv, ch. 2 (vol. i, p. 223).
[3] *ibid.*, bk. vi, ch. 1 (vol. ii, p. 593).

ment for a time, but in supposing a change impracticable, and not incessantly looking forward to its accomplishment.'[1]

It can hardly fail to suggest itself that Godwin is here sketching out in advance the technique of propaganda which, rendered a thousand times more effective by modern science, has been employed in our own day to accomplish political changes. The difference is that his methods are now generally used to extinguish liberty, whereas it never occurred to Godwin that any cause could be so promoted except the true one. It is, however, in some cases still open to the friends of liberty, as well as their opponents, to propagate their opinions in the way Godwin suggested, although in certain quarters the machinery for 'suppressing the activity of mind' is so much more efficient than that of 1793 as to make the attempt highly dangerous.

What kind of truths, then, should be disseminated, in order to prepare for the unbinding of Prometheus? It is in Godwin's answers to this question, especially, that the characteristic teachings of 'Godwinism' make their appearance. The guiding principle has been best stated, perhaps, by Wordsworth and by Hazlitt. It was first put by Wordsworth into the mouth of Oswald, the Godwinian Iago of *The Borderers* (1795-6):

> To-day you have thrown off a tyranny
> That lives but in the torpid acquiescence
> Of our emasculated souls, the tyranny
> Of the world's masters with the musty rules
> By which they uphold their craft from age to age:
> You have obeyed the only law that sense
> Submits to recognize; the immediate law,
> From the clear light of circumstances, flashed
> Upon an independent Intellect.[2]

And again in *The Prelude*, describing the brief period of his full acceptance of these doctrines, he exclaims:

> the dream
> Flattered the young, pleased with extremes, nor least

[1] *ibid.*, bk. i, ch. 7 (vol. i, p. 70).

[2] *The Borderers*, 1488.

With that which makes our Reason's naked self
The object of its fervour. What delight!
How glorious! in self-knowledge and self-rule,
To look through all the frailties of the world,
And, with a resolute mastery shaking off
Infirmities of nature, time, and place,
Build social upon personal Liberty,
Which, to the blind restraints of general laws
Superior, magisterially adopts
One guide, the light of circumstances, flashed
Upon an independent intellect.[1]

'He places the human mind,' says Hazlitt,

> 'on an elevation, from which it commands a view of the whole line of moral consequences; and requires it to conform its acts to the larger and more enlightened conscience which it has thus acquired. He absolves man from the gross and narrow ties of sense, custom, authority, private and local attachment, in order that he may devote himself to the boundless pursuit of universal benevolence.'[2]

Rejecting the 'supplementary aids of an imperfect virtue', Godwin would have us take Reason as our sole guide and abstract Good as our sole end. 'The genuine and wholesome state of mind,' he writes (and this is probably one of the passages versified by Wordsworth in the above quotations),

> 'is to be unloosed from shackles, and to expand every fibre of its frame according to the independent and individual impressions of truth upon the mind.'[3]

We must accordingly teach, and practise, universal benevolence and justice; in every situation that presents itself we must determine our course of action, not by any prejudice or maxim of traditional morality, but by the sole consideration of what will produce the greatest benefit to society. 'Love your neighbour as yourself', for example, is a rule which, admirable as it is, and pointing in the right

[1] *The Prelude*, bk. xi, 232. [2] *The Spirit of the Age*, *loc. cit.*
[3] *Political Justice*, bk. v, ch. 23 (vol. ii, p. 569).

direction, is not 'modelled with the strictness of philosophical accuracy'. One 'neighbour' may be a 'being of more worth and importance' than another. Godwin's illustration of Fénelon and his chambermaid has become classical:

> 'The illustrious bishop of Cambrai was of more worth than his chambermaid, and there are few of us that would hesitate to pronounce, if his palace were in flames, and the life of only one of them could be preserved, which of the two ought to be preferred.'[1]

It would have been 'just' in the chambermaid herself to prefer Fénelon's life to her own. But if she had been 'my wife' or 'my mother'—what then? 'What magic is there', Godwin rejoins,

> 'What magic is there in the pronoun "my" to overturn the decisions of everlasting truth? My wife or my mother may be a fool, or a prostitute, malicious, lying or deceitful. If they be, of what consequence is it that they are mine?'

Similarly, 'gratitude', like filial affection, is no part of justice or virtue; it is merely 'a sentiment which would lead me to prefer one man to another from some other consideration than that of his superior usefulness or worth'. I ought to be 'constantly and carefully enquiring into the deserts of all with whom I am connected'. To do all the good in my power is what is 'just' for me. Generosity is not a virtue, it is simply a duty; it is 'impossible for me to confer upon any man a favour, I can only do him a right':

> 'My neighbour is in want of £10 that I can spare—his claim is as complete as if he had my bond in his possession, or had supplied me with goods to this amount.'

This principle, which can obviously work both ways, was one of those which Godwin never abandoned, and in later life, during long years of financial embarrassment, he in-

[1] *ibid.*, bk. ii, ch. 2 (vol. i, pp. 82 ff.).

cessantly urged upon his friends (especially Shelley) the completeness of his claim to the many hundreds of pounds of which he was always in want.

> 'My neighbour has just as much right to put an end to my existence with dagger or poison as to deny me that pecuniary assistance without which I must starve, or as to deny me that assistance without which my intellectual attainments or my moral exertions will be materially injured.' [1]

From these Micawberish utterances it is somewhat of a relief to turn to Godwin's remarks on the penal laws, and still more to those on war and patriotism. We must work for the reform of the penal laws, because our whole theory of punishment is wrong. It is based upon the notions of 'retribution' or deterrent example, whereas our sole care should be for the reformation of the criminal and the benefit of society. A crime is simply an error, for which in most cases society itself is finally responsible; and punishment is not the best way of correcting men's errors. It is 'a menace of violence made use of to persuade them of the truth or falsehood of a proposition'; it has little chance of making them wise, and can scarcely fail to make them 'timid, dissembling, and corrupt'. Godwin's most telling point is perhaps this:

> 'What . . . can be more shameless than for society to make an example of those whom she has goaded to the breach of order, instead of amending her own institutions which, by straining order into tyranny, produced the mischief?' [2]

The argument widens into a general condemnation of the use of violence in human relationships. He enunciates the most advanced (as well as the oldest) truths about non-violence—here (as so often) translating Gospel maxims into Godwinese. 'Resist not him that is evil' becomes:

> 'the powers of reason and truth are yet unfathomed. . . . Who shall say how far the whole species might be improved, were they

[1] *ibid.*, bk. ii, ch. 6 (vol. i, p. 112).
[2] *ibid.*, bk. vii, ch. 3 (vol. ii, p. 713).

accustomed to despise force in others, and did they refuse to employ it for themselves.'

Coercion, for 'example', fails of its effect; 'the whole scope of gloomy invention is exhausted in vain'. Our prisons, too, are known to be nurseries of vice, and even Howard's proposed 'solitary confinement' is objectionable. However, Godwin admits that in the present state of humanity 'human beings are such tyros in the art of reasoning' that we cannot simply dispense with punishment; we must first abolish selfishness and vice, and prepare the field for reason. But though we must put up with second-bests during the period of transition, we must remember that the true remedy for our present plight is not more coercion, but simplification of the vicious complexities of the present system. In a small ideal community such as Godwin desires, we should all live under our neighbours' eyes, and be subject only to coercion derived from 'the system of the universe'.

Godwin's advocacy of non-violence is wholehearted; he applies it not only to personal human relations and to internal revolution in a state, but also to international politics. On the subject of war his view is almost that of absolute pacificism. War is justifiable, if at all, only to repel invasion, not to forestall it, and still less 'to impart a healthful and vigorous tone to the public mind'.[1] The wars which desolate mankind would probably nearly cease if they were supported only by the voluntary contributions of those who approved of their principles, and there would be less discussion about 'justifiable' causes of war,

'if we were accustomed, along with the word, to call up to our minds *the thing which that word is intended to represent*.'[2]

'We can have no adequate idea of this evil, unless we visit, at least in imagination, a field of battle.' He will have none of the usual excuses—that another nation is pre-

[1] *ibid.*, bk. v, ch. 16 (vol. ii, p. 516).

[2] *ibid.*, bk. v, ch. 16 (vol. ii, p. 519). (My italics. The same argument has been effectively used by Mr Aldous Huxley.)

paring, or that national honour must be vindicated. The supposed distinction between private and international morality is an error: 'the morality that ought to govern the conduct of individuals and of nations is in all cases the same'. During the transition-time wars—if we must have them—should be conducted with the utmost magnanimity and humanity, as an intermediate stage towards their abolition. It is a fallacy to think that war may be abolished by making it more and more terrible:

> 'The direct contrary of this is the truth. . . . It is a most mistaken way of teaching men to feel that they are brothers, by imbuing their minds with perpetual hatred.' [1]

Godwin sees only the bad effects of soldiering, also, upon the minds of individual men: 'the man that is merely a soldier, must always be uncommonly depraved'. How can the man who has been trained to regard a loaded weapon as his argument 'entertain all that confidence in reason and distaste of violence which severe truth prescribes'? 'It cannot be a matter of indifference for the human mind to be systematically familiarized to thoughts of murder and desolation.' Let us especially eschew the fallacy of 'national glory'; individuals are everything: society, abstracted from its component individuals, nothing. Do not be deceived by the cant of 'benefits to the whole' for which no single individual is the better. Patriotism, or the 'love of our country', is

> 'another of those specious illusions, which have been invented by impostors in order to render the multitude the blind instruments of their crooked designs.' [2]

For the wise man, 'wherever there are men who understand the value of political justice and are prepared to assert it, that is his country'. Do I owe gratitude and reverence to the British Constitution as such? No: whoever wants me to respect it must rely on one of two motives

[1] *ibid.*, bk. v, ch. 18 (vol. ii, p. 531).
[2] *ibid.*, bk. v, ch. 16 (vol. ii, p. 512).

—'it has a claim upon my support, either because it is good, or because it is British'. Godwin's views were here so 'advanced' as to seem, in his own time, merely perverse; and nationalism is to-day, in some countries, more exorbitant than he would have thought conceivable. Nevertheless, in his usual way, he is anticipating some of the most hopeful developments of thought in our own time—in this case, what is being urged by the supporters of 'Federal Union'. He sees clearly that 'the much-vaunted independence of the European states is an object of an equivocal nature'; 'the despotism which at present prevails among them, is certainly not so excellent as to make us very anxious for its preservation'. He desiderates the 'united states of Europe', and even suggests that freedom might have a better chance in a 'mighty empire' (to-day, a union of the great democracies?).

One of Godwin's most firmly held convictions was (the Pecksniffian doctrine) that Truth must prevail, and Virtue be triumphant—or, as he puts it,

> 'We should not be creatures of a rational and intellectual nature, if the victory of truth over error were not ultimately certain.'

Magna est veritas et praevalebit: it will prevail, but it is for us to make it prevail by incessantly propagating it—'saturating men with argument', in Leslie Stephen's phrase. Men always act upon 'apprehensions of preferableness'; if, therefore, we show them what is truly preferable, they will follow it; and they will not only love the highest when they see it, but, 'having thus gained one step in the acquisition of truth, it cannot be easily conceived of as lost'. It was from this sense of the supreme duty of broadcasting Truth on all occasions that Godwin deduced his celebrated teaching on the importance of Perfect Sincerity. Here, as elsewhere, he seems to anticipate the methods and ideals of the 'Oxford' Group; he proposes that every man should make himself a kind of missionary Alceste, telling everybody everything about himself and themselves, for the purpose of doing them good. Let us outdo the Papists by turning the whole world into our confessional! If every man would tell all the truth he knows, there would be no more falsehood in three years. This sincerity (not cynicism) would clarify and ennoble all our social intercourse. It should be followed out in every detail; for example, we should not teach our servants to exclude unwanted visitors by saying 'not at home', if we are really there.

'Throw aside your books of chemistry', Wordsworth is reported to have said to a young student, 'and read Godwin on Necessity.' We, however, after reading Hartley, Holbach, and Priestley on the subject, may perhaps be excused if we do no more than glance at Godwin's version of the creed. In the infancy of science, men flew for explanations to 'chance', but the more their 'improvements extended' the more convinced they became that 'everything takes place in Nature according to necessary and universal laws'. The same laws of causation, which admittedly govern the universe, govern mind as well; 'thought' is a link in the chain of necessity. Nothing in Nature could have happened otherwise than it has actually happened, and similarly it was 'impossible for a man to act in any instance otherwise than he has acted'. Like the other eighteenth century necessitarians, Godwin tries to eat his cake and have it; nothing could have been otherwise, yet we both can and must make it otherwise! The value of the idea of necessity, for Godwin, is threefold: it enables him to exonerate the criminal from the crime which not he alone, but the whole system of things, has produced; it enables him to preach truth and justice, and the duty of so preaching (because like effects follow like causes, and men must 'necessarily' be improved by hearing good sermons); and it enables him to believe in perfectibility, because 'reason', 'truth', 'justice' are equivalent, for him, to 'that which *must* prevail'. As workers for mankind, we are to regard mind as a chief link in the chain of causes, and work incessantly upon other minds in order to release them from their bondage. Once truth is seen, it must convince: the laws of necessity will ensure that. But occasionally Godwin relapses into the fatalistic type of Necessitarianism: 'the assassin cannot help the murder he commits any more than the dagger', he says; or, to take a more respectable example: 'our disapprobation of vice will be of the same nature as our disapprobation of an infectious distemper'. The element of resentment in the punishment of criminals should be eliminated by Necessitarianism (as later in Butler's *Erewhon*), and a general tolerant acceptance of human failings generated. A 'virtue', or a 'vice', is not a subject for praise or blame, it is merely a characteristic, like a knife's capacity to cut. A knife is made 'good' by sharpening; a man is made 'virtuous' by persuasion. In persuading, a necessitarian will not exhort or threaten, as if the listener were free to choose; he merely 'represents' and 'elucidates'; Truth will do the rest. There is in all this the usual strange blend of active and passive, effort and relaxation. It may seem queer that the missionary whose main concern, after all, is in converting men and improving the world, should have based his gospel upon the very philosophy which enables the assassin to excuse himself, and might give every man a pretext for staying as he is. Necessity, 'the tyrant's plea', gives the bad man too easy an acquittal, and good and bad men alike too little incentive to bestir themselves. But, as we have already suggested, 'necessity' was an essential part of the intellectual outfit of 'enlightened' persons at that time; it was too useful a weapon against religion, superstition, and the supernatural dogmas and claims of the Church, for its inconveniences to be much felt. To acknowledge it was part of your Roman virtue, your Stoic dignity; it marked your disdain for the magic of sacrament, holy water or rosary, and your kinship with Nature. Nevertheless, I doubt whether Godwin, or any of our necessitarians, would have found their philosophy so satisfying if they had not retained, as unconscious presuppositions, certain axioms derived from religion: man's capacity to be born again, for instance; the 'duty' of loving our fellows, and of working unsparingly for their betterment. The Calvinism in which Godwin had been brought up minimized, in theory, the value of good works, but silently admitted them in practice; and his later Necessitarianism remained moral only because he tacitly admitted that *someone*, even if it were only himself, could be an originating 'cause' of reformative action.

Godwin's political ideal was a kind of philosophic anarchism. Government is an unnecessary evil, perpetuating historic imposture and injustice, and he hoped it would at length wither away altogether. The annihilation (of course by argument and persuasion) of the 'quackery' of government will be one of the most memorable stages of human improvement:

> 'With what delight must every well-informed friend of mankind look forward to the auspicious period, the dissolution of political government, of that brute engine, which has been the only perennial cause of the vices of mankind, and which . . . has mischiefs of various sorts incorporated with its substance, and no otherwise to be removed than by its utter annihilation!'[1]

He dwells upon the inefficacy of all attempts to produce virtue by government regulation, and upon the ill effects of the political superintendence of opinion. 'Erroneous' opinions on politics or religion must not be suppressed; they are probably just criticisms of a corrupt establishment, and in any case Truth has nothing to fear. 'Reason and good sense will not fail to augur ill of that system of things which is too sacred to be looked into.' In spite of his passion for education Godwin opposes state education as yet another means of rendering permanent the existing order of things. If every child could receive the education of an Emile, all would be well, but 'public educa-

[1] *ibid.*, bk. v, ch. 24 (vol. ii, p. 578).

tion has always expended its energies in the support of prejudice'.

> 'It has commonly been observed of universities and extensive establishments for the purpose of education that the knowledge taught there is a century behind the knowledge which exists among the unshackled and unprejudiced members of the same political community.'[1]

In Godwin's anarchist Utopia, equalization of property is an indispensable condition, and he cites Plato, More, Swift, and Mably in support of his equalitarian principles. At present a King's income may be equivalent to the earnings of 50,000 labourers: 'is this a state of human beings that must be regarded as the last improvement of political wisdom?' Both the favoured and the deprived classes are 'corrupted by their unnatural situation';[2] the juxtaposition of extreme poverty with ostentatious wealth is a main source of crime. Aristocracy is a system for rendering permanent the inequality of mankind, whereas men, considered as sentient and percipient beings, are by nature approximately equal. The feudal system was a 'ferocious monster devouring, wherever it came, all that the friend of humanity regards with attachment and love', and empty titles still preserve the name and style of territorial overlordship without the thing—'history labours under the Gothic and unintelligible burden'. Burke has invested the existing order with a halo of awe and reverence, but 'it is strongly to be suspected that that regulation which dares not rest upon its own reasonableness, conduces to the benefit of a few at the expense of the many'. No man has a right to superfluities while others lack necessities; moreover, superfluous wealth ruins the health and happiness of its possessor. In his novels Godwin dilates with truly Rousseauistic sentiment upon scenes of patriarchal simplicity, generally in mountainous country—as the Fleetwood home in Merionethshire, or the Swiss

[1] *ibid.*, bk. vi, ch. 8 (vol. ii, p. 667).
[2] *ibid.*, bk. v, ch. 12 (vol. ii, p. 485).

retreats of Ruffigny and St Leon; and these scenes are characteristically contrasted with pictures of riot and misery in 'high' life—

> that voluptuous life
> Unfeeling, where the man who is of soul
> The meanest thrives the most; where dignity,
> True personal dignity, abideth not;
> A light, a cruel and vain world cut off
> From the natural inlets of just sentiment,
> From lowly sympathy and chastening truth.[1]

'Let us at length dismiss artificial tastes', cries Marguerite to the repentant St Leon (after he has wasted his patrimony in riotous living at Paris, and retired upon a pittance to a Swiss fastness):

> 'and idle and visionary pursuits, that do not flow in a direct line from any of the genuine principles of our nature! . . . Here we may live in true patriarchal simplicity. What is chivalry, what are military prowess and glory? Believe me, they are the passions of a mind depraved, that with ambitious refinement seeks to be wise beyond the dictates of sentiment or reason! There is no happiness so solid, or so perfect, as that which disdains these refinements. You, like me, are fond of the luxuriant and romantic scenes of nature. Here we are placed in the midst of them. How idle it would be, to wish to change our arbours, our verdant lanes and thickets, for vaulted roofs, and gloomy halls, and massy plate! Alas, Reginald! it is, I fear, too true, that the splendour in which we lately lived has its basis in oppression; and that the superfluities of the rich are a boon extorted from the hunger and misery of the poor. Here we see a peasantry more peaceful and less oppressed than perhaps any other tract of the earth can exhibit. They are erect and independent, at once friendly and fearless. Is not this a refreshing spectacle?'[2]

Marguerite continues in this vein for a considerable time, extolling the joys of rustic moderation, innocence, and freedom. But it soon appears that Godwin (as might be supposed from what we have seen) does not hold with the alleged 'primitivism' of Rousseau; the rustic joys are to

[1] *The Prelude*, bk. ix, 345.

[2] *St Leon* (1831 ed.), p. 85.

be tasted by the sophisticated mind. An honest ploughman, he had taught in *Political Justice*, cannot be as virtuous as Cato unless he is also an educated man, for 'virtue consists in a desire of the benefit of the species', and 'that desire only can be denominated virtuous, which flows from a distinct perception of the value, and consequently of the nature, of the thing desired'. 'Though I love the sight of peasants, I would not be a peasant', Marguerite declares with commendable frankness; 'I would have a larger stock of ideas, and a wider field of activity. . . . I would not sacrifice in prone oblivion the best characteristics of my nature. I put in my claim for refinements and luxuries, but they are the refinements and purifying of intellect, and the luxuries of uncostly, simple taste.' It was in this manner that Godwin tried to combine 'Primitivism' with belief in 'progress', 'Nature' with 'cultivation'; and he supposes himself, perhaps wrongly,[1] to differ from Rousseau on this point. The savage state was not the genuine and proper condition of man, as he assumes that Rousseau believed; it was, however, by a very slight mistake that Rousseau 'missed the opposite opinion, which it is the business of the present volume to establish'.[2] He had at least seen, and been the first to teach, that the imperfections of government have been 'the only permanent source of the vices of mankind'. Godwin's ideal society would have been a small community or parish inhabited by a cultured peasantry, each family subsisting upon small holdings of equal size, and attending with equal devotion to the husbandry of the soil and of the mind. It is an attractive ideal, and has allured other social experimenters besides the Pantisocrats. But he insists that an intellectual acceptance of the principles of reason is the indispensable precondition of the equalization of property. For there must be no state-superintendence; even accumulation will not be prohibited, but it will be regarded as so absurd that no

[1] Cf. Lovejoy, *The Supposed Primitivism of Rousseau's Discourse on Inequality* (*Modern Philology*, xxi, 1923).

[2] *Political Justice*, bk. v, ch. 15 (vol. ii, p. 503).

one will attempt it. Our present respect for mere possessions will be transferred to intrinsic worth. Men will have a 'right' only to what they need, or can use; anything further, even if made by themselves, will be passed on. There will still be some division of labour, but much less than now. Godwin's equality and fraternity, of course, must be strictly consistent with Liberty in the bourgeois sense; he wants no communism—particularly of house or meals; individuality must at all costs be preserved. Marriage, however, will disappear, along with other forms of exclusive appropriation, and so will parental affection, which is contrary to the principles of Political Justice (tender care of the young will of course continue, but their exact parentage will be a matter of no account). Towards the end of the book Godwin gives the reins to his imagination, and forecasts a time when, as Franklin had said, mind will be omnipotent over matter, and men may conquer disease and even lengthen their lives indefinitely by so willing. Even now, cheerfulness and serenity of mind have incalculable physical effects, and a relapse into vacancy, sleep, or melancholy is so much cut off from life. Let no one fear that if men become too happy they will multiply too rapidly; beings who can control death will be able to control the birth-rate. The first step towards the realization of these visions is the removal of the present odious governments of Europe. But argument, writing, and persuasion are to be the means employed, not incitement to tumult; we must await, in calm confidence, the arrival of the great crisis of human affairs, the day of ultimate hope for humanity.

Such, in briefest outline, are some of the contents of that celebrated book, which immediately won for its author the fame he had thirsted for, and influenced some of the best heads of the generation. Within a few weeks of its appearance, and for some years afterwards, Godwin 'blazed as a sun in the firmament of reputation; no one was more talked of, more looked up to, more sought after, and wherever liberty, truth, justice was the theme, his name was not far off'.[1] Almost as remarkable as his meteoric ascent, and quite as significant, was his later obscuration; 'now he has sunk below the horizon', wrote Hazlitt twenty-five years afterwards, 'and enjoys the serene twilight of a doubtful immortality'. The reasons for this change have already been hinted at, and indeed a mere summary of the contents of *Political Justice* is perhaps enough to suggest its likelihood. Godwin caught the ardent tone of 1793, and uttered what was then in the hearts of the young and the eager, but the tide that carried him was just about to turn, and his fame was lost in the opposite currents that now began to flow steadily, bringing in the nineteenth century. The development of Wordsworth and Coleridge is often described in terms of 'Godwinism' and 'Reaction', but it is not so often remembered that Godwin himself moved in the new direction almost as quickly, though never so completely. Godwin, like the poets, was caught at the meeting-point of the two centuries, but, unlike them, he had done his best work in the eighteenth century tradition, and for all his later development, he never ceased to be thought of as a voice from the past. The younger men were able, before age and other causes silenced them, to identify themselves with 'the revolt of the human mind against the philosophy of the eighteenth century', and to reveal what had been undreamed of in that philosophy.

4

It is not my purpose to follow Godwin through his years of twilight, but a word may be said about his own crossing of the dividing watershed between 1793 and 1800. He, like Wordsworth, came to see 'Nature' as 'Feeling', and not merely as 'Reason'. 'I am filled with grief', he wrote in his memoranda,

'when I reflect on the possibility that any extravagances or over-

[1] Hazlitt, *loc. cit.*

sights of mine should bring into disrepute the great truths I have endeavoured to propagate. But thus my mind is constituted. I have, perhaps, never been without the possession of important views and forcible reasonings; but they have ever been mixed with absurd and precipitate judgments, of which subsequent consideration has made me profoundly ashamed.' [1]

The theoretic basis of *Political Justice* was defective, he came to believe, in not yielding enough importance to feeling:

> 'the voluntary actions of men are under the direction of their feelings. . . . Reason, accurately speaking, has not the smallest degree of power to put any one limb or articulation of our bodies into action. Its province, in a practical view, is wholly confined to adjusting the comparison between different objects of desire, and investigating the most successful mode of attaining those objects.'

Similarly, the *family affections* are not objects of moral censure:

> 'The benefits we can confer upon the world are few. . . . The benefits we can confer upon those with whom we are closely connected are of great magnitude, or continual occurrence. It is impossible that we should be continually thinking of the whole world, or not confer a smile or a kindness but as we are prompted to it by an abstract principle of philanthropy.'

'But it seems equally certain', he adds, in a rather pathetic effort to stick to his old guns, 'that utility, though not the source, will be the regulator' of a good man's actions, and that 'however ardent be his parental, domestic, or friendly exertions, he will from time to time examine into their coincidence with the greatest sum of happiness in his power to produce'. Again, education remains a most powerful instrument, but he came to allow more weight to 'differences of the highest importance' existing between human beings from their birth.

[1] Quoted by F. K. Brown, *op. cit.*, pp. 135-6.

As early as in the Preface to the second edition (dated October 29, 1795) he says that he has 'in several instances detected error', and speaks of the 'duty of a severe and assiduous revisal'. He had, in fact, rewritten the first four and the last books, and had modified many of the extremer views, notably on Property, on Marriage, on Personal Virtue and Duties, on Promises, on Sincerity, on Longevity, and on Political Change. He had said, for example, that nearly all private property was unjust; now (perhaps thinking of what he had earned for *Political Justice* and *Caleb Williams*) he allows the individual the disposal of property earned by service to the human species. Sincerity might sometimes be infringed on grounds of utility; after marriage is abolished there should still be permanent attachments; political change should be brought about, not only without violence, but by almost imperceptible degrees. 'No man can more fervently deprecate scenes of commotion and tumult than the author of this book', he says, and he hopes that his work will be found favourable to 'the increase and preservation of genuine kindness and benevolence'. Finally, in the Preface to *St Leon* (1799), there occurs the following passage:

> 'Some readers of my graver productions will, perhaps, in perusing these little volumes, accuse me of inconsistency; the affections and charities of private life being everywhere in this publication a topic of the warmest eulogium, while in the *Enquiry Concerning Political Justice* they seemed to be treated with no great degree of indulgence and favour. In answer to this objection, all I think it necessary to say on the present occasion is, that, for more than four years, I have been anxious for opportunity and leisure to modify some of the earlier chapters of that work in conformity to the sentiments inculcated in this. Not that I see cause to make any change respecting the principle of justice, or any thing else fundamental to the system there delivered, but that I apprehend domestic and private affections inseparable from the nature of man, and from what may be styled the *culture of the heart*, and am fully persuaded that they are not incompatible with a profound

and active sense of justice in the mind of him that cherishes them.'[1]

(Marguerite, the heroine of this novel, it may be remembered, was an idealized portrait of Mary Wollstonecraft.) I have italicized the phrase 'culture of the heart' to bring out the analogy between Godwin and his spiritual kinsman of the next century, J. S. Mill, who, describing his recovery from the arid intellectualism and nervous collapse of his youth, tells us that he found in Wordsworth's poetry 'the very culture of the feelings, which I was in quest of'.[2] Much has been made, and rightly, of the anti-Godwinian theme in *The Borderers* and in *Lyrical Ballads*, but even while Wordsworth was writing against the meddling intellect, and in praise of parental love, gratitude, love of home and personal possessions, and all the 'supplementary aids of an imperfect virtue', Godwin was making the same criticisms on his earlier self. That he was capable of such self-criticism is to his credit (and perhaps also to Mary Wollstonecraft's), but it is not surprising that he lost his influence with those who had revered him solely as the voice of Immutable Truth, the Truth that makes us free. *Political Justice*, whatever its perversities, had at least had some distant affinity with the Gospels; it was, indeed, in Hazlitt's phrase, 'a metaphysical and logical commentary on some of the most beautiful and striking texts of Scripture'. One recalls: 'Who is my mother? and who are my brethren? . . . whosoever shall do the will of my Father which is in heaven, he is my brother, and sister and mother'; or the injunction to leave house, and wife, and brethren, and parents, and children for the Kingdom of God's sake. It is not commonly suggested that the Kingdom of Heaven, because difficult of access, is not worth trying to enter; but many, including Godwin himself, came to think the Godwinian heaven a worse place than this imperfect world. There was 'a want in all his

[1] *St Leon* (1831 ed.), pp. ix-x. (My italics.)
[2] Mill's *Autobiography* ('World's Classics' ed.), p. 125.

system of the mild and persuasive tone of the Gospel', and perhaps the rationalist's arguments, addressed exclusively to the head (and so, to the few who can understand), are more liable to perversion than the exhortations of religion, which humble the pride of intellect and use the heart's affections in obedience to an absolute command. And what might not the foolish or unscrupulous do with the maxims of universal benevolence! 'There was danger', says Hazlitt, 'that the unseasoned novice might substitute some pragmatical conceit of his own for the rule of right reason, and mistake a heartless indifference for a superiority to more natural and generous feelings', or the 'perfectibility code' might turn out in practice to be a scheme 'for the accommodation of the enterprising and cunning, at the expense of the credulous and honest'. It might be that average humanity was unequal to the strain of living the life of pure reason—as indeed Swift had hinted by making his ideal creatures, not philosophers, but horses. Perfected humanity could perhaps dispense with the poor, irrational 'virtues' of gratitude, filial and parental affection, patriotism, or piety. But supposing we dispensed with them, and yet failed of perfection, might we not discover too late that these virtues are what alone prevent us, not from advancing to perfection, but from sinking into brutality?

Misgivings of this kind were in Wordsworth's mind when he composed *The Borderers* (1795-6), and similar fears, though relating to the Jacobin philosophy and not to Godwin, led Burke to write the *Reflexions on the Revolution in France* (1790). In order to show how, in 'the revolt of the human mind against the philosophy of the eighteenth century', 'Nature' in the sense of 'the historical and the actual' came to be used in opposition to 'Nature' in the sense of 'the abstract and potential', I shall conclude with some observations on these two representatives of the new way of thought.

II. EDMUND BURKE

I see him,—old, but vigorous in age,—
Stand like an oak whose stag-horn branches start
Out of its leafy brow, the more to awe
The younger brethren of the grove . . .
While he forewarns, denounces, launches forth
Against all systems built on abstract rights,
Keen ridicule; the majesty proclaims
Of Institutes and Laws, hallowed by time;
Declares the vital power of social ties
Endeared by Custom; and with high disdain,
Exploding upstart Theory, insists
Upon the allegiance to which men are born—

[*The Prelude*, bk. vii, 519.]

No writer, says Leslie Stephen, has received or deserved more splendid panegyrics than Burke. The above-quoted passage from *The Prelude* represents Wordsworth's mature attitude, and not the state of mind in which he heard Burke in the year 1791, nor the mood in which he wrote the *Letter to the Bishop of Llandaff* (1793). But even Hazlitt, who almost alone of his literary compeers resisted the master-current of his time, and said, 'I would rather quarrel with my best friend than admit the right of the Bourbons to the throne of France'—even Hazlitt said of Burke, 'It has always been with me a test of the sense and candour of anyone belonging to the opposite party, whether he allowed Burke to be a great man'; 'in arriving at one error he discovered a hundred truths'. It is not my purpose to enlarge in any detail upon Burke's political philosophy, but merely to give him the place which seems his due in our particular story.

All down the eighteenth century, both in England and France, there had been a succession of novels, plays, poems, and treatises exalting the natural over the artificial man, the primitive (as being fresher from the hands of God or Nature) over the sophisticated, the rustic over the urban.

One could mention, as all belonging in some sense to this tradition, Shaftesbury, Addison, Thomson, Rousseau, Cowper, Brown (of the *Estimate*, 1757), Henry Brooke, Lord Kames, Thomas Day, Mary Wollstonecraft, Holcroft, Bage, Mrs Inchbald, and many others. Much of this body of literature, especially in England, remained on the level of sentimental reverie or 'escapism'; some of it may be characterized as a cultivated blend of classical (especially Horatian) with Christian feeling against luxury and in favour of simplicity. But the principle so concisely stated by Rousseau in the opening sentence of the *Contrat Social*, and by Diderot in the *Supplément au Voyage de Bougainville* (cf. above, p. 14), was capable, as we have seen, of being turned towards revolutionary ends if—like most of the French philosophers of the century—you were sufficiently indignant with the existing order. When the French Revolution broke out, it was received in England (as has been said) with mingled astonishment and sympathy. Fox's exclamation has become classical, but it should be remembered how far, in much contemporary popular literature, the 'Jacobinical' values were being taken for granted. In the novels of Day, Holcroft, Bage, and Mrs Inchbald, virtue is found in the cottage, vice in the palace. 'What is a peer of the realm', asks Holcroft, 'but a man educated in vice, nurtured in prejudices from his earliest childhood, and daily breathing the same infection as he first respired?' Or again: 'Men are rendered selfish and corrupt by the baneful influence of the system under which they live. . . . They are not in love with baseness, it is forced upon them.' In Mrs Inchbald's *Nature and Art* the theme is the contrast between two cousins, one of whom has been pampered by rich parents, and goes to the dogs, while the other—the hero of the book—has had the good fortune to be cast ashore upon a tropical island in infancy, and to be brought up by the noble savages. Further back, in Cowper and in Brown's *Estimate*, one encounters a sense of the contrast between the corruption in high places, and the health and wholesomeness which dwelt among the poor—a great reservoir of vital energy which would at last overflow and renovate the world by washing away the tawdry ruins of the ancient régime. It is no wonder that, to the considerable body of opinion here represented, the Revolution seemed 'nothing out of Nature's certain course'. 'What temper at the prospect did not wake To happiness unthought of?' asks Wordsworth. The answer is simple: that of Edmund Burke did not. It was precisely in 1790, when Europe was still 'thrilled with joy', and many could still regard the Revolution as the triumph of Nature and Reason over ancient wrong, that Burke uttered his solemn warning, and made those prophecies whose speedy fulfilment caused him to be admired as an oracle of prescience. In the 'eighties, as Fanny Burney tells us, Burke's name had been unmentionable at Court, because he had supported the Americans, because he had proposed to reform the King's Kitchen, and because he was prosecuting Warren Hastings. But when the *Reflexions* appeared, he found himself for the first time the darling of the dynasts, and George III is reported to have said that this was 'a good book, a very good book, and every gentleman ought to read it'. In spite of such praise, however, and the approval of all who had vested interests in the 'social ties endeared by Custom', the *Reflexions* must always command respect as an exploration of the one avenue which was shaded from the eyes of the reformers. Burke sees so far into what was missed by the Holbachs and the Godwins, and states his case with such rhetorical opulence, that he has perhaps been overpraised at their expense.

In a passage already referred to, J. S. Mill takes Bentham as typical of the sort of mind which questions things established, asking of any ancient or received opinion, 'Is it true?' Coleridge, on the other hand, seeing so much further into the complexities of the human intellect and feelings, asks rather 'What is the meaning of it?' and considers 'the long or extensive prevalence of any opinion as a presumption that it was not altogether a fallacy'.[1] Coleridge is with Burke in this, and indeed he had learnt much from him. The central instinct of Burke, as Morley rightly insisted, was his preference for that which has *grown* to that which is *made*; it was this which gave unity to his superficially diverse attitudes, especially on the American and French Revolutions. The colonists had grown into an independent people, and they claimed not the 'rights of man', but the rights of Englishmen, which had been the same since the beginning of history. It was the narrow imperialism of George III and his ministers which, in the name of mere abstract 'right', was misshaping this fine natural growth. The French Revolutionists, on the other hand, were sweeping away, in the names of 'reason' and 'abstract right', nothing less than the whole complex organism of society, the product of centuries of development and adaptation, on which alone depended the possibility of civilized living. Destroy rank, privilege, established religion, property, and the reverence with which prescription had invested them, and you destroy the only framework within which poor human nature had proved capable of virtue. Set up 'reason' in their place, and you are setting up something essentially feeble and fallible, and, moreover, liable to become enslaved by the very passions it claims to rule; you are opening the way to 'calculators' and exploiters, and banishing 'the unbought grace of life' which lingers amongst the feudal forms. 'Politics', said Burke, 'ought to be adjusted, not to human reasonings, but to human nature; of which the reason is but a part, and by no means the greatest part.'[2] This celebrated remark illustrates the manner in which Burke counters 'Nature' the abstraction with 'Nature' the actuality, the metaphysical with the historical, *natura naturans* with *natura naturata*, and it may stand as a symbol of the transition from the eighteenth century mental climate to that of the nineteenth. Burke belongs to the eighteenth

[1] Mill, *Dissertations and Discussions*, vol. i, p. 394.

[2] Quoted by A. Cobban, *Edmund Burke and the Revolt against the Eighteenth Century*, p. 77.

century in his acceptance of a divine purpose as immanent in the existing order of things:

> 'the awful Author of our being is the Author of our place in the order of existence; and . . . having disposed and marshalled us by a divine tactic, not according to our will, but according to His, he has, in and by that disposition, virtually subjected us to act the part which belongs to the place assigned us.'[1]

In this and similar pronouncements Burke seems to return, though admittedly with a much finer sense of history and a greatly strengthened imaginative power, to the standpoint of 'whatever is, is right'. What has actually come into being must be 'right' and 'natural', because it must accord with the Will that has permitted it. But Burke belongs also to the 'romantic' reaction inasmuch as he rejects the abstract intellectualism into which the eighteenth century had evolved, and which in his time was being pushed to revolutionary conclusions. As a believer in what is felt in the heart rather than in what is excogitated by the brain he is with Rousseau as well as with Wordsworth. But Rousseau had excluded human societies from the 'Nature' he worshipped; 'Nature' had been adorable because it was untainted by the 'mean and vulgar works of man', and man-made things, for him as for the rest of the revolutionary school, were bad because 'artificial'. Burke, on the contrary, includes human society in his conception of 'Nature'; the political organisms evolved by history are as venerable to him, therefore, as mountains, forests, and lakes were to Rousseau. For Rousseau the principle of evil lay in the 'artificial' system which, by some unexplained process, had been foisted from outside upon unspoiled, instinctive man; for Burke it lay in the meddling intellect which presumes to interfere with the mysterious march of God in the world. Burke was of the company of those who are continually conscious of the weight of all this unintelligible world; he was more aware of the complex forces which hem us in and condition all

[1] *ibid.*, p. 94.

we do, than of any power in us to act back upon and modify the very environment that limits us.

> 'The nature of man is intricate; the objects of society are of the greatest possible complexity: and therefore no simple disposition or direction of power can be suitable either to man's nature, or to the quality of his affairs.... [The revolutionists] are so taken up with their theories about the rights of man, that they have totally forgotten his nature.'[1]

But if the unaided reason is feeble, and productive of nothing but cobweb-abstractions—as Bacon had taught—the reason need never be unaided, for it has at its disposal, not what Bacon had meant by 'Nature', but what was truly 'Nature' for Burke: the funded wisdom of the ages. The individual is foolish, but the species is wise. The present order of society, like a great forest tree, has grown with the majestic slowness of Nature herself, and its present shape, as the result of natural adaptation to environment, is more 'natural' than it could be after any lopping and pruning that men could inflict upon it. Men may, indeed, remove from it any ivy or mistletoe which is checking its growth, and so leave it freer to develop its own nature, but if they apply the axe or the saw they can only deface it, and may destroy its life altogether.

It was, of course, comparatively easy for Burke to accept the English Constitution as part of the order of Nature; with all its defects it was a living organism of proved adaptability and power of growth, whereas in France the Constitution could be likened, if to any biological form, only to the fossil of an extinct creature. But probably what Burke really reverenced was less the English Constitution as it actually was in the reign of George III, than an ideal English Constitution, stripped of its ugly incrustations, and working freely according to its inner intention: an ideal almost, but not quite, as remote as Plato's city which is in heaven. The distance between idea and reality can be measured by comparing his noble eulogies of the idea

[1] *Reflexions*, pp. 59 and 62 ('Everyman' ed.).

of our Constitution, and of our aristocracy, with his own account of the state of both in *Thoughts on the Present Discontents*. But his conviction always was, like Dante's or Langland's, that the organism was healthy at the core, and that it only needed wise direction to ensure the harmonious working of its parts. Burke takes pleasure in comparing the state with the family; we in England, he tells his French friend, have managed to combine our political and domestic instincts. The perfections of our Constitution, he writes, are

> 'the happy effect of *following nature*, which is wisdom without reflection, and above it. . . . By a constitutional policy, working *after the pattern of nature*, we receive, we hold, we transmit our government and our privileges, in the same manner in which we enjoy and transmit our property and our lives. . . . Our political system is placed *in a just correspondence and symmetry with the order of the world*, and with the mode of existence decreed to a permanent body composed of transitory parts; wherein, by the disposition of a stupendous wisdom, moulding together the great mysterious incorporation of the human race, the whole, at one time, is never old, or middle-aged, or young. . . . Thus, by *preserving the method of nature* in the conduct of the state, in what we improve, we are never wholly new; in what we retain, we are never wholly obsolete. By adhering in this manner and on those principles to our forefathers, we are guided not by the superstition of antiquarians, but by the spirit of philosophic analogy. In this choice of inheritance we have given to our frame of polity the image of a relation in blood; binding up the constitution of our country with our dearest domestic ties; adopting our fundamental laws into the bosom of our family affections; keeping inseparable and cherishing with the warmth of all their combined and mutually reflected charities, our state, our hearths, our sepulchres, and our altars.' [1]

All this has been achieved by 'a conformity to nature in our artificial institutions', and by 'calling in the aid of her unerring and powerful instincts, to fortify the fallible and feeble contrivances of our reason'. He challenges the

[1] *Reflexions*, pp. 31-2. (My italics.)

sophisters of France to produce any better plan than we have followed—we 'who have chosen our nature rather than our speculations, our breasts rather than our inventions, for the great conservatories and magazines of our rights and privileges'. 'You think you are combating prejudice, but you are at war with nature.' It is thus that Burke rescues 'Nature' from its professed disciples—the Nature which he feels to be real, because deeply rooted, far below the probings of superficial analysis, in history, in the unconscious mind of man, and ultimately in the purposes of God. In spite of the 'importunate chink' of Dr Price, and the other English revolutionary grasshoppers, the thousand great cattle, 'reposed beneath the shadow of the British oak, chew the cud and are silent'. This is Burke's imagery for expressing the contrast, so constantly present to his mind, between the transitory and the permanent, the specious and the real; the same thought is expressed in the even more characteristic image of the 'proud keep of Windsor, rising in the majesty of proportion, and girt with the double belt of its kindred and coeval towers', contrasted with the 'pickaxes of all the levellers of France'. And so he would have us reverence tradition, prescription, even prejudice:

> 'We are not the converts of Rousseau; we are not the disciples of Voltaire; Helvetius has made no progress amongst us. Atheists are not our preachers; madmen are not our lawgivers. We know that *we* have made no discoveries, and we think that no discoveries are to be made, in morality; nor many in the great principles of government, nor in the ideas of liberty, which were understood long before we were born, altogether as well as they will be after the grave has heaped its mould upon our presumption, and the silent tomb shall have imposed its law on our pert loquacity. [1]

The tone is more forensic, the rhythm less subtle, and the afflatus more windy than in Browne or Taylor, but it is clear nevertheless that we have left the eighteenth century

[1] *ibid.*, p. 83.

that we knew, and are back amongst the imaginatives, at the line where men and mountains meet. Burke continues:

> 'We fear God; we look up with awe to Kings; with affection to Parliaments; with duty to magistrates; with reverence to priests; and with respect to nobility. Why? Because when such ideas are brought before our minds, it is *natural* to be so affected.'[1]

And then follows the defence of prejudice, which, in its anticipation of Wordsworth and Coleridge, reads more like an answer to Godwin than (what it actually was) an occasion for one of Godwin's most celebrated pronouncements (cf. above, pp. 219-22):

> 'We are afraid to put men to live and trade each on his own private stock of reason; because we suspect that this stock in each man is small, and that the individuals would do better to avail themselves of the general bank and capital of nations and of ages. Many of our men of speculation, instead of exploding general prejudices, employ their sagacity to discover the latent wisdom which prevails in them. If they find what they seek, and they seldom fail, they think it more wise to continue the prejudice, with the reason involved, than to cast away the coat of prejudice, and to leave nothing but the naked reason; because prejudice, with its reason, has a motive to give action to that reason, and an affection which will give it permanence. Prejudice is of ready application in the emergency; it previously engages the mind in a steady course of wisdom and virtue, and does not leave the man hesitating in the moment of decision, sceptical, puzzled, and unresolved. *Prejudice renders a man's duty his habit; and not a series of unconnected acts.*'[2]

It is Burke's main distinction that, in an age which was willing to abolish history and amend human nature, he was alive to the inescapable power of both. According to the Jacobin philosophy, which derives from Locke, man brings nothing into the world with him except a sensitive

[1] *ibid.*, pp. 83-4. (Burke's italics.)

[2] *ibid.*, p. 84. (My italics: contrast Godwin's 'the genuine and wholesome state of mind,' etc., p. 222 above.)

percipience on which any sort of impressions may be inscribed. Heredity, history, physical environment, count for nothing. The rules of justice and reason (the laws of Nature) are therefore applicable to all times and all places. If history has been for a long time inscribing erroneous impressions on the blank sheet of the mind, let us 'abolish' history—as d'Alembert suggested. Let us only begin to write reason and justice where history has written prejudice, slavery, and superstition, and we shall change human nature in one generation. To all this Burke replies by an appeal to psychological fact, and to history itself. Man is not a blank sheet at birth; he is born with a mass of predispositions inherited from an incalculable past, and these vary according to place and time. There is therefore no one, universal, 'natural', and best form of society or of government; 'I cannot', Burke writes, 'stand forward, and give praise or blame to anything which relates to human actions, and human concerns, on a simple view of the object, as it stands stripped of every relation, in all the nakedness and solitude of metaphysical abstraction. Circumstances (which with some gentlemen pass for nothing) give in reality to every political principle its distinguishing colour and discriminating effect.' These inherited predispositions, call them prejudices if we will, are in fact the fountain-light of all our day. The effort to wipe them out, and live by unsupported reason, will result, not in truly rational and virtuous conduct, but in moral anarchy. Ideally, perhaps, man may aspire to a fully rational consciousness, but actually reason is by no means the most important part of his nature, and thus to try to live by it will mean catastrophe. The events of the Terror gave point to Burke's teaching, and readers of Wordsworth will recognize that he repeated, in his revolt from France and from Godwin, Burke's general revolt against the revolutionary creed. The famous eighteenth century alliance between Nature and Reason had begun to crumble; Reason, it was found, could lead one way, and Nature another. Or, putting it another way, the

'Nature' to which the century had so confidently appealed could have two main sets of meanings: it could mean the head, or it could mean the heart; ideas or facts; theories or history; what is congenial to abstract reason, or what is dear to the heart. The nineteenth century went on believing in 'Nature', but not without misgivings due to the inherent contradictions of the creed. Was Nature best expressed in the 'march of mind', or in the heart's affections—including its new-found affection for mossy ruins? These things, it was found, could conflict. The dilemma was thus expressed by George Eliot:

> 'Is not the striving after something better and better in our surroundings the grand characteristic that distinguishes man from the brute? . . . But Heaven knows where that striving might lead us, if our affections had not a trick of twining round those old inferior things—if the loves and sanctities of our life had no deep immovable roots in memory.'[1]

The 'truth', it seemed, was not all upon the side of Burke, nor all upon the side of Godwin. It would be a poor and chaotic world, no doubt, in which men were put to live and trade each upon his private stock of reason. But what sort of world should we get if existing systems were always to be regarded as 'too sacred to be looked into'? Because custom and prejudice are often wise, because in them is often embodied the accumulated wisdom of ages for the guidance of the erring individual, is the light of reason never to be directed upon them? Burke is in many ways a spiritual progenitor of the nineteenth century. It has been truly said that Scott, in his novels, translated into the dialect of fiction Burke's basic principles; and the attempts of Coleridge, Carlyle, Green, and Ruskin to reintroduce a conception of the state as a spiritual and not merely an economic partnership derive in part from him. So, too, does the corollary of that attempt—the recognition that the Middle Ages had in some sort realized that ideal; for Burke was one of the first philosophic admirers of the

[1] *The Mill on the Floss*, p. 173. ('World's Classics' ed.)

'age of Chivalry'. For us it is of more concern that he was the first to formulate the principles of the nineteenth century brand of patriotic 'nationalism', believing that this was the only weapon with which to fight an 'armed doctrine'. The French, 'become oppressors in their turn', and their revolutionary élan deflected into conquest and Napoleonism, could be effectively met by no mere combination of effete dynasties, but only by the awakening of a national spirit as ardent as their own. As Mr Cobban says, 'Pitt was waging a nineteenth century war on eighteenth century methods', and 'Burke, and for a long time Burke alone, comprehended that a new system was needed'.[1] All through the era of struggles for national independence and liberty, and down to the Treaty of Versailles, the authority of this idea has seemed absolute. It has been reserved for our own unhappy generation to see nationalism itself become an armed doctrine, as aggressive as Napoleonism, and more sinister. In face of this dangerous degeneration of the nationality principle we may have to return for deliverance, behind Burke and the 'concrete', to the grand leading abstractions of the eighteenth century—to liberty, equality, and fraternity, to the Rights of Man, and the Laws of Nature. Dr Catlin (in a book on the Anglo-Saxon Tradition, just published at the time of writing), has said of the present situation that 'Unless there is an emotion for this free community of ours more powerful than that aroused in the Marxist for class war, or in the Hitlerian for his race, then these and not we will shape the world's future'.[2] Unfortunately it is far harder to fight armed nationality with an abstract doctrine than an armed doctrine with nationality, particularly when, as now, the militant nationalities are 'armed doctrines' as well. The question of our time is whether the liberal tradition (now mainly represented by the three great democracies) can hold its own against militant racialism—by Federal Union or other means—without invoking its own

[1] *op. cit.*, p. 129.
[2] Quoted in *Times Lit. Supp.* review, Aug. 12, 1939.

race-passions and so becoming the very thing it opposes —*propter vitam vivendi perdere causas*. If this can be achieved,[1] the eighteenth century will not have existed in vain. The alternative is to leave the future to be shaped by war and the ensuing revolution.

[1] See Clarence K. Streit, *Union Now* (Cape, 1939).

CHAPTER XII

'Nature' in Wordsworth

I

WORDSWORTH'S importance in the history of the Idea of Nature is not likely to be underestimated, and it will not be expected that much can be added to what he himself and numerous critics and biographers have written on the subject. Nevertheless it is essential to the rounding-off of our story that Wordsworth's 'Nature' should be seen in its relation to the background we have been describing, and particularly in relation to the political thought of his age. The divinization of Nature, which began in the modern world at the Renaissance, and proceeded during the eighteenth century in the way we have seen, culminates for English literature in Wordsworth. This is commonly agreed; but why it culminated in the particular form of a passion for 'mute, insensate things', for 'green grass and mountains bare', for Man 'ennobled outwardly' by mergence with the inanimate (Michael, the Leech Gatherer, 'Nature's Lady') —all this can only be fully understood by tracing the growth of Wordsworth's political sympathies between 1790 and 1798. Much else is, of course, necessary besides this, especially an understanding of his childhood and youth, of his love-affair in France, and of the influence of Dorothy Wordsworth and Coleridge. But in the present context it seems most relevant to fix our attention on what I have called the vital transition of his life, when, after his early attachments to France and to Godwin, he came to share Burke's evaluation, and to regard the Revolution as made by man, not evolved by 'Nature'. This transition is of special importance as a symbol of the transference, then in progress, from the eighteenth century senses of 'Nature' to the nineteenth. In the development of Wordsworth during the last decade of our century we can see, what we have hitherto found mainly in separate minds, 'Nature' turning from a revolutionary into a conservative principle, and the emphasis shifting from the abstract to the concrete, from reason to feeling. For Wordsworth's generation it was political emotion, above all, which gave warmth to that conception of a divine Nature which had hitherto been held mainly as an intellectual abstraction. In Wordsworth himself it was reaction from politics which gave the special fervour to the poetry of his 'inspired decade', and led him back to those 'grand and permanent forms' in which the wisdom and spirit of the universe seemed most unmistakably manifest. Wordsworth is thought of mainly as a recluse, yet Harper can describe him as, with the exception of Milton, the most political of our poets. This may be so, and we must believe Wordsworth when he said (in 1833) 'that although he was known to the world only as a poet, he had given twelve hours' thought to the conditions and prospects of society, for one to poetry'. Yet it was not when he was most political—whether in youth or in later life—that he was most 'poetical'. What breathes in his best work is rather the rapture of an escape from uncongenial political preoccupations, and the joy of the discovery that amidst

> the calm oblivious tendencies
> Of Nature, 'mid her plants, and weeds, and flowers,
> And silent overgrowings,[1]

he could correct his despondency and find tranquil restoration. In a passage now incorporated in Book IV of *The Excursion*, but written by March 1798 (that is, at the time of his most intense communing with 'earth and every common sight'), he explains, more explicitly than in *Tintern Abbey*, how he has found in Nature (in the sense of 'all that we behold from this green earth') the anchor

[1] *The Excursion*, bk. i, 928.

of his purest thoughts, the guide and guardian of his heart:

For, the Man—
Who, in this spirit, communes with the Forms
Of Nature, who with understanding heart
Both knows and loves such objects as excite
No morbid passions, no disquietude,
No vengeance, and no hatred—needs must feel
The joy of that pure principle of love
So deeply, that, unsatisfied with aught
Less pure and exquisite, he cannot choose
But seek for objects of a kindred love
In fellow-natures and a kindred joy.
Accordingly he by degrees perceives
His feelings of aversion softened down;
A holy tenderness pervade his frame.
His sanity of reason not impaired,
Say rather, all his thoughts now flowing clear,
From a clear fountain flowing, he looks round
And seeks for good; and finds the good he seeks.

. . . . .

So build we up the Being that we are;
Thus deeply drinking-in the soul of things,
We shall be wise perforce.[1]

At the very same time (April 1798) Coleridge, quoting Wordsworth's lines and expressing their conjoint sentiments in those ecstatic Alfoxden days, wrote to his brother that he had 'snapped his squeaking baby-trumpet of sedition' and withdrawn himself totally from 'French metaphysics, French politics, French ethics, and French theology', in order to meditate upon the '*causæ causarum*':

'I devote myself to such works as encroach not on the anti-social passions—in poetry, to elevate the imagination and set the affections in right tune by the beauty of the inanimate impregnated as with a living soul by the presence of life—in prose to the seeking with patience . . . what our faculties are and what they are capable of becoming. I love fields and woods and mountains

[1] *The Excursion*, bk. iv, 1208-66

> with almost a visionary fondness. And because I have found benevolence and quietness growing within me as that fondness has increased, therefore I should wish to be the means of implanting it in others, and to destroy the bad passions not by combating them but by keeping them in inaction.'[1]

And in a phrase which seems to glance at Wordsworth's *Borderers*, he adds that he is regulating his mind so as to prevent 'the passions from turning the reason into a hired advocate'. There was nothing new, it may be remarked, nothing very startling, in the discovery that one can find peace and contentment in rural retirement: from Horace to Cowper (to go no further afield) there had seldom lacked poets, satirists, and moralists to recommend plain living and high thinking. But the 'Nature' of Wordsworth and Coleridge was apprehended with a new kind of intensity. In a sense, like Burke, they return to 'whatever is, is right', but it is on a higher level of insight—the level of Plotinus, Spinoza, and the mystics. And the passion with which they mingled themselves with landscape was derived, partly indeed from their rejection of the mechanical philosophy which had yielded 'a universe of death', but primarily from the deflection into imaginative channels of their thwarted political ardours. They had thought to see human nature born again, and the millennium realized, whether in Europe or on the banks of the Susquehanna. Defeated of these hopes by the Terror, the war, and 'the chain of harsh necessity', they found deliverance in transforming the world, not by political action, but by the 'modifying colours of the imagination'. That this was possible, they felt, was owing to the existence of a bond between Nature and the soul of man. So exquisitely was Nature fitted to the mind, and the mind to Nature, that the creation which they 'with blended might accomplish' must needs be both beautiful and 'true'. It was thus to the achievement of a 'fine balance of truth in observing, with the imaginative faculty in modifying the objects

[1] *Letters of S. T. C.*, ed. E. H. Coleridge, vol. i, p. 244. (Quoted in L. Hanson, *Life of S. T. C., The Early Years*, p. 275.)

observed' (a balance already reached by Wordsworth in *The Female Vagrant*; in Coleridge's view) that the two poets dedicated themselves during those happy months of intimacy between Alfoxden and Stowey. The Quantock Hills, transfigured by the mind's 'auxiliar light', replaced for them the vanished France and the impossible Pantisocracy. Let us then, in the hope of capturing some faint echo of the emotions of 1798, briefly retrace the path that led Wordsworth from France to Racedown and Alfoxden.

It is needless to recapitulate in detail the familiar tale, so graphically told in *The Prelude*, and so amply filled out by the critics, of Wordsworth's early enthusiasm for the Revolution, at the time when 'a homeless sound of joy was in the air', and the political scene took on, for ardent youth, 'the attraction of a country in romance'. I shall dwell mainly upon the theme suggested above—his acceptance and rejection of Godwin. Of his first revolutionary sympathies during the summer tour of 1790, he himself has said that he 'was touched, but with no intimate concern'. The memorable passage in Book VI, which describes that tour, is not the account of the Festival of the Federation, of which he saw the gaudy 'reliques'—'flowers left to wither on triumphal arcs'—but the description of the crossing of the Alps, with the apocalyptic vision which ensued. It is instructive, by the way, to compare this passage, written ten years afterwards, when the experience had had time to incubate in his mind, with a letter written in September 1790 to Dorothy, in which he blandly informs her—like any other 'picturesque' tourist of the eighteenth century—that he is 'a perfect enthusiast in my admiration of nature in all her various forms'.[1] Wordsworth was always more responsive to single impressions, whether great or small, than to the chequered human scene, and just as the Simplon Pass meant more to him than the rejoicing millions of France, so in describing London he succeeds best when he can fuse its multitudinousness into a unity—when at night he

[1] Harper's *Life*, vol. i, pp. 93-5.

sees 'moonlight and stars, and empty streets', and hears sounds 'unfrequent as in deserts', or when at dawn 'all that mighty heart is lying still'. Even when he was enjoying the 'heart-bracing colloquies' of Beaupuy (1791-2) on their walks in the Touraine, and feeling a fervour in part genuine and in part 'less genuine and wrought up within myself', he allowed his imagination, at the sight of royal castles and dismantled convents, to mitigate the 'bigotry of a youthful patriot's mind'. In George Eliot's phrase, he indulged in 'a little Toryism on the sly', and in his own, 'on these spots with many gleams I looked Of chivalrous delight'. The quality of his revolutionary ardour at its height is best expressed in the factitious rhetoric of *Descriptive Sketches* (mostly written on the banks of the Loire in 1791-2), a poem whose forced accents betoken a Wordsworth still far from his true anchorage. He tells us, in the tones of conventional poetic dejection, that

> Me, lur'd by hope her sorrows to remove,
> A heart, that could not much itself approve,
> O'er Gallia's wastes of corn dejected led,

and we hear how, at the destruction of the Chartreuse, 'Blasphemy the shuddering fane alarms', while 'start th' astonish'd shades at female eyes', and 'the thundering tube the aged angler hears'. Coming to the Alps and the pastoral Swiss, he indulges in a passage of old-style 'primitivism'. In these peasants, though fallen indeed from the bliss of the legendary Golden Age of the Alps, he sees 'the traces of primaeval Man appear'; guarded by 'vestal Nature' they still enjoy the blessings 'only given to uncorrupted hearts'.

> Once Man entirely free, alone and wild,
> Was bless'd as free—for he was Nature's child.
> He, all superior but his God disdain'd,
> Walk'd none restraining, and by none restrain'd,
> Confessed no law but what his reason taught,
> Did all he wish'd, and wish'd but what he ought.

From this Rousseauistic Eden man has, of course, been largely driven by his oppressors:

> Still have my pilgrim feet unfailing found,
> As despot courts their blaze of gems display,
> Ev'n by the secret cottage far away,
> The lily of domestic joy decay.

But he concludes with a *redeunt saturnia regna* addressed to emancipated France: 'all nature smiles' as 'Freedom spreads her pow'r'; the very cocks crow 'with ear-piercing power till then unheard', and in spite of warlike threats from the enemies of liberty,

> Nature, as in her prime, her virgin reign
> Begins, and Love and Truth compose her train.

The poem ends in a rhetorical prayer, bristling with personifications, for the success of the cause and arms of Freedom, and the destruction of the dynasts:

> Oh give, great God, to Freedom's waves to ride
> Sublime o'er Conquest, Avarice, and Pride,
> To break, the vales where Death with Famine scow'rs,
> And dark Oppression builds her thick-ribb'd tow'rs;
> Where Machination her fell soul resigns
> Fled panting to the centre of her mines;
> Where Persecution decks with ghastly smiles
> Her bed, his mountains mad Ambition piles;
>
> . . . .
>
> And grant that every sceptred child of clay,
> Who cries, presumptuous, 'here their tides shall stay',
> Swept in their anger from th'affrighted shore,
> With all his creatures sink—to rise no more.

This 'Nature', which now begins her virgin reign, is the abstract goddess of the eighteenth century, not the Nature of Wordsworth's maturer communings. If tone and diction are indications, as much as sense, of the 'sincerity' of poetic speech, then we may trust the statement in *The Prelude*, spoken in Wordsworth's authentic voice—that much of this emotion was 'wrought up within myself'—

rather than the strident ventriloquisms of *Descriptive Sketches*.

Wordsworth returned to England 'a patriot of the world', and therefore unable at once to 'glide into communion with her sylvan shades'. For about six months 'it pleased me more To abide in the great City'. In *The Prelude* he speaks of his period of discipleship to Godwin as following his abandonment of hope for France, when

> become oppressors in their turn
> Frenchmen had changed a war of self-defence
> For one of conquest, losing sight of all
> Which they had struggled for. [Bk. xi, 206.]

Yet it is clear from several of his writings that he was familiar with *Political Justice* from the time of its publication in 1793, at the very time, that is, when his sympathies were all with the 'Herculean Commonwealth' then engaged in 'throttling with an infant godhead's might The snakes about her cradle' (including the British forces). His most 'Godwinian' compositions belong to 1793, 1794, and 1795, and by 1795 he was at work on *The Borderers*, which we must recognize as marking his partial revolt from Godwin. We are therefore compelled to suppose that during those important but obscure years Wordsworth passed rapidly through a series of phases. In 1793-4, though demonstrably steeped in Godwinian notions and phraseology, he had only surrendered himself to those parts of *Political Justice* which fitted in—as so much of it did—with the 'heart-bracing colloquies' of Beaupuy: the passion for justice and equality, the humanitarianism, the hatred of privilege, of caste, of war, and of the penal code, the determination to judge all things, not in the light of tradition and prejudice, but by the fixed standards of justice and utility. All this was common heritage from eighteenth century revolutionary theory, and it may be said that Wordsworth had already absorbed it in France. Probably *Political Justice* served at first chiefly to clarify and systematize his ideas on these subjects, and it certainly had an immediate effect on his vocabulary, as we may briefly illustrate from his *Letter to the Bishop of Llandaff*[1] and his correspondence of 1794-5. The Letter to Bishop Watson, written in 1793, is the completest statement of Wordsworth's early revolutionary principles. Watson, who may be regarded as a sort of third-rate Burke, had been formerly known as the 'levelling Prelate' and the 'Bishop of the Dissenters', but had recently published a recantation of his liberal principles, praising the British Constitution and recommending contentment with the status quo. Wordsworth's reply, which was never published in his lifetime, can be classed among the best of the counterblasts to Burke's *Reflexions*.

Watson had expressed horror at the execution of Louis XVI, just as Burke had bewailed the sufferings of Marie Antoinette. All this, says Wordsworth, is mere 'modish lamentation'. The only rational sorrow would be for the sufferings of twenty-five millions of French people, and for the unnatural folly of a system which forces one man into a position of irresponsible authority, demanding from him more than human virtue and ability, 'and at the same time precludes him from attaining even a moderate knowledge of common life'.[2] As for the confiscation of Church property, deplored by Watson as by Burke, we may console ourselves for the sad fate which has deprived the hero of the diamond necklace of 1,300,000 *livres* per annum, by reflecting that part of the spoil has gone to preserve some thousands of poor curés from famine. You say that in a republic men live under the most odious of all tyrannies, that of their equals. What we should rather regret is that oppression by so-called 'superiors' is *not* odious to so many, owing to their breeding in slavery. The great advantage of a republic is, to Wordsworth (as to Godwin), that the governors have not an interest separate from that of the governed. He pauses to consider the objection that the people are unfit to govern themselves, and

[1] In Knight's *Prose Works of W. Wordsworth*, vol. i, pp. 1-27.
[2] Cf. *Political Justice*, vol. ii, bk. 5, ch. ii.

we here see him wrestling with the difficulties described in *The Prelude*, Book X. This was the period when any sanguine view of human nature and of human capacity for freedom and self-rule seemed refuted by the present fact of the Terror. Wordsworth admits that probably every European state is so corrupt that 'if the original power of the people should be restored only a change of tyranny would result'. But what is accountable for this state of affairs? Not human nature, but customs and institutions, and in particular the institution of monarchy. Here we find Wordsworth, like Holbach, Godwin, and all the party, refusing to see institutions as the expression of something in human nature, even if it be only of its wickedness; while Burke and the traditionalists on their side over-emphasized the fixity of both, and in insisting that institutions were fitted to man's nature if not to his reason, ignored the possibility that an evolving humanity might have outgrown its institutions. As a proof of the capacity of Church and King to debauch the popular mind, Wordsworth asks: 'left to the quiet exercise of their own judgment, do you think that the people would have thought it necessary to set fire to the house of the philosophic Priestley?', or that they would now be crying out for a war which will only increase their already intolerable burdens? Like Godwin, he argues that a philosopher should look beyond such considerations, and not labour to perpetuate injustice. The terrific reservoir of guilt once emptied —alas, not without violence and chaos—the stream of public affairs will steadily become clearer. In the republic there will be no Machiavellian diplomacy; all will be conducted in the daylight. It will no longer be the interest of the governors to keep the people in ignorance, hence 'a moderate portion of useful knowledge would be universally disseminated'. The penal code, now full of disproportionate penalties, will be reformed. As for property, the present system of fixed inequality is pernicious, and must go. In protecting property, our laws have forgotten the property of a labourer, which is his power to support himself and his family. Wordsworth deplores the immense salaries annexed to useless and hereditary offices, and points out the debasing effect of titles, stars, ribbons, and garters—all the apparatus of 'nobility', and the social hypocrisy and snobbery to which it leads. In his peroration he denounces the Bishop for having 'aimed an arrow at liberty and philosophy, the eyes of the human race', and for having tried to divert men from fruitful enquiry by telling them that perfection has already been attained. Finally, from the Bishop's silence about the war, Wordsworth assumes that he supports 'that infatuation which is now giving up to the sword so large a portion of the poor, and consigning the rest to the more slow and more painful consumption of want'.

If any further proof were needed of the extent to which Wordsworth had absorbed *Political Justice* one might take these remarks from letters written in 1794 to Mathews, in which not only the ideas but also the phraseology of Godwin are echoed:

> 'The enlightened friend of mankind should let slip no opportunity of explaining and enforcing those general principles of social order which are applicable to all times and places. . . . He should diffuse by every method a knowledge of those rules of political justice from which the further any government deviates the more effectually must it defeat the object for which government was ordained. . . . You know perhaps already that I am of that odious class of men called democrats, and of that class I shall for ever continue. . . . I disapprove of monarchical and aristocratic governments, however modified. Hereditary distinctions and privileged orders of every species I think must necessarily counteract the progress of human improvement: hence it follows that I am not amongst the admirers of the British Constitution.' [1]

The poem now entitled *Guilt and Sorrow* was in part composed during the summer of 1793, and is full of the gloom of that troubled year. Busy with the thoughts just summarized, and with other uneasiness in his heart, Wordsworth watched from the Isle of Wight in July the

[1] Cf. Harper's *Life*, vol. i, pp. 242-4.

naval preparations against France, and the sound of the sunset cannon filled him with 'melancholy forebodings'. Afterwards, when he was wandering over Salisbury Plain, the sight of Stonehenge made him think of old, unhappy, far-off things, and he wondered whether the ancient savage rites had caused as much suffering as the wars of modern times. These thoughts, mingling with a story he had heard some time before (that of the 'Female Vagrant'), were the origin of the poem, of which the main purpose was 'to expose the vices of the penal code and the calamities of war, as they affect individuals' [1]—particularly the poor. The poem as we now have it has undergone successive revisions, and a comparison between *Guilt and Sorrow* as published in 1842 with that portion printed as *The Female Vagrant* in *Lyrical Ballads* shows that it was precisely the most 'Godwinian' passages which Wordsworth softened down. A returned sailor is shown driven to crime, and a soldier's widow to destitution, after the American War, and Wordsworth deploys all his rhetoric to paint the horrors of war and the callousness of society towards those whose lives it has ruined. The Vagrant is made to exclaim,

> Or in the streets and walks where proud men are,
> Better our dying bodies to obtrude,
> Than dog-like, wading at the heels of war,
> Protract a curst existence, with the brood
> That lap (their very nourishment!) their brothers' blood.

—a description of soldiering which was omitted from all editions after 1800. A band of gypsies are represented as the first to treat the Vagrant kindly on her return (compare the highway-robbers' entertainment of Caleb Williams after his escape from prison). In *The Female Vagrant* the beginning of all the woman's woes is the tyranny of a greedy landlord who buys out the neighbouring cottagers and persecutes those who, like her father, refuse 'the proffered gold'; while in *Guilt and Sorrow* this is sum-

[1] Letter to Wrangham, Nov. 20, 1795. Harper's *Life*, vol. i, p. 272.

marized as 'severe mischance and cruel wrong'. Originally, if the letter to Wrangham may be credited, the poem must have been meant to end in an indictment of capital punishment, whereas the revised version ends incongruously with the sailor's submission to it as a religious expiation.

Two other poems composed at the end of this period may be briefly noted, both of which reflect the same Godwinian humanitarianism, and imply bitter criticism of the social system. The first is *The Convict*, published in *Lyrical Ballads* and never reprinted by Wordsworth. It illustrates one of the main themes of *Political Justice* and of *Caleb Williams*—the cruelty and injustice of the penal laws. Two points are relevant: first, the original version of the poem, which appeared in the *Morning Post* of December 14, 1797, contained these two stanzas—

> When from the dark Synod, or blood-reeking field
> To his chamber the Monarch is led,
> All soothers of sense their soft virtue shall yield
> And silent attention shall pillow his head.
>
> If the less guilty Convict a moment would doze
> And oblivion his tortures appease,
> On the iron that galls him his limbs must repose,
> In the damp-dropping vault of disease.[1]

A reference to this poem as it appeared in *Lyrical Ballads* shows that although the contrast between monarch and convict is retained, its sting has been lost through the omission of the Godwinian imputation of greater guilt to the monarch. (The vapidity of this solemn doggerel compels the passing remark that it is not through the Godwinian fire and whirlwind that Wordsworth's true voice is heard.) Secondly, Godwin's proposal to substitute transportation and a fresh start in life for penal servitude and death is embodied in the last verse. The other poem I referred to is *The Ruined Cottage*, or the story of Margaret, also composed at this time, though now to be found

[1] Cf. Harper's *Life*, vol. i, p. 301, and *Lyrical Ballads* (1798), p. 198.

in Book I of *The Excursion*. This story bears some resemblance to that of *Guilt and Sorrow* in that it tells of the misery befalling the wife of a man who enlists in desperation and leaves her destitute. It may be classed with that group of Wordsworth's works which deal, in a Godwinian spirit, with the evils of war, though Godwin is here but a shadowy recollection, and Wordsworth has already begun to write with his own 'noble bareness'.

It must be remembered that a considerable part of this body of notions was retained by Wordsworth (in a modified form) to the end of his life.[1] It is not from the republican, humanitarian, pacifist Godwin that he records his deliverance in Book XI of *The Prelude*, nor is it these teachings that he renounces in *The Borderers* and in *Lyrical Ballads*. In 1804 he could still say of the whole system of Godwin that it was

> A noble aspiration! *yet* I feel
> (Sustained by worthier as by wiser thoughts)
> The aspiration, nor shall ever cease
> To feel it. . . . [*The Prelude*, bk. xi, 255.]

Throughout 1793 and 1794 he was clinging desperately to his faith in France as the embodiment of the aspiration, and suffered the double misery (so vividly described in Book X) of resisting patriotic sentiment and of seeming to condone the Terror. After a time, he hoped, the violence would abate—if only it were left to itself. But the dynasts would not leave it to itself, and they were therefore morally accountable for the excesses of 1793-94, and the endless war which followed. Wordsworth loved England, but at this time of interference abroad and persecution of liberals at home he was compelled to accept Godwin's view of patriotism as a specious illusion. The death of Robespierre (July 28, 1794) revived his hopes for a while, so that we are brought to the threshold of 1795 before we

[1] See, on this subject, *The Later Wordsworth*, by E. C. Batho (Cambridge, 1933), e.g. pp. 196 ff., and p. 200 ('I have a great deal of the Chartist in me').

can be sure that he had renounced France in favour of the *whole* Godwinian doctrine. This means that he was only under the full dominion of Godwin for the first six months of that year, for by September 1795 he had already realized some of the dangers of his doctrine. What were these teachings which he adopted in disillusionment and rejected again so soon? One would suppose, from the brevity of their hold upon him, that they were theories essentially hostile to his inmost nature, and that is precisely what we find. As suggested above, what temporarily attracted him were the 'speculative schemes that promised to abstract the hopes of man out of his feelings'; it was Godwin's abstract individualism, which made 'our Reason's naked self the object of its fervour'. He sought escape not only in Godwin's abstract world, but even in mathematics, 'where the disturbances of space and time find no admission'.

This brief phase of Wordsworth's development marks a temporary denial of his normal mood, which was one of trust in instinctive and spontaneous living, and of confidence in what Keats calls 'the holiness of the heart's affections'. Up to a point, 'Nature' had seemed to be realizing itself in the course of public events—the ideal expressing itself in the actual. When events became too much for him he for a time rejected the actual, and took refuge in pure abstraction. This amounted to an admission that ideal and actual belonged to separate regions, and for Wordsworth, in whom distrust of abstractions was innate, this could only be the first stage of a return to the actual. And the 'actual' to which he did in fact return was 'Nature', now finally identified with the English landscape to which he had long ago dedicated his heart. By the summer of 1795 the effort to rise superior to 'infirmities of nature, time and place' had landed him in moral scepticism, and he reached 'the crisis of that strong disease' in which he 'yielded up moral questions in despair'. Recovering from this crisis in the congenial atmosphere of Racedown, he composed *The Borderers*, which may be taken to represent his convalescence, and which embodies his verdict upon Godwinian ethics. He wrote this tragedy chiefly to show that the attempt to live by the naked reason, though it might be a noble aspiration, is apt to produce monsters rather than supermen. His own experience had taught him that the process of dragging all precepts and maxims to the bar of reason led to moral chaos; might not the heart, then, be a safer guide than the head? When we strip off the traditional affections and inhibitions ('prejudices' though they may be called), what happens? the reason is left supreme? No, the *passions* gain

> the privilege to work
> And never hear the sound of their own names—
> [*The Prelude*, bk. xi, 232.]

reason becoming their slave and not their master. In the 1842 note to *The Borderers*, Wordsworth says that he wrote the tragedy while he had fresh in his memory examples of this process from the events of the French Revolution, where sin and crime had been seen to result from the most exalted principles. The interest of *The Borderers* centres in the complex character of Oswald, Wordsworth's Godwinian Iago. His prefatory essay, long mislaid and only republished in 1926 by Professor de Selincourt,[1] is entirely devoted to a subtle analysis of this character (no doubt he realized that he had not fully succeeded in exhibiting it dramatically). Oswald is a young man of acute intellect who uses his reason to rise superior to conventional morality, and Wordsworth wishes to show that this superiority may quite easily become the source of evil. At the beginning of his career Oswald has been betrayed into the commission of a terrible crime, that of leaving a man to starve upon a desert island, on suspicions which he afterwards finds to be groundless. Instead of repenting, he banishes remorse by adopting

[1] In *The Nineteenth Century*, Nov. 1926, p. 723.

a moral sophistry which condemns all human feelings as weaknesses. 'His feelings are interested in making him a moral sceptic'; 'he disguises from himself his own malignity by assuming the character of a speculator in morals'. 'Remorse', he exclaims,

> Remorse—
> It cannot live with thought; think on, think on,
> And it will die.[1]

He examines established opinions, and rightly finding many of them unreasonable, he is confirmed in his sense of superiority. Oswald exerts his intellect and asserts his moral freedom by poisoning the mind of Marmaduke with an atrocious story about his betrothed, and thereby leading him virtually to repeat his own crime. In so doing, he is not acting as a disinterested Godwinian who desires to confer upon his friend the blessings of moral emancipation. He is acting from the more complex motives of an Iago—from pride, restlessness, and indeed 'motiveless malignity', and though Wordsworth means his behaviour to illustrate the abuse and not the true intention of Godwinism, he also means that it is a perversion into which that philosophy easily degenerates. The general moral, Wordsworth says explicitly, is 'to show the dangerous use which may be made of reason when a man has committed a great crime', and also to show 'that from abuses interwoven with the texture of society a bad man may be furnished with sophisms in support of his crimes which it would be difficult to answer'. The new philosophy exposes ordinary unsuspecting folk to exploitation by unscrupulous sophists.

It was thus that Wordsworth was preparing, in *The Borderers*, the foundations of the faith of his great decade. Once he could convince himself that pure intellectualism in morals was more likely to produce or justify crime than virtue, then with what 'deep power of joy' he could regain

[1] *The Borderers*, 1560.

a 'saving intercourse' with his own past, and allow himself to be led, by Dorothy, and by 'Nature's self'—

> back through opening day
> To those sweet counsels between head and heart
> Whence grew that genuine knowledge, fraught with peace.
>
> [*The Prelude*, bk. xi, 352.]

2

William Hale White ('Mark Rutherford'), a lesser-known but true Wordsworthian, has written with insight about Wordsworth's recovery from Godwinism. Wordsworth's temporary subjugation by *Political Justice*, he suggests, was due, not to pure intellectual conviction, but to that 'hypochondriacal graft in his nature' which was remarked more than once by Coleridge, and which must have held him most strongly in those unhappy years from 1793 to 1795. 'Certain beliefs', he writes, 'at any rate with men of Wordsworth's stamp, are sickness', and 'with the restoration of vitality and the influx of joy they disappear'; and again—'There is no evidence that Wordsworth attempted any reasoned confutation of *Political Justice*. It was falsified in him by Racedown, by better health, by the society of his beloved sister, and finally by the friendship with Coleridge'.[1] Mark Rutherford's understanding of Wordsworth's case was due to his own experience, for he had known himself (and has described with a power like Bunyan's in *Grace Abounding*) what it was to be pierced 'with the fang of some monomaniacal idea which cannot be wrenched out', and he had also known sometimes how, when 'the clouds rolled off with the south-west wind into detached, fleecy masses, separated by liquid blue gulfs, in which were sown the stars', there would come 'a kind of flush in the brain and a momentary relief', together with 'a sense of the infinite, extinguishing

[1] *More Pages from a Journal*, p. 214.

all mean cares'.[1] In any attempt to understand what 'Nature' meant to Wordsworth due weight should be given, I think, to the healing power of the impersonal over a sick mind. It was when the 'fretful stir Unprofitable, and the fever of the world' had long 'hung upon the beatings of my heart' that Wordsworth turned to the sylvan Wye, and found 'for this uneasy heart of ours a never-failing principle of joy'. Wordsworth speaks so often of 'dim sadness and blind thoughts', of 'listlessness from vain perplexity' and 'the heavy weight of many a weary day Not mine', and on the other hand of 'tranquil restoration' and 'renovation'—indeed, 'Despondency Corrected' is so much his central theme—that we are left in no doubt upon this point. He found, amongst the 'calm oblivious tendencies of Nature', both stimulus and anodyne:

> I well remember that those very plumes,
> Those weeds, and the high spear-grass on that wall,
> By mist and silent rain-drops silvered o'er,
> As once I passed, into my heart conveyed
> So still an image of tranquillity,
> So calm and still, and looked so beautiful
> Amid the uneasy thoughts which filled my mind,
> That what we feel of sorrow and despair
> From ruin and from change, and all the grief
> That passing shows of Being leave behind,
> Appeared an idle dream.[2]

By 1795 the 'later sinkings' of the French cause had made it vain to keep up any longer the unprofitable strife, and vain too (as he probably felt with relief) to torment himself with further thoughts of duty to Annette. With Raisley Calvert's legacy as an economic deliverance, with Dorothy, with Racedown, and 'long months of ease and undisturbed delight' in prospect, he could forget France, and Godwin, and 'all the ways of men, so vain and

[1] *Autobiography of Mark Rutherford*, pp. 98, 95, 37.
[2] *The Excursion*, bk. i, 942.

melancholy'. Like his own Ruth (if one may adapt the lines)

> Among the fields he breathed again:
> The master-current of his brain
> Ran permanent and free—

that 'current' which was native to the hills, and had only lost its direction for a while in political and emotional meanderings. It is perhaps worthy of remark that those who have felt most powerfully the healing influence of 'Nature' have often been those who were most subject, in their ordinary moments, to gloom and nervous depression. One thinks of Cowper, and Rousseau, and Gray, Wordsworth himself, Tennyson, Arnold, and Mark Rutherford. Moreover, remarking that all these men belong to the later eighteenth and the nineteenth centuries, we may conjecture that it was owing to the commanding authority of the idea of Nature at that time, as well to the more obvious sanative virtues of the open-air, that they could find amongst fields and mountains a substitute religion—even, as with Cowper and Rutherford, a *cure* for religion, or at least for religious melancholy. That ease of heart which religion had formerly given—which a Bunyan could find at the foot of the Cross—could now best be derived from 'the silent looks of happy things, Or flowing from the universal face Of earth and sky'. Wordsworth says of his Wanderer (i.e. himself) that though he had early learnt to reverence the Bible, yet 'in the mountains did he *feel* his faith . . ., nor did he believe,—he *saw*'. What Wordsworth saw in mountains was due, most assuredly, to what his eyes brought means of seeing; but we may also say that neither he nor others of his time might have lifted up their eyes to the hills for such help if the eighteenth century had not so unfalteringly directed them towards the visible universe as the clearest evidence of God.

It is sometimes argued that Wordsworth's belief in the moral value of the love of fine scenery is a fallacy; that communion with mountains does not generate any 'pure principle of love', but is only a form of self-glorification, leading to an anti-social habit of mind and producing the 'egotistical sublime'. Hazlitt remarked with bitterness that Wordsworth himself could sympathize only with objects that could enter into no sort of competition with him. From another angle Mr Aldous Huxley attacks Wordsworth's Nature-religion as the product of 'the cosy sublimities of Westmorland', and reminds us that Nature in the Tropics is apt to produce worship of the devil rather than of God. And Mr Empson can dismiss Wordsworth with the remark that 'Wordsworth frankly had no inspiration other than his own use, when a boy, of the mountains as a totem or father-substitute'. With all these and other reasons for suspecting that Wordsworth's particular faith or philosophy is now inaccessible to many, the question arises once more, can we separate his 'poetry' from his 'philosophy'? Can we say, with Matthew Arnold, that the 'poetry' is the reality, and the 'philosophy' the illusion? In saying this, Arnold must have been referring only to Wordsworth's passages of *explicit* moralizing (such as led Leslie Stephen to praise him as a systematic ethical philosopher), for he himself believed in Wordsworth's central doctrine, namely that 'the source of joy from which he draws' (Nature) 'is the truest and most unfailing source of joy accessible to man'. Arnold praises Wordsworth for 'the extraordinary power with which, in case after case, he shows us this joy, and renders it so as to make us share it'. But suppose that, lacking Wordsworth's sense of the sacredness of the created world, of the dignity of the human spirit, and of the affinity between Nature and the soul, we are incapable of sharing it? 'How shall he fully enjoy Wordsworth', said Coleridge (in *Table Talk*) 'who has never meditated on the truths which Wordsworth has wedded to immortal verse?'—or, shall we say, for whom they have ceased to be truths? I do not propose here to enter into the highly complicated question of 'poetry and beliefs', but it may perhaps be hazarded that what most readers want from a poet is his 'experience', not his beliefs, though their appreciation of him is likely to be greater if they also regard his beliefs—however secondary in interest—as being 'true'. Many readers, I think, are now retaining their respect for Wordsworth by trying to separate, in his poetry, what they feel to be genuine 'experience' from what they feel to be false or 'dated' belief. They are virtually using the distinction made by Dr Richards in reference to the poetry of D. H. Lawrence: Wordsworth is genuine (it is felt) when he is 'feeling something', and often relatively false, for us, when he is 'feeling *that* so-and-so'. Can we, then, by separating experience from intellectual superstructure, detect where Wordsworth has 'felt something' and communicated it, and define what it is that he has felt? To answer this question fully would take us far beyond the limits of the present study. I can only indicate a possible method of procedure, namely to make a collection of the passages in which Wordsworth seems to be communicating imaginative experience, and then by collating them to discover, as far as may be, what was the quality of that experience. I think we should find that the experiences *preceded* the beliefs which Wordsworth later (with Coleridge's assistance) elaborated out of them, and that they can therefore be shared by the reader for whom those beliefs are no longer 'immortal truths'. Let us take a few examples; first, the familiar episodes from Book I of *The Prelude*:

(*a*) I heard among the solitary hills
Low breathings coming after me, and sounds
Of undistinguishable motion, steps
Almost as silent as the turf they trod. [321.]

(*b*) Suspended by the blast that blew amain,
Shouldering the naked crag, oh, at that time
While on the perilous ridge I hung alone,
With what strange utterance did the loud dry wind
Blow through my ear! the sky seemed not a sky
Of earth—and with what motion moved the clouds!
[334.]

(*c*) but after I had seen
That spectacle, for many days, my brain
Worked with a dim and undetermined sense
Of unknown modes of being ; o'er my thoughts
There hung a darkness, call it solitude,
Or blank desertion. No familiar shapes
Remained, no pleasant images of trees,
Of sea or sky, no colours of green fields;
But huge and mighty forms, that do not live
Like living men, moved slowly through the mind
By day, and were a trouble to my dreams.

[390.]

With these may be taken the passage from Book XII, which commemorates an experience of similar quality. The child is lost on the hills, and is suddenly terrified by coming upon a place where a murderer had been hanged in chains, and seeing his name carved in huge letters in the grass:

(*d*) A casual glance had shown them, and I fled,
Faltering and faint, and ignorant of the road:
Then, reascending the bare common, saw
A naked pool that lay beneath the hills,
The beacon on the summit, and, more near,
A girl, who bore a pitcher on her head,
And seemed with difficult steps to force her way
Against the blowing wind. It was, in truth,
An ordinary sight; but I should need
Colours and words that are unknown to man,
To paint the visionary dreariness
Which, while I looked all round for my lost guide,
Invested moorland waste, and naked pool,
The beacon crowning the lone eminence,
The female and her garments vexed and tossed
By the strong wind. [246.]

In all these recollections there is one common experience: the child is startled by terror or suspense into a heightened state of consciousness, through which he sees surrounding objects in a preternatural light. It was not always fear which worked the magic; 'the coarser pleasures of my boyish days and their glad animal movements' could also do it, as when in skating

(*e*) with the din
Smitten, the precipices rang aloud;
The leafless trees and every icy crag
Tinkled like iron; while far distant hills
Into the tumult sent an alien sound
Of melancholy not unnoticed, while the stars
Eastward were sparkling clear, and in the west
The orange sky of evening died away. [Bk. i, 439.]

Or the more rarefied excitement of mimicking the owls across the lake, and when a pause of silence came—

(*f*) Then sometimes, in that silence while he hung
Listening, a gentle shock of mild surprise
Has carried far into his heart the sound
Of mountain torrents; or the visible scene
Would enter unawares into his mind,
With all its solemn imagery, its rocks,
Its woods, and that uncertain heaven, received
Into the bosom of the steady lake. [Bk. v, 364.]

There is no reason to suppose that what the boy Wordsworth felt on these occasions arose from anything but that simple 'animism', as W. H. Hudson has called it, 'that sense of something in Nature which to the enlightened or civilized man is not there, and in the civilized man's child, if it be admitted that he has it at all, is but a faint survival of a phase of the primitive mind',[1] and which in Wordsworth (as in Hudson) persisted throughout life. So far no question of intellectual superstructure or belief has arisen. But when we ask why Wordsworth valued these recollections so highly, or what were his explicit reasons for commemorating them, we at once encounter such beliefs. We find the primitive animism being refined into pantheism; and we find that 'Nature' has been acting as a sort of glorified parent or schoolmistress. He gives 'thanks to the means which Nature deigned to employ'

[1] *Far Away and Long Ago* (Hudson's '*Prelude*'), pp. 224 ff.

—the discipline of fear and joy through which her benign Hartleian curriculum has been fulfilled. The first three passages quoted above are given by him as examples of Nature's 'ministries' and 'interventions', whereby she reproved his childish delinquencies. It is at this point that we begin to see the cleavage between experience and belief; what matters, for us (and, we feel, for Wordsworth too), is simply that he should have had these moments of imaginative energy, in which the earth and every common sight were apparelled—not only in celestial light, but also sometimes in visionary dreariness, and that he should have been able, as few others have done, to remember and communicate them. The theory about Nature's Education, no doubt attributable to Hartley via Coleridge, can be disregarded if we will. But Wordsworth himself gives other interpretations of his own experiences, other reasons for cherishing his recollections, and some of them give us still further confidence in our winnowing process. One of them is given at the beginning of the passage from which extract (*d*) above is taken:

> There are in our existence spots of time
> Which with distinct pre-eminence retain
> A renovating virtue, whence . . . our minds
> Are nourished and invisibly repaired.
>
> [Bk. xii, 208.]

Certain recollections have the power to evoke in him the dormant imaginative energy, so that he can literally fetch 'invigorating thoughts from former years' [Bk. I, 620]. At the time when he is writing *The Prelude* he appears already as the historian, rather than the present possessor, of the visionary power. The regular action of the world has already had its effect, and he is turning for stimulus to the past. After he has drawn his moral from passage (*d*), he continues:

> The days gone by
> Return upon me almost from the dawn
> Of life: the hiding-places of man's power
> Open; I would approach them, but they close.

> I see by glimpses now; when age comes on,
> May scarcely see at all; and I would give,
> While yet we may, as far as words can give,
> Substance and life to what I feel, enshrining,
> Such is my hope, the spirit of the Past
> For future restoration.
>
> [Bk. xii, 277.]

By the time that this passage was composed (probably 1802) Wordsworth was fighting a rearguard action against the adult consciousness, against the matter-of-factness in himself, and against Nature's own irresistible tendency to turn the enchanted moonbeams of Alfoxden into the light of common day. He wrote *The Prelude* chiefly in order to 'rescue from decay' his early 'visitings of imaginative power' and to brace himself for the composition of his great unwritten philosophical poem. Here too no unacceptable beliefs are involved; Wordsworth was an imaginative child; as a man he can best revive his flagging energies by evoking past moments of creativeness; and, as all his deepest emotions have been associated with natural objects, it is through them that he can best recapture what was so fugitive.

But Wordsworth has a further point to make. Why were these recollections invigorating? By the time that he was ready to answer this question Wordsworth had acquired, partly through conversation and collaboration with Coleridge and partly from reflexion on his own experience, a set of theories about the imagination, the relationship of the Mind with Nature, and the psychology of poetic creation. In the light of these theories he offers the following explanation:

> This efficacious spirit chiefly lurks
> Among those passages of life that give
> Profoundest knowledge to what point and how
> The mind is lord and master, outward sense
> The obedient servant of her will.
>
> [Bk. xii, 219.]

In the ceaseless interplay of Mind and Nature sometimes

the one and sometimes the other is predominant. He speaks of two main states of his own soul, one the uncreative, in which he is under the 'despotism of the eye', and the mind is 'prostrate, overborne', a mere passive 'pensioner on outward forms', the other the creative, in which 'the mind is lord and master', and through its own 'plastic power' can transfigure without distorting all it contemplates, adding the 'visionary' quality to natural objects, darkening the 'midnight storm', or adding 'new splendour' to the setting sun. Passage (*d*) from Book XII is of particular interest here, because Wordsworth interprets the 'visionary dreariness' episode entirely in the light of this theory, and we are not confused, as in Book I, by the suggestion that Nature is acting in a disciplinary way. At first sight it is not too obvious how the recollection of the pool, the beacon, and the girl with a pitcher can be so invigorating, or can illustrate the principle of the mind's predominance over the senses. But, of course, the clue is in the 'visionary' quality of the scene; surprised by fright, just as when he had been bird's-nesting or stealing the boat, his mind had been aroused, and had impressed its own mood upon the 'vulgar forms of present things'. Later, when 'in the blessed hours of early love' he revisits the same scene with Mary Hutchinson, there is shed upon pool and beacon another sort of light, 'a spirit of pleasure and youth's golden gleam'; but his joy even in this is enhanced by the old remembrances, and by 'the power they had left behind'.

So feeling comes in aid
Of feeling, and diversity of strength
Attends us, if but once we have been strong.
[Bk. xii, 269.]

To have been 'strong' means, here, to have been imaginatively creative, to have had the power of conferring the visionary quality upon an ordinary sight. With his unique gift for reading the palimpsest of his own memory, he remembers how he had felt as a frightened child, and how the scene had looked in the light of that feeling, and recognizes that then, unknown to himself, he had exercised the modifying power which he has since come to regard as the master-faculty. And so infrequent have the moments of vision become—'I see by glimpses now; when age comes on, may scarcely see at all'—that he now cherishes with a miser's care each recollected 'spot of time' in which he had been 'strong'. Not that he was unable still to exercise the power: in a poem like *Resolution and Independence* we can see the transforming process actually at work, as the figure of the old leech-gatherer passes successively into stone, sea-beast, and cloud, and finally evaporates into a spirit of lonely places. But none the less he knows that a glory is passing from the earth, and he comes more and more to feel the superiority of the child's endowment over the man's:

> Oh! mystery of man, from what a depth
> Proceed thy honours. I am lost, but see
> In simple childhood something of the base
> On which thy greatness stands.
>
> [Bk. xii, 272.]

The child possesses what the adult is toiling to find, and so becomes for him the type and symbol of creative strength. 'To that dream-like vividness and splendour which invest objects of sight in childhood, everyone, I believe, if he would look back, could bear testimony', says the prefatory note to the 'Immortality' *Ode*. In his own childhood, he there further tells us, his mind was so predominant over the senses that he had frequently to grasp at a tree or stone to rescue him from the 'abyss of idealism', and assure himself of their existence outside himself. Later, he has had reason to deplore, as we all have, 'a subjugation of an opposite character'; the world has resisted the plastic power more and more stubbornly; and with the fading of the vision has come the need to cherish those 'shadowy recollections' which are the 'fountain-light of all our day'. We may recoil, as even Coleridge did, from some of Wordsworth's idealizations of the child ('mighty prophet, seer blest', etc.), but in what has just been summarized there is otherwise little but introspection and accurate psychology. Both as child and as man Wordsworth possessed unusual sensibility, and had associated his inner life, far more than most men, with natural objects; but no 'dated' beliefs are involved, and nothing which need antagonize a modern reader.

It would appear, then, that as long as Wordsworth is communicating experiences of this kind, and not merely discussing or rationalizing them, his poetry can still be read with unabated interest. Sometimes he is doing both at once, and sometimes, again, one can see the 'join' where an ethical superstructure has been cemented on to an imaginative foundation (the ending of *Resolution and Independence*, for example). One may perhaps venture to guess that the elements in him which will now be found least congenial by most people are precisely those for which he was once most valued: his optimism—his 'cheerful faith, that all that we behold is full of blessings'; his 'spilt religion' (in T. E. Hulme's phrase):

> Far and wide the clouds were touched,
> And in their silent faces could he read
> Unutterable love....
>
> Rapt into still communion that transcends
> The imperfect offices of prayer and praise....
>
> [*The Excursion*, bk. i, 203-15.]

(I include these extracts with hesitation, for I think their magnificence must be acknowledged by the most hardened unbeliever in 'natural religion'); his belief in the moral influence of Nature:

> But he had felt the power
> Of Nature, and already was prepared,
> By his intense conceptions, to receive
> Deeply the lesson deep of love, which he,
> Whom Nature, by whatever means, has taught
> To feel intensely, cannot but receive.
>
> [*The Excursion*, bk. i, 191.]

or,

> Thus deeply drinking-in the soul of things
> We shall be wise perforce.
>
> [*The Excursion*, bk. iv, 1264.]

and perhaps his Coleridgean belief in the bond between Nature and the soul of man:

> How exquisitely . . .
> The external World is fitted to the Mind;
>
> [*Preface* to *The Excursion*, 63 ff.]

—all these, it will be observed, being examples of 'feelings *that* so-and-so'. (I exclude his later religious orthodoxy, for that is not under discussion.)

If, with these considerations in mind, we now return in imagination to 1795-8, the period of Wordsworth's vital transition, we shall perhaps be able to recapture something of the meaning which 'Nature' had for him then, whatever it may mean or not mean to us now. Let us remind ourselves, first, of all that he had passed through in the years 1790-5, of the emotional and intellectual distress he had experienced. When he came to Racedown he was in the condition of that youth to whom he wrote advice in the *Letter to The Friend* (1809), unsettled, perplexed, and adrift from his moorings. His greatest needs were to recover contact with his own past self and to resolve the inner discords set up in him by the revolutionary period. And his peaceful retirement with Dorothy, who gave him eyes and ears, and an 'exquisite regard for common things', satisfied both these needs. He seeks Nature now, 'not as in the hour of thoughtless youth', not for the sake of the old animistic thrills and the 'glad animal movements', but with the longing of a sick man for the sources of health. His dealings with Nature are now those of a man who has been depressed 'by false opinion or contentious thought', who has lived 'amid the many shapes of joyless daylight', and known 'the dreary intercourse of daily life'. It is in this spiritual context, and after such knowledge, that Nature acquires for him her great soothing and cheering power, and revives for him with new significance those dormant emotions which have been linked with her by long association. Thus Nature's healing power, which for some may be merely an outworn doctrine, was for him a fact of experience, and the rapture of that experience, which glows through *Tintern Abbey* and much of his best poetry, can be caught by any reader, without reference to the ethical and philosophical theories which Wordsworth evolved from it. Two main characteristics of Wordsworth's poetry can now perhaps be viewed with somewhat fuller understanding: his reverence for childhood, and his passion for mergence with 'mute insensate things'. I will comment briefly on these.

On the passage already referred to, W. H. Hudson makes these relevant observations:

> 'It is difficult, impossible I am told, for any one to recall his boyhood exactly as it was. It could not have been what it seems to the adult mind, since we cannot escape from what we are, however great our detachment may be; and in going back we must take our present selves with us: the mind has taken a different colour, and this is thrown back upon our past. The poet has reversed the true order of things when he tells us that we come trailing clouds of glory, which melt away and are lost as we proceed on our journey.'[1]

Perhaps it is the adult nostalgia which really imparts the glory and the freshness to recollections of early childhood —the celestial light being, in truth, the symbol of a yearning for the pre-adult consciousness. Early experiences came back to Wordsworth with a new intensity when he recollected them in the context I have sketched; now that he sees it across a waste of unprofitable years he realizes his own childhood as a 'golden time', a 'visible scene, on which the sun is shining'. Moreover, his childhood's experiences are now re-interpreted in the light of the philosophy which he is building up out of his return to

[1] *Far Away and Long Ago*, pp. 225-6.

Nature, and its accompanying emotions; he is forming a system of beliefs about the imagination—'the vision and the faculty divine'—and each imaginative moment is welcomed, each past one remembered, as an evidence, not only of his own continued vitality, but of the sublime power and dignity of the human soul.

A comparison between the 'spots of time' passage in *The Prelude* and the 'Immortality' *Ode* provides a useful illustration of the contrast in Wordsworth between 'experience' and 'superstructure'—if we will, between 'truth' and 'falsification'—and raises further questions of importance. In the *Prelude* passage, as we saw, Wordsworth not only attempts to communicate one of his vital experiences (with only partial success: 'I should need colours and words that are unknown to man, to paint the visionary dreariness'), but also makes a serious attempt to explain, in purely scientific and psychological terms, the importance of the experience. Wordsworth seems to have felt that this account was 'true' to his experience; indeed, I doubt whether he could have yielded full intellectual assent to any other sort of account. In *The Prelude* he expressly disclaims any attempt to ground a mystical faith on such experiences.

> I guess not what this tells of Being past
> Nor what it augurs of the life to come,

he writes (Book V, 510); and his reference to the

> isthmus, which our spirits cross
> In progress from their native continent
> To earth and human life.
> [Bk. v, 536.]

seems clearly made in full consciousness that this is 'mere' metaphor. What, then, is to be said of the *Ode*? I think it must be allowed that the *Ode* is greatly superior, as poetry, to its 'psychological' counterpart in *The Prelude* (Book XII), and yet at first sight it seems to contain a serious falsification of Wordsworth's essential experience. This 'falsification' comes in with the mythology of the *Ode*, which, by shifting back all the 'glory' into pre-existence and super-nature, forces Wordsworth to degrade earth into a foster-mother, and Nature into a medium to which the heaven-born visitant is gradually subdued. Is not this a denial of his most central certainties, that Nature needs no glory from 'worlds not quickened by the sun', and that the child is in fact exquisitely *fitted* to its environment by

> those firstborn affinities that fit
> Our new existence to existing things.
> [*The Prelude*, bk. i, 555.]

It has been plausibly argued[1] that if the *Ode* is admitted to be finer poetry than most of *The Prelude*, it must necessarily be in some sense 'truer'. And yet the semi-Platonic machinery of pre-existence, reincarnation, and recollection by flashes seems intrusive, and foreign to Wordsworth; and we know from the Fenwick note that he used it with no more than a momentary suspension of disbelief, and for a 'merely poetic' purpose. The *Ode*, in fact, has the air of being a departure from Wordsworth's general practice of making verse deal boldly with substantial things; he appears here to have admitted what he normally eschews—a piece of mythology which intervenes between him and his object. I think, however, that we can trust our sense of the poem's superiority, indeed of its unique position among Wordsworth's works, while granting that he has departed from his customary asceticism. For what, after all, is the real subject of the poem? What is it that he is trying—in this case successfully—to communicate? Not one of the 'spots of time'; not a particular mystical or imaginative moment. The poem is an impassioned celebration of childhood as the period of most intense vitality, written by a man who realizes that 'the hiding-places of man's power' are closing. It derives its passionate quality from a sense of loss and alienation, in spite of the claims of the concluding lines. What Wordsworth had to express

[1] By Prof. G. Wilson Knight, in an article in the Toronto University Magazine (alas, 'full early lost, and fruitlessly deplored'!), of which the substance, he tells me, appears in his *Christian Renaissance*.

here was his sense of vast distance from the sources of energy and vision. The 'philosophic mind' is but consolation; it is a poor substitute for the splendour in the grass and glory in the flower. This sense of estrangement, of loss, of subjugation by the adult consciousness and the frost of custom, had become so insistent that Wordsworth could only convey it by ascribing a *supernatural* endowment to childhood, and a supernatural authority to the surviving gleams that reached him through recollection. He had written *The Prelude* in order to rescue from decay the essential 'spots of time', but that work, both from its great length and from the circumstance of its being written for Coleridge, was inevitably couched in a discursive and analytic style, and represents an effort to give the 'philosophical' or 'scientific' account of his mind's growth ('Not in a mystical and idle sense, But in the words of Reason deeply weighed'—Book II, 230). But in the *Ode* he gathers all his strength together, and in one concentrated utterance bids farewell to the past which he has so carefully explored. What suffuses the *Ode* almost throughout with unwonted power and warmth is, I think, this sense that he is giving final and definitive expression to the most poignant experience of his poetic life. He is not trying, as often elsewhere, to convey the ineffable; he is lamenting his inability to experience it any more. This is partly why the poem succeeds; such sorrow *can* be uttered, while the ineffable moments of vision can only be hinted at and discussed. Moreover, the unique passion behind the *Ode* has driven him to adopt, for once, a myth. It happened that this particular one was available for him, and it was free from the objectionable associations connected with most of the classical machinery used by eighteenth century poets. It looks as if Wordsworth had found in this Platonic or Oriental fiction a symbolism which, though a falsification of 'psychological truth', yet enabled him to embody his experience objectively, and elevate it to a degree of impersonality normally beyond his reach. For by using it he has turned his personal experience into a universal journey of man away from the East, and inland from the sea. The comparative strength and concentration of the feeling behind this poem can be gauged by the 'concreteness' of its diction; the vagueness and abstractness of the 'psychological' *Prelude* here gives place to a profusion of precise images. In a word, he is creating or 'realizing', not merely describing and analysing; he is creating a sense of the splendour and inaccessibility of childhood, when viewed, from within the 'prison-house', by one who remembers *how* he felt, but can no longer experience *what* he had felt.

But even though the *Ode* be his most 'splendid' poem, its very uniqueness renders it not wholly characteristic of him. We find the more typical 'Wordsworthian' quality in those passages where he has recorded, not loss of vision, but his more successful dealings with the world of eye and ear. And it is here that we meet with the second characteristic mentioned above: his passion for mergence with impersonal things. As we have seen, his most urgent needs, when he 'returned to Nature', were tranquillity and restoration. And he could find these best by assimilating himself and other men as closely as possible with the landscape, and with the goings-on of the elements. He could best forget his 'old remembrances' and 'all the ways of men, so vain and melancholy' by fusing himself, and mankind in general, with natural backgrounds and processes. He loved to think of himself as 'clothed with the heavens and crowned with the stars', and this explains his need for solitude as a condition of inspiration. Mergence of the human figure with Nature gave it that degree of dignity, of separation from the mere social crowd, in virtue of which alone it could become, for Wordsworth, a worthy symbol of human life as he understood it. So viewed, the figures are seen in abstraction from all that in everyday humanity is disturbing, distressing, or uninteresting, and take on something of

> the silence and the calm
> Of mute insensate things.

Three Years She Grew (from which this phrase is taken) communicates with special force this passion for the fusion of the human with the impersonal—a passion which is concentrated, perhaps most intensely of all, in the 'Sublime Epitaph':

> Rolled round in earth's diurnal course
> With rocks, and stones, and trees.

But the same thing is occurring constantly. I have referred already to the de-humanizing of the old man's figure in *Resolution and Independence*; in *The Thorn*, again, the finest passage is that in which the tragic figure comes nearest to union with the elements:

> And she is known to every star
> And every wind that blows.

The Knight in *Hartleap-Well* is introduced to us riding

> down from Wensley Moor
> With the slow motion of a summer's cloud.

Michael owes much of his impressiveness to the statement that

> When others heeded not, he heard the South
> Make subterraneous music.

The Shepherd in Book VIII of *The Prelude*, seen against a mountain background, is

> man
> Ennobled outwardly before my sight,

and Wordsworth thanks the God of Nature and of Man that

> men before my inexperienced eyes
> Did first present themselves thus purified,
> Removed, and to a distance that was fit.

In *Tintern Abbey*, addressing his sister, he exclaims:

> Therefore let the moon
> Shine on thee in thy solitary walk;
> And let the misty mountain-winds be free
> To blow against thee. . . .

> thy mind
> Shall be a mansion for all lovely forms,
> Thy memory be as a dwelling-place
> For all sweet sounds and harmonies.

What was amiss with Peter Bell, and made him (in his unregenerate days) a moral monster, was that

> At noon, when by the forest's edge
> He lay beneath the branches high,
> The soft blue sky did never melt
> Into his heart; he never felt
> The witchery of the soft blue sky!

Examples need not be further multiplied; it is recognized that Wordsworth's typical human figures—The Highland Girl, Lucy, the Wanderer, the Old Cumberland Beggar—are those which are most intimately 'engaged' with their natural background. And he felt a special exaltation when he could feel himself, also, mingled with the cosmic processes; it gave him a sense of release from responsibility, from the weight of separate existence; a feeling of 'grandeur in the beatings of the heart'. It may be remarked, as a kindred characteristic in Wordsworth, that it seems to have been necessary for him to 'distance' an object—particularly a distressing or tragic object—in space or time, in order to think and feel freely about it. His need to see man 'removed to a distance that was fit' is analogous to his need to recollect emotion in tranquillity. The music of humanity comes restoringly to him only when it is still and sad—purged by distance, just as he can feel most fully the

> old unhappy far-off things
> And battles long ago,

or the

> Sorrow barricadoed evermore
> Within the walls of cities.

The story of Margaret is related as a happening of many years ago.

These soothing and cheering influences are probably as available now as they were in Wordsworth's time, though the communings of the modern Nature-lover with the 'misty mountain-wind' will probably lack the sacramental unction imputed to them by Wordsworth. It may be doubted, too, whether a modern father would treat his squalling infant as Coleridge (then at his most Wordsworthian stage) treated Hartley;

> once, when he awoke
> In most distressful mood . . .
> I hurried with him to our orchard-plot,
> And he beheld the moon, and, hushed at once,
> Suspends his sobs, and laughs most silently,
> While his fair eyes, that swam with undropped tears,
> Did glitter in the yellow moon-beam! [1]

No wonder Coleridge 'deemed it wise' to make the infant 'Nature's playmate', and in another poem could thus address him:

> For I was reared
> In the great city, pent mid cloisters dim,
> . . . . .
> But *thou*, my babe, shalt wander like a breeze
> By lakes and sandy shores, beneath the crags
> Of ancient mountain, and beneath the clouds,
> . . . so shalt thou see and hear
> The lovely shapes and sounds intelligible
> Of that eternal language, which thy God
> Utters, who from eternity doth teach
> Himself in all, and all things in himself.[2]

The prophecy was fulfilled, but the results of Nature's schooling, in Hartley's case, failed to come up to expectations.

The tranquil restoration and the renewal of faith which Nature brought to Wordsworth was brought by his own poetry to certain nineteenth century readers.

[1] Coleridge, *The Nightingale*, 98 (1798).
[2] *Frost at Midnight*, 51 (1798).

Mark Rutherford may be quoted once more here; he is speaking of his discovery of *Lyrical Ballads* while struggling for release from theological fetters:

> 'It conveyed to me no new doctrine, and yet the change it wrought in me could only be compared with that which is said to have been wrought on Paul himself by the Divine apparition.... God is nowhere formally deposed, and Wordsworth would have been the last man to say that he had lost his faith in the God of his fathers. But his real God is not the God of the Church, but the God of the hills, the abstraction Nature [after what has been said the reader will not be misled by this use of "abstraction"], and to this my reverence was transferred. Instead of an object of worship which was altogether artificial, remote, never coming into genuine contact with me, I had now one which I thought to be real, one in which literally I could live and move and have my being, an actual fact before my eyes. God was brought from that heaven of the books, and dwelt on the downs in the far-away distances, and in every cloud-shadow which wandered across the valley. Wordsworth unconsciously did for me what every religious reformer has done,—he re-created my Supreme Divinity; substituting a new and living spirit for the old deity, once alive, but gradually hardened into an idol.' [1]

For many another escaped Puritan or overwrought intellectual in the nineteenth century, and for many a sufferer from the strange disease of modern life, looking up from amongst the dark Satanic mills of the industrial age, the authority of the Wordsworthian Nature-religion has seemed absolute. Nevertheless it was probably only relative to a certain passing phase of civilization: for an age, and not for all time. Vestiges of the Wordsworthian impulse still survive in the activities of bodies like the National Trust or the Society for the Preservation of Rural England, and amongst the hordes of hikers and cyclists who wander weekly over the countryside in search of they know not what (I have recently seen Wordsworth and Dorothy praised as the 'first hikers'). All these, like the poet of Wordsworth's *Epitaph*, have viewed 'the outward shows

[1] *Autobiography*, pp. 18-19.

of sky and earth, of hill and valley', but it may be doubted whether 'impulses of deeper birth have come to them in solitude'. With the scientific 'neutralization' of Nature (in Dr Richards's phrase) the heart of her mystery has been plucked out, and the joy which she still spreads in wider commonalty than ever, and will doubtless continue to spread, is for the most part that of physical and nervous regeneration rather than of spiritual assurance. As Pascal long ago saw, Nature proves God only to those who believe in Him already on other grounds. And the religious roots from which the Nature-worship of Wordsworth sprang have, I think it must be admitted, largely withered away. One further observation of a different order may here be added: perhaps the healing power of Nature is only felt to the full, as Ruskin found, by those who return to it at intervals after being long 'in populous cities pent'. Even to Wordsworth Nature meant most as long as he could retain a sense of *escape* into it; when he had long been domiciled there it lost its glory and freshness. In his callow Jacobinical days he had written: 'Cataracts and mountains are good occasional society, but they will not do for constant companions'. His later life perhaps proved the truth of this statement, though he would never have admitted it. It is significant that Wordsworth to some extent abandoned Nature himself, as if he had discovered its inadequacy; abandoned it first for 'Duty', and then for Faith. Wordsworth wrote much excellent poetry to the end of his life, but his best powers were spent in expressing the rapture of his reunion with Nature after exile, and of the 'high moments' which followed—moments which in the nature of things were bound to recur less frequently once he had regained his equilibrium, and which in any case are probably the special privilege of youth. Much of his later poetry deals with experiences and subjects other than the moments of vision which are admittedly his special prerogative, and is consequently felt to be of less importance. But, as Miss Batho has shown, it is incorrect to attribute 'arrested development' or 'decay' to Wordsworth. There is, indeed, a certain pathos in the circumstance that his most splendidly sustained utterance should have been a farewell to his own visionary power. But the power had lasted as long as the best period of most poets, who in general are not blamed (as Wordsworth has been) for doing their finest work before the age of forty. The *Ode* occurred at a unique climacteric moment in Wordsworth's history, and in his later work the 'worlds not quickened by the sun' approximate more and more to the orthodox heaven. But though he may always be valued as the poet of the first and not the latter phase, this change is the natural development of a mystic who wishes to 'improve those transient Gleams of Joy . . . into an inviolable and perpetual State of Bliss and Happiness'.[1] Men cannot live by gleams alone, and though Wordsworth may have been a worse poet as he grew older, it has been argued (by a Dean, it is true) that he was a better 'man'. This cannot be expected to impress those whose only concern is with his poetry. But from the point of view of this book it is of much interest and importance to note, in the later life of our greatest 'Nature' poet, that there is a steady retreat towards the religious sources of his mysticism, and grace supplants the visionary gleam.

[1] Addison, *Spectator*, 393.

INDEX